Roy Jenkins' Gallery of
Twentieth Century
Portraits
and Oxford Papers

DAVID & CHARLES
Newton Abbot   London

I am grateful to *The Observer* for permission to reproduce numerous excerpts throughout the book. Acknowledgements are also due to the *Spectator*, the *Sunday Telegraph*, the *Sunday Times* and the *Times Literary Supplement*.

British Library Cataloguing in Publication Data

Jenkins, Roy, *1920–*
    Roy Jenkins' gallery of 20th century portraits.
    1. Statesmen, 1900 – Biographies – Collections
    I. Title
    909.82'092'2

    ISBN 0–7153–9299–9

Typeset by Typesetter (Birmingham) Ltd
and printed in Great Britain
by Billings & Sons, Worcester
for David & Charles Publishers plc
Brunel House Newton Abbot Devon

Distributed in the United States by
Sterling Publishing Co. Inc,
2, Park Avenue, New York, NY 10016

Contents

CONTENTS

Preface

The idea for this book came from David St John Thomas, its publisher. It has mostly been put into shape by Diana Fortescue, my research assistant form 1984 to the summer of 1988. It is nonetheless very much my own book. Every single word of it, with the sole exception of the Latin versions of the Oxford allocutions, started life by being laboriously written out in my own longhand, which is the only method I know of not using at least twice as many words as necessary.

Thirty-five of the pieces are essays on individuals, in some cases covering mainly special aspects of their lives, such as Asquith and his correspondence with Venetia Stanley or Roosevelt and his relations with Churchill. In two cases (Hugh Gaitskell and Harold Macmillan) the essays are split into two parts, written at different times and seeing the subjects from different perspectives. In one case (Beatrice and Sidney Webb) a married couple is considered together. In another two groups about whom collective biographies have been written (six American pro-consuls of the imperial age and six British Lord Chancellors) are similarly treated.

The longer essays at the end, Presidents and Prime Ministers, Modern Political Biography, Changing Patterns of British Leadership, and Should Politicians Know History?, are based on lectures, mostly given to academic audiences. I have also included my Oxford ceremonial addresses as Chancellor, because they have never been published outside the University, and brief speeches about four distinguished authors at the Royal Society of Literature.

To all those who have been concerned with the putting together of the book, including those who gave permission for the use of copyright material, I am grateful, but particularly so to Diana Fortescue, without whose work it could not have existed.

Roy Jenkins
East Hendred, July 1988

7

Introduction

My interest in political biography has developed only gradually. I did not read much of it as a boy or even as an undergraduate. Indeed at the end of my time at Oxford I remember being rather badly caught out in my Schools *viva* by a personal/factual question which was presumably asked because my papers exhibited some weakness in that direction. 'Do you know who was British Foreign Secretary in 1869?', K. C. Wheare, later Gladstone Professor of Government and Rector of Exeter College, asked me, 'Granville', I hesitantly hazarded. 'No, Clarendon', he said sadly, and I thought that my chance of a First had gone.

This was ironical, for if there is one subject on which I could hope today to avoid humiliation in a *Mastermind* contest it would I suppose be that of rather useless details of who held what office exactly when and for how long. This framework of knowledge I began to acquire in a concentrated three months at the end of 1945, when the war was over and I was still in the army, although with practically nothing to do. I then read nearly all those two or three volume 'tombstone' lives of the main British figures of the late nineteenth and early twentieth centuries.

The perhaps surprising result of this period of pre-Christmas fattening up with these heavy and stodgy meals was that I became addicted to the diet and have never since tired of it. I extended its range both across the Atlantic and beyond the tombstones to memoirs and diaries and to the mounting spate of new works in all these categories which have poured out from the 1950's onwards. And in seven books (only two of them of medium size and none of them very big) spread over forty years I have marginally contributed to the flood myself. The writings on which this book is based were however in most cases stimulated by the biographies or autobiographies of others. They add up to a fairly dense but by no means complete coverage of twentieth century political figures of this country, a much more partial but none-theless substantial coverage of their American counterparts, and a few isolated forays into continental Europe. In contrast with the closeness of transatlantic links in this respect connections within the cross channel biographical industry remain exiguous. It is perhaps easier to create a single market for goods than for words.

The next question is whether from the substantial gallery of portraits, reviews and sketches there can be drawn any significant lessons either about the biographer's art or about the nature of political leadership in the twentieth century world. First, is biography an art or is it just competant journeyman's work, involving no more than the readable stringing together of a more or less accurate narrative?

My answer here is somewhat hesitant. Biography is certainly not a purely mechanical process of assembling and presenting facts. Its rules are too irregular to be easily taught. Word processors are unlikely to be able to take over the task from authors. It involves a certain constructive tension between the writer and his subject (neither antipathy nor identification are in my view desirable, but adequate sympathy and respect are), and for this reason professional biographers at large who ply for hire like taxicabs or barristers lose in rapport and background knowledge at least as much as they gain in technique.

Yet I cannot wholly convince myself that biography is a high literary art form. If one takes semi-contemporary lives of nineteenth century figures in order to seek greater objectivity it would I suppose be widely considered that Froude's *Carlyle*, Morley's *Gladstone* and Ward's *Newman* stood very high. But I do not think they could be placed in the same category of artistic excellence as Gibbon's *Decline and Fall* or Carlyle's own *French Revolution* or the poetry of Tennyson, Browning or Matthew Arnold or the novels of Austen, the Brontes, Thackeray, Trollope or George Eliot.

My conclusion is that biography, while capable of varying enormously in quality, is better designated as a craft than as an art. The meanings of the two words are of course fairly close together, but the difference which I wish them to signify is that the craft of biography is like making a very good pair of shoes, whereas the art of creating poetry or a novel or even a great work of history can be infused with a touch of genius which transcends gradations of quality. Trollope tried to pretend, because he liked throwaway remarks, that all writing was cobbler's work. It is not true of imaginative writers, although perhaps nearer to the truth with him than with most of his fellow novelists because of the almost cartographical precision which he imported into his work. But it is true of nearly all biographers, including the best.

The man who strove hardest to demonstrate that it was not so was Lytton Strachey. He was as resolved to miniaturise biography as any Japanese woman ever has been to constrict her feet, and by achieving this by a preference for aphorism over fact thought he could make each small picture an iconoclastic work of art. To a remarkable extent he succeeded, but his work was sterile as well as brilliant.

He believed himself to have far more daring and insight than his occasionally close friend Keynes, and would have been dismayed to know that Keynes's *magnum opus* (published six years after Strachey's death) changed the assumptions of his subject for at least a generation, whereas Strachey's own breaking of the mould merely caused a few gasps of shocked admiration before subsequent waves of biographers got back to writing even longer and less selective books than they had done before. As Andrew Sinclair has pointed out in a recent collection of essays entitled *The Troubled Face of Biography*, 'modern biographers are both drowned by their material and stranded without it'. There has been far too much of a trend (stemming from America) to value biographies, as though they were fat cattle, by dead weight on the hoof.

Patterns of political leadership have changed considerably over the seven-eighths of a century covered by this book. The two causes of change which might be expected most strongly to exhibit themselves would be the gradual shift from oligarchic to democratic politics associated with the broadening of the franchise and the advent of television, effectively from just after the mid-century mark. The first it must be said, so far at least as the background of those holding the highest offices is concerned, has worked itself out remarkably unevenly, even perversely.

The century began with a handover which was both oligarchic and nepotic. Arthur Balfour succeeded his uncle, the 3rd Marquess of Salisbury, as Prime Minister in 1902. He was the fourth successive Etonian Prime Minister. But when, after $3^1/_2$ years, the Government of which he was leader ended in despairing resignation followed by ignominious electoral defeat, there began a full half-century of drought for the playing fields of Eton, for by far the greater part of which time 10 Downing Street was occupied by 'new men'. Campbell-Bannerman and Asquith, who provided the Liberal revolution with not very revolutionary leadership had been respectively at Trinity, Cambridge and Balliol, but had preceeded those governing class establishments with day schools in Glasgow or London. Then, almost entirely sustained by Conservative majorities, there was a run of Prime Ministers to most of whom the ancient universities were as unfamiliar as were the water-meadows of the middle Thames: Lloyd George, Bonar Law, Ramsay MacDonald, Baldwin (the exception) and Neville Chamberlain.

This was strange and probably largely accidental (in the sense that Lloyd George's touch of political genius was an accident of genes rather than a symbol of social change), and the style and composition of Cabinets remained more oligarchic and striped-trousered than democratic and informal. Curzon was as symbolic a figure of the early Twenties as Halifax was of the late Thirties.

Then came Churchill, who while a product neither of Eton nor of an ancient university, could equally well (although less crucially) have presided over an eighteenth or nineteenth century Cabinet, and Attlee, who led the Labour revolution but was, if anything, less of a 'new man' than Asquith had been. And then, rather amazingly, nearly forty years into universal suffrage (counting from before the 'flapper' enfranchisement of 1928 because it was only a demographic adjustment), well after the seismic social change of 1945, and in the third quarter of the 'century of the common man', the old order suddenly got up from its bed and walked, producing between 1955 and 1964 another three Etonian Prime Ministers in a row (Eden, Macmillan and Home). But they have so far been the last, and although three of the next four (Wilson, Heath and Mrs Thatcher) have been Oxonians they have none of them been of patrician style or background. Nor is anyone in this category currently on the somewhat distant horizon.

It therefore seems to me very difficult to see British political leadership during the twentieth century broadening down steadily, or even jerkily, from aristocracy to plebeianism. The most than can be said is that it would be difficult to imagine Arthur Balfour leading a popular party in the past twenty years, or Mrs Thatcher in 10 Downing Street in 1910.

The impact of television has been less elusive. There was the intermediate stage of sound radio only, and two of the Prime Ministers of this penumbra (Baldwin and Churchill) became in vastly differing styles master of this medium. Whether they would have survived the transition to full visual exposure is difficult to say. (Churchill of course experienced the edge of the television age, but never enough of it either for him to have to make obeisance to its demands or for performance within its techniques to determine political success. He and his 'squalid nuisance' Aneurin Bevan were the last great orators who could ignore the demands of the small screen.) My guess is that Baldwin would have been better with television cameras than Churchill, which may say more about the limitations of the medium than about the virtues of 'Honest Stan'.

What I am more certain about however is that there are several Prime Ministers of the first half of this century, some of them good, some of them bad, who simply could not have functioned in a television-dominated age. I cannot imagine Salisbury or Asquith surviving its intrusions. Balfour I can just see achieving a highly stylized throwaway success, a sort of earlier and perhaps less 'ham' version of Harold Macmillan. But Salisbury and Asquith would never have got where they did, and Bonar Law, Neville Chamberlain and Attlee would have found full television exposure a very considerable handicap. None of them however would have been quite as crippled by its demands as would Truman, who only just escaped its imprint in America. He was one of the best Presidents but his corncrake voice, following the mellifluous and confidence-giving tones of Franklin Roosevelt, was enough of a handicap on sound radio. To have added to it his haberdasher's appearance, natty and cocky but neither authoritative nor reassuring, would have been fatal.

Television has not insisted upon the fluent politician. If it had it would be difficult to explain the success of President Reagan or the failure of Mr Kinnock. but it has insisted upon the packageable and not too fastidious politician, and as a result is coming to exclude many who would earlier have been eligible. While I am against a constant moaning that everything in the world is getting worse, which is neither interesting nor true, I doubt if this particular change is likely to be for the good.

Part I
Individual Portraits

Asquith As Letter Writer

Herbert Henry Asquith was born in 1852. His father died when he was eight and in 1863 he was sent by his mother to live with relations in London where he attended the City of London School. He subsequently went to Balliol College, Oxford as a classical scholar in 1870.

In 1877 he married Helen Melland (who died in 1891), with whom he had four sons and one daughter, amongst whom three, Raymond Asquith, Cyril Asquith (a law lord) and Violet Bonham Carter, were notable. In 1894 he married Margot Tennant and of their five children only one son (Anthony Asquith the film director) and one daughter (Princess Elizabeth Bibesco) survived infancy.

He was MP for East Fife 1886–1918 and for Paisley 1920–24.

He was Home Secretary 1892–95, Chancellor of the Exchequer 1905–08, Prime Minister 1908–16. He was created Earl of Oxford and Asquith and died in 1928.

When, in the autumn of 1959, I decided to write a biography of Asquith, I was partly influenced in my choice of subject by my knowledge of the existence and availability to me of the Venetia Stanley letters. This was not, of course, the only or even the dominant consideration. Had there instead been (perhaps an improbable thought) a similar stock of letters from, say, Bonar Law or Austen Chamberlain, it would not have swung me into making one of them my choice. *Sir Charles Dilke: A Victorian Tragedy* had been published in the autumn of 1958, and part of the intervening years had been occupied by my writing an ephemeral Penguin Special (*The Labour Case*) for the 1959 General Election. In spite of the persuasive powers of that tract, the election had been well and truly lost, and there was clearly another full Parliament of Conservative government ahead.

In these circumstances I wanted to plan another substantial biography. I wanted it to be set in the late nineteenth and/or early twentieth centuries, the period on which my historical expertise, such as it was, was concentrated. I wanted it this time to be about a major figure, for Dilke had been relatively minor, even though of exceptional and mysterious interest. I wanted it to be a Liberal rather than a Conservative, and about a figure who commanded my general sympathy and admiration; for while there is much to be said for short polemics, it would be perverse, in my view, and even corrupting to spend five years trying to get inside the life of someone who is antipathetic.

All this meant that Asquith almost chose himself as a subject. But there was bound to be one other consideration, which was the extent to which the half-chosen subject was an overtilled field, with the quality of the soil almost exhausted. Asquith was not overtilled. There had at that time been only two posthumous biographies - the first a two volume 'tombstone' life published soon after his death and written mainly by J.A. Spender with some chapters by Asquith's fourth son (later Lord Justice Asquith), and the second a slim 1946 essay by R.B. McCallum, Master of Pembroke College, Oxford. There were also four remarkably uninformative volumes of memoirs by Asquith himself. And the existence of the letters to Miss Stanley meant that there would be at least some fresh nutrient in the soil.

These letters posed, however, considerable problems as well as being a great potential bonus. They were physically in the possession of Venetia's daughter, who some years earlier had allowed copies to get into the hands of Lord Beaverbrook. Beaverbrook had become something of a crazed Monopoly player in his approach to political papers of the period. Moreover, in the main hobby of his old age – the constant refighting of the battles of his political youth – he was firmly anti-Asquith. However, he was inhibited from doing more than gossip about the letters by the fact that their copyright, which will not run out until 2015, did not go with their physical possession. This remained with the Asquith family, most forcefully represented by Lady Violet Bonham Carter.

Beaverbrook was convinced that Lady Violet's motive in encouraging me to write a biography of her father was, as it were, to ease the letters into public knowledge and thus pre-empt him from doing a 'shock-horror' publication. The dates do not quite fit, for he could hardly have expected to live until 2015, but I vividly recollect on what was probably the last occasion that I saw him, his sitting behind a guttering candle, his face wreathed in mischief, and saying, 'Lady Violet lets you have the letters because she knows how much more damaging would be the use I would make of them.'

The position was, however, more complicated than this, because Lady Violet did not know of the existence of the letters, or at any rate their content, until she saw the completed typescript of my book. Nor, she strenuously claimed, was she aware of the relationship from which they sprang. On the face of it this was unlikely. Venetia was her exact contemporary and close friend. Nor was Lady Violet unworldly. However, the terms in which she expressed her surprise have left me always convinced of its genuineness. She did not say 'It cannot be true. My father would never have done it.' She said, 'It cannot be true. Venetia was *so plain.*'

There was then a period of difficulty. My book was in no way an official commissioned biography. I was not beholden to Lady Violet. But I liked and respected her. There was also the question of copyright. Fortunately Lady Violet behaved admirably. There were a number of aspects of the book that she did not like, and she would, of course, have greatly preferred it to be published without the letters. But she quickly saw that this was impossible. Instead she asked for some excisions to be made. These mostly related not to Asquith's attachment to Venetia but to the effect that the break-up of the relationship had upon his firmness of grip during the formation of the first Coalition in May 1915.

We argued a little and eventually reached an accommodation. This led to some sporadic post-publication accusations that under family pressure I had bowdlerised the truth. Formally this was, I suppose, the case, but only tangentially so. When, 13 years later, with Lady Violet, Lord Beaverbrook, and even Venetia's daughter all dead, I came to do a second edition, I thought it right to revert to the original manuscript, except where I had been convinced by Lady Violet's arguments rather than merely responsive to her pleas. The changes created hardly a ripple, for the truth had not been seriously doctored.

These were the extraneous difficulties about using the letters. The internal ones were in some ways greater. But both their nature and the reason why it was so worthwhile to overcome them depend upon explaining the volume and historical value of the correspondence. It began with a faint trickle of letters in 1910 and 1911. It became substantially more in 1912. For 1913 there are about 50 letters, most of them of substantial length, 500 words or so. By 1914 the trickle had become a flood. From July of that year Asquith rarely wrote less than once a day, and sometimes more often. On one memorable day in March 1915, he wrote four times, a total of over 3,000 words. This flow continued until May 1915, and then, with Venetia's sudden swoop into marriage with Edwin Montagu, Financial Secretary to the Treasury and protégé and close friend of Asquith's, it stopped.

For three years the correspondence gave an almost hour-by-hour account of the pattern of Asquith's life. It told us whom he saw, what happened at his meetings – for he was uninhibited by any thought of official secrets – what was his daily and sometimes fluctuating view of the performance of his colleagues, where he lunched, where he dined, what he read, and how he filled in his substantial hours of leisure, which stemmed not from laziness, unless a lack of taste for scaling ideological heights be so counted, but from an extraordinary skill and speed in the dispatch of official business. From what other politician's correspondence would we get the following vignette?

> [21 January 1915]. After writing to you, and writing my Cabinet letter [i.e. to the King, and in those days the only written account of the business] and disposing of a lot of smaller things, I walked across after 6 to the Athenaeum, and took up a novel, 'Sir Perryworm's Wife' (a good title), which with judicious skipping I read from cover to cover . . . I found it readable and rather soothing.

He would have been back in Downing Street by 8 p.m.

In three sentences we get a picture of his speed at the writing table, of a Prime Minister still able to walk alone through London in the dark and never thinking of official transport, of his desire for a private refuge where he could be uninterrupted by private secretaries, of his casual and eclectic reading tastes, and of his need to detach his mind.

A diary might have performed almost the same function. But a diary remains under the control of the diarist. It can be altered, it can be expurgated, and it is frequently written several days after the events. Asquith's letters were all in the pillar-box within half an hour. (Thanks to the postal services of those days they were in the hands of the recipient – if in London – within three or four hours.) They were then out of his control. There was no opportunity for afterthoughts.

That he was infatuated with Miss Stanley cannot be denied, although quite how deeply so is open to question. That may have been unfortunate, particularly for the leader of a largely Nonconformist party, although as revelations mount about figures of the genius of Franklin Roosevelt or Lloyd George, it can hardly be regarded as evidence of a fatal flaw in his statesmanship. What is more to the point is whether the relatively innocent form in which he chose to express that infatuation was compatible with leaving him either the time or the intellectual concentration to run the country.

The answer, I am convinced, is that it constituted no interference. Throughout his last three or four decades Asquith poured out letters to one female correspondent or another. In the early 'nineties he did so to Lady Horner (who became the mother-in-law of Raymond Asquith), with whom he was not in love, and then a little later to his second wife, Margot, with whom he was. In his last years he wrote to Mrs Harrisson a series of letters which were later edited by Desmond McCarthy into two volumes of agreeable published correspondence. Kathleen Scott (later Kennet), the widow of the explorer, and Nan Tennant, one of his wife's relations, were among others who received his epistolary attention.

These letters were for him a necessary form of intellectual and emotional release. They interfered with his duties no more than did Churchill's brick-laying or painting or late-night conversation. For most people such a volume of writing would have been an immense burden. For him it was not so. In his flowing classical hand he wrote easily, casually, economically, and as a relaxation. If he had a spare half-hour between meetings, or even during one, it was no effort for him to produce a quick three pages of comment on his recent doings.

This was so because his mind was not obsessed by politics. He was not always planning the next move, always thinking how he would outwit his enemies or his colleagues at the next encounter. The price was that he was not innovative. But he was fair, generous, tolerant, loyal and remarkably free from the vice of intrigue.

21

His judgement was good and he could exercise it with exceptional speed and precision.

Obviously he was a better Prime Minister in peace than in war. But this was nothing to do with Miss Stanley. Indeed, he was a better Prime Minister when he was writing to her than he was when he had just ceased to do so, when after seven years of presiding over a Liberal Government he failed to accommodate himself to coalition and moved into the declining authority which led to the palace revolution of December 1916.

The unfortunate thing, I believed when I wrote my book, was that his relationship with her should have collapsed when he was in deep and difficult negotiations over the formation of the 1915 Coalition and that this may have been responsible, among other things, for his uncharacteristically ungenerous treatment of Haldane, his oldest political ally. This, it may be recalled, was the major point of my dispute with Lady Violet Bonham Carter.

Now I am not so sure. Perhaps she was right after all. For I did not then know that within a few days he was writing a similar volume of letters to Miss Stanley's sister, Sylvia Henley, who lived into the 1980s. So perhaps the infatuation was not too deep. Perhaps it was the pillar-box and not the recipient which exercised the compulsion.

Margot Asquith

Margot Asquith was born in 1864, the sixth daughter and eleventh child of Sir Charles Tennant, 'the bart', who acquired great wealth and launched a remarkable family of great fashion. She was educated by governesses and tutors until she was fifteen when, after a short period at finishing school in London, she went to study in Dresden.

She married Herbert Henry Asquith as his second wife in 1894.

As Countess of Oxford she lived through a long widowhood until her death in 1945.

Margot Asquith was the best known, most outrageous, and, some would say, least suitable Prime Minister's consort since Lady Caroline Lamb. Lady Caroline, of course, did not survive to darken the doors at 10 Downing Street. Lady Oxford, on the contrary, was the longest lasting chatelaine of the residence since the second Lady Liverpool. And she did much more enlivening of the atmosphere than darkening of anything except for the characters of those she (often temporarily) took against. She had remarkable qualities of wit and spontaneity, recklessness and charm, loyalty and indiscretion. She surpassed Dame Margaret Lloyd George as a hostess of the *beau-monde*, Mrs Baldwin as a leader of fashion, Mrs Attlee as a political partisan and Mr Denis Thatcher as a letter-writer, although perhaps not as a golfer.

She was born Margot Tennant in 1864, the daughter of a rich, partially self-made Liberal baronet, whose numerous children erupted into social prominence with unusual force. She did not marry Asquith (as his second wife) until she was 30 and he was already Home Secretary. But from the age of 19 or 20 she had been used to being the centre of attention in almost any *milieu*. Her speciality, particularly on a first meeting, was the unexpected provocative remark. Her particular gift was that it rarely failed to intrigue rather than offend. Lord Randolph Churchill, then in his heyday, rashly asked her if she knew any politicians. She replied, by no means wholly inaccurately, that 'with the exception of himself (she) knew them all intimately'. She then told him that 'he had resigned more out of temper than conviction' and was repaid with an invitation to meet and sit next to the Prince of Wales at a supper party, which she attended wearing what most of the women present thought was her nightgown. She told General Booth (of the Salvation Army) that he did not believe in hell any more than she did, and then knelt with him, praying, on the floor of the railway compartment in which, by chance, they were travelling together. She suggested to Tennyson that she thought he was dirty and was rewarded with a long reading from 'Maud' and 'The Princess'.

She was an appalling lion-hunter, but her success owed as much to the co-operation of the lions as to her own intrepidity and determination in their pursuit. When Gladstone, during his third premiership and aged 77, came to luncheon with her parents she was afraid that her father 'might resent my wish to take (him) up to my room after lunch and talk to him alone'. Whether or not there was resentment, Mr Gladstone was duly led up several floors. Her boast to Randolph Churchill was wholly justified. Before Asquith it was rumoured that she was going to marry first Lord Rosebery and then Arthur Balfour. The former prickly pederast was rather offended that she did not deny it with sufficient vehemence or speed. The latter merely said that, on the contrary, he had rather thought of having a career of his own. She also provoked Balfour into one of his best languid *mots*. When she accused him of being so self-contained that he would not mind if all his close women friends including herself died, he paused for reflection and then said: 'I think I should mind if you *all* died on the same day.'

Her marriage with Asquith was a most remarkable event to the world, and an equally remarkable decision on both their parts. He was a recent widower with five young children, and much less part of her circle than any of those previously mentioned, except for General Booth. Brilliant though his prospects already were (and she was never indifferent to success) she was undertaking a formidable challenge. He, much infatuated, was determinedly taking a substantial risk and also reversing a rather common human pattern. Instead of being discontented with one wife and then, when an

24

opportunity for fresh choice presents itself, proceeding to marry a near copy, he claimed complete happiness while his first marriage lasted, but followed this by the early acquisition of a second wife who was in almost every respect the direct opposite of the first.

The marriage was a moderate success. It lasted for 34 years until Asquith's death in 1928. In the early years she suffered from bursts of neurasthenia, insomnia and depression, punctuated by five appallingly difficult pregnancies, only two of which produced children who lived. Asquith probably found her less exhilerating and satisfying than he had hoped. Her expectations may have been less high, except for Downing Street, in which respect they were abundantly fulfilled, although not satiated. Even after $8^{1}/_{2}$ years the wrench of leaving was appalling for her, worse than for him, and until well into *his* seventies she sustained herself with wholly illusory dreams of getting back. This was partly out of fierce personal and political loyalty, and partly out of an unquenchable desire for the limelight, which was part of her essentially theatrical personality. Asquith sustained the indiscreet exhibitionism which flowed from her with remarkable tolerance and equanimity. She sustained his potentially impoverished old age with extravagance, money and vitality. She then lived on through 17 years of widowhood, with the money running short but not the flow of coruscating witticisms, until she died at the age of 81 on the day after Attlee replaced Churchill as the occupant of the house she had left so reluctantly.

Nancy Astor

Nancy Astor was born in 1879, the daughter of Chiswell Dabney Langhorne of Greenwood, Virginia. She married Robert Gould Shaw in 1897, with whom she had one son. They were divorced in 1903. In 1906 she married William Waldorf (later 2nd Viscount) Astor who died in 1952 and with whom she had four sons (William, later 3rd Viscount, David, long editor and proprietor of the Observer, Michael and John Jacob (Jakie) and one daughter (Countess of Ancaster). She was the first woman to sit in the House of Commons where she represented the Sutton division of Plymouth from 1919 to 1945. She died in 1964.

Nancy Astor was essentially a figure of the inter-war years, as much so as King Edward VIII or Stanley Baldwin, P.G. Wodehouse or C.B. Cochran. There is no evidence that she ever knew the last two. But they none the less all lived their lives and achieved their fame as firmly linked to the same slice of English history and social climate as was she. And it is perhaps a pity that, of the four, Cochran was the most remote from her, for among her many attributes she was a great musical comedy actress *manquée*. She had all the requisite vitality, verve, exhibitionism, and capacity to make vivid the words of others.

Although it is impossible to separate her from the England of those two decades, she was born long before (in 1879), lived well afterwards (until 1964), and was not English. She was a Virginian married to a deliberately English scion of one of the grandest New York families of the 'gilded age'. Although the first Astor was a century and a half late for the *Mayflower*, the family were amongst the earliest wave of American settlers on the shores and rivers of England. When two Mrs Astors quarrelled in the tight Edith Wharton world of the New York of the 'eighties, the husband of one did not hesitate to take his fortune to the virgin lands of Cliveden and Hever. He became a peer against the wishes of his son (Nancy's husband) and established a family as remarkable in a different way in England as the one he had left behind him in Manhattan.

Nancy Astor's background was not at all the same. Her father was a post Civil War Southern gentleman of fluctuating fortune. His name, Chillie Langhorne, is in itself almost a concentrated description of his life and character. His daughter was always known in Virginia as Nannie, Nannie Langhorne, then Nannie Shaw, then Nannie Astor, which small change from Nancy seems to alter her whole character. The 'Shaw' came from an unsuccessful first marriage with a Bostonian alcoholic. It lasted barely a year and produced one son.

It was six or seven years after this before she met Waldorf Astor and then married him at the age of 28. She had previously spent a great deal of time in England mainly for hunting seasons in Leicestershire. As with Margot Asquith, a comparison with whom is constantly in mind when thinking about Nancy Astor, she was briefly obsessed by the sport.

Christopher Sykes, whose biography *Nancy: The Life of Lady Astor* was published in 1972, develops this comparison and comes to a surprising conclusion:

> They both enjoyed a reputation for wit which in both cases was largely undeserved. Both had the gift of quick, uninhibited, often boisterous repartee, a different thing . . . The fact is that they were both so talkative and said so much on so many subjects that they could hardly avoid saying something good sometimes about something. Nancy was by far the more rewarding to talk to. She had the art of conversation. Margot was without it.

Nancy Astor was therefore not without experience of England at the time of her second marriage. She immediately moved into a powerful social position. She became the chatelaine of Cliveden, of a large house in St. James's Square, of a seaside villa at Sandwich, of another in Plymouth, where her husband became parliamentary candidate, and later of a holiday house on a Scottish island. With these resources, she and Waldorf Astor, who between them combined social responsibility, fashionable gullibility, political concern, and desire to startle, began a 40-year pattern of entertainment of the great and the good, the rulers and the commentators, the friends and the acolytes.

Yet to see Nancy Astor as a rich but frivolous hostess who only amused herself with politics would be to get the whole picture out of perspective. She was a relentless proselytiser, anxious to improve, imbued with a deep social conscience. Her religious beliefs – Christian Science after 1914 – went to her core. There was much more of the Salvation Army lass than of the society lady in her.

In 1910 Waldorf Astor became an MP, a reformist Tory. Nancy Astor explained her canvassing technique: 'Some would say, "But I am a Liberal", and then I would explain how Waldorf was too, at heart, but that he thought the Conservative platform was the best and so was fighting on that'. Throughout her life she believed in trying to get the best of both worlds, and to a large extent succeeded, although not without considerable public and private vicissitudes.

In 1919 her father-in-law died and the unwanted peerage devolved upon her husband. She became candidate in his place, and after an adequate victory became the first woman to sit in the House of Commons. (Countess Markievicz had been elected for an Irish seat in 1918, but a combination of her incarceration in Holloway and the boycott by Sinn Fein of the 'Imperial Parliament' prevented her from taking her seat.) Nancy Astor was introduced by Lloyd George and Arthur Balfour. A painting of her historic introduction, flanked by the short and the tall and wearing a semi-uniform of her own invention, which was appropriately halfway between that of a Lady Mayoress and an officer in the WRNS, was presented to the House of Commons, then removed, and has since remained an object of controversy.

She remained in Parliament for 26 years, surviving six general elections in an uncertain seat, and achieved a mixture of success and failure. Although more feminine than feminist, she was, no doubt inevitably in the circumstances, self-consciously a *woman* MP. She at once traded upon and limited herself by her sex. She clucked over the instruction and welfare of later women members, independently of their parties. She made herself, without much difficulty, a 'character' rather than a mainstream member. She was never in the long years of Conservative Government a serious candidate for office, which her husband, had he not been snatched to the House of Lords, would certainly have been. But she could pursue a cause with great tenacity; her contribution to the establishment of nursery schools was almost unique.

She began better in the House of Commons than she continued and in her last 10 years or so of parliamentary life made a number of remarkably silly interventions. She was always fond of the erratic gesture, and having enthusiastically supported Chamberlain throughout the appeasement period (although the alleged evil power of the 'Cliveden Set' was almost totally a press invention), marched imperturbably through the lobby against him after the 1940 debate. At the end her husband decided firmly that enough was enough, and skilfully vetoed her standing in 1945.

Her life was never bounded by the House of Commons, and she should not be judged primarily by her parliamentary performance. She was a highly idiosyncratic character of great courage if little subtlety, whose wealth gave her the opportunity, which she abundantly seized, to imprint her personality upon an adopted country.

Clement Attlee

Clement Richard Attlee was born in 1883, the fourth son of Henry Attlee, a City solicitor who lived in Putney. He was educated at Haileybury and University College, Oxford. In 1922 he married Violet Miller and they had one son (the present earl) and three daughters. He served in the First World War in France and Gallipoli. He was the first Labour Mayor of Stepney in 1919 and 1920.

He was elected MP for Limehouse in 1922 and represented that seat until 1950, when he moved for 5 years to West Walthamstow, was Chancellor of the Duchy of Lancaster 1930, Postmaster-General 1930–31, Lord Privy Seal 1940–42, Secretary of State for the Dominions 1942–43, Lord President of the Council 1943–45, Prime Minister 1945–51. He had been Deputy Prime Minister 1942–45. He was leader of the Labour Party from 1935 to 1955.

He was created first Earl Attlee in 1955 and died in 1967.

Attlee was leader of a party for 20 years, longer than any other man this century. He was only Prime Minister once, unlike Baldwin, MacDonald, Churchill and Wilson, but it was for a $6^1/_4$ year continuous spell, a length exceeded in this century only by Asquith, Macmillan and Mrs Thatcher. It was certainly not a Government of undistinguished ministers. The Prime Minister apart, it would be difficult to think of another team to match Bevin, Cripps, Morrison, Bevan, Dalton and Gaitskell as a band of formidable politicians. And its lasting impact upon both the social structure and the international orientation of Britain is equally unrivalled.

Few who could begin to make one would therefore miss Attlee from a list of Prime Ministers. Nor is Attlee now in any way under-regarded by the cognoscenti. He is indeed very much a politicians' politician, and to some considerable extent a political commentators' one as well. I suspect that if, as is rather a habit for ranking Presidents in the United States, a sort of electoral college of, say, 250 politicians (including many Tories, the successors of those who bitterly and sometimes contemptuously opposed him at the time) and of political journalists (whose forbears found him appallingly lacking in both charisma and indiscretion) were asked to vote for the best recent Prime Minister, Attlee might easily win outright, and would certainly be put very high.

Where I think he would score badly is in the public's recognition of what sort of man he was, what he looked like, what was his life and his background. He was just before the television age. But so of course was Churchill. However, there has been no Attlee reconstruction, no series entitled 'the Stanmore Years', no Lloyd George-like sexual dramas, not even the tangential screen coverage which, mainly because of the Abdication crisis, Baldwin has received. Nor has he been recently available for reminiscent television reflection, unlike most of his successors. He is in a crack between those who have the fame of history, and those who in retirement are still able to burnish their own image.

Attlee was probably the last Prime Minister who could have moved about the country, and lunched, say, in a provincial town hotel, without automatic recognition. It is easy to underestimate how great is the change in this respect. Asquith was surprised when, visiting a Stratford-on-Avon church in 1914, the verger recognised him. Mrs Thatcher would be amazed if the reverse were to be the case.

The respect in which Attlee is an unknown Prime Minister is essentially the personal. If intelligent members of his grandchildren's generation were asked to write a 200 word sketch of the work of his Government, they would probably do quite well: India, the second wave of social security, the National Health Service, public ownership of utilities, maybe NATO, the resistance to the Berlin blockade, and the decision to manufacture a British nuclear A-bomb. If they were asked to write a 200 word essay about his personal characteristics, they would be defeated. They could probably do better on Palmerston, MacDonald or Eden, let alone the obvious 'greats'. This stems more from Attlee's character than from any deficiency of his biographers. At least until he retired, he was an exceptionally taciturn man, and his taciturnity extended to the written as well as the spoken word, to his private as well as his public habits. There just is not much personal material available.

31

I found this when, in 1946 and '47, I was rashly writing an 'interim biography' of a man who was not only alive but the Prime Minister of the time, and it is still true today. Rather surprisingly, as it now appears to me, Attlee allowed me to rummage alone in his Downing Street study and to go through such few boxes of private papers as he had kept. They were a very haphazard collection: engagement books, a few odd jottings (including cricketing elevens made up of politicians!) and a very limited number of incoming letters of interest. My book covered only the less publicly important part of his life - up to 1945, and for this period the main source now available which I missed were his frequent but laconic letters to his elder brother.

After he retired in 1955 Attlee became somewhat more conversationally expansive (although never garrulous; he always retained his staccato economy of words) and happy at least to give his views about others. Kenneth Harris, in his 1982 biography, was even successful in making him stray a little way towards self-revelation. I doubt if anyone else would have got him to say that while he liked the ethics of Christianity he was not really 'a believer'. Nor perhaps to have expressed his slightly dejected awareness of the jejuneness of his own autobiography, appropriately entitled *As It Happened*. Mr Harris however did not solve the enigma of Attlee. That is not easy to do. He was a pillar of the constitution but he had a strong, simple, collectivist socialist faith. He was rather partisan and never believed in letting the Tory dogs get the best of it. He collected great honours like a fly-paper collects flies. No other Prime Minister except for Balfour has had an earldom, a Garter and an Order of Merit. Attlee had a C.H. as well, and he commemorated them all in a limerick at once satisfying and deflating which he wrote about himself when he was an old man:

> Few thought he was even a starter
> There were many who thought themselves smarter
> But he ended PM
> CH and OM
> An earl and a knight of the garter.

In everything except politics Attlee was profoundly conservative. He liked and respected almost every institution with which he was ever associated, from Haileybury to the National Executive Committee of the Labour Party. He was remarkly family orientated. He had almost no iconoclasm and little vanity. He confined his daily newspaper reading to the *Daily Herald* and *The Times* (mostly the non-political columns), thus insulating himself in the most effective way possible from the vagaries of day-to-day criticism. But he had just enough conceit to hold on when others wanted him out of the way, and thus to enable his sound sense and high social conscience to make him a formidable Prime Minister.

Arthur James Balfour

Arthur James Balfour was born in 1848, the eldest son of James Maitland Balfour and Lady Blanche Cecil, sister of the 3rd Marquess of Salisbury. He was educated at Eton and Trinity College, Cambridge. He never married.

He was MP for Hertford 1874–85, for East Manchester 1885–1906 and for the City of London 1906–22, when he was created Earl of Balfour.

He served as President of the Local Government Board 1885–86, Scottish Secretary 1886–87, Chief Secretary for Ireland 1887–91, Leader of the House of Commons and First Lord of the Treasury 1891–92, Prime Minister 1902–05, First Lord of The Treasury and Leader of the House of Commons 1895–1905. He resigned as Conservative Leader in 1911, but was First Lord of the Admiralty 1915–16, Foreign Secretary 1916–19, and Lord President of the Council 1919–22 in the Lloyd George Coalition. He was again Lord President of the Council 1925–29 under Baldwin.

He died in 1930.

Judged by the standards of popular appeal, Arthur Balfour was the least successful Prime Minister of the century. He was one of the four who never won an election. (The others are Neville Chamberlain, who never fought one, Alec Home and James Callaghan.) But, far worse than that, his short three-and-a-half year reign, during which ministers resigned under him like leaves falling in November, ended in a Conservative holocaust.

He lost his own Manchester seat, as well as those of 200 of his supporters, but returned to the House of Commons for the not very challenging constituency of the City of London, and led his party to a further two lost elections. By then he had established a record of defeat never previously or since surpassed by any party leader since parties assumed a coherent shape.

Yet when, nine months later, he eventually gave up the leadership he did so with a veneer of public grace but an underlying feeling of grievance and self-regard. 'As you know I am not given to brooding over my wrongs,' he wrote in the run-up. 'But last Friday and Saturday I could think of nothing else: a thing which has not happened to me since I was unjustly "complained of" at Eton more than 40 years ago!' But he comforted himself with the thought that 'a slower brain would often be more welcome to the Party as a whole'.

In these circumstances it may seem remarkable that 11 years later Lloyd George and Lord Birkenhead (neither of them notable for lack of ability to denigrate others) were able to agree that 'taking it all round he (Balfour) was at that moment the most distinguished figure in the world'. Perhaps Mr Heath, who also had a three and a half year premiership which ended in apparent failure, who also showed a penchant for losing elections and a certain reluctance for giving up the leadership, might take some comfort from this judgement. It must be said, however, that common bachelorhood apart, it is difficult to imagine two characters and personalities who are less alike. Delicacy of constitution and of mind, elegance of phrase and supple indecisiveness of execution, feline charm exercised over an adoring, mainly female, family and wider social circle were Balfour's most obvious characteristics. I do not think that any of these are the descriptions which would spring most readily to the minds either of Mr Heath's best friends or of his worst enemies.

There are, I think, three reasons for the renaissance of Balfour's reputation. First, the failure of his premiership, while in a sense real, was concentrated on the surface. Despite the tergiversation on tariff reform which was the main political topic of the day, despite the electoral débâcle, there were underlying successes. He passed one of the two great constructive Education Acts of the past hundred years. He achieved the Anglo-French entente, which for good or ill wrenched British foreign policy out of its previous course and gave it its dominant direction for the next 40 years. And he began inter-Service co-ordination in defence policy. It was a considerable constructive record, but it lacked popular appeal and was detached from the more superficial issues of politicians' politics.

Second, he had an extra-political distinction which sprang from

an unusually wide range of intellectual interests and scientific connections. He published two philosophical treatises – a 'Defence
of Philosophic Doubt' when he was a young man of 31, and
the 'Foundations of Belief' 16 years later. His main concern was
to reconcile science with a yearning desire for the immortality of
man. His works may not have been in the highest philosophical
category, but they were of a much higher quality than, for example, Gladstone's forays into theology. And 'Foundations of Belief'
contained a hauntingly written passage about the purposelessness
of a purely determinist world:

> We sound the future, and learn that after a period, long
> compared with the individual life, but short indeed com-
> pared with the divisions of time open to our investigations,
> the energies of our system will decay, the glory of the sun
> will be dimmed, and the earth, tideless and inert, will no
> longer tolerate the race which has for a moment disturbed its
> solitude. Man will go down into the pit, and all his thoughts
> will perish . . . Nor will anything that is be better or worse
> for all that the labour, genius, devotion and suffering of man
> have striven throughout countless generations to effect.

Third, Balfour had longevity. There was a quarter of a century
between the end of his premiership and his death. This in itself
would not have turned things round. Rosebery had even longer
– 35 years – but they were sulking years, and his reputation went
the other way. Balfour's long evening was interspersed with frequent periods of subordinate office. He was First Lord of the
Admiralty for 18 months, Foreign Secretary for three years and
Lord President of the Council for eight. Somewhat surprisingly,
he loved office, and was always willing to serve under those – Lloyd
George, Baldwin – whose political style seemed in most marked
contrast from his own. To think otherwise was one of Asquith's
great miscalculations in 1916.

Balfour was not a great believer in personal political alliances.
From most of those to whom he was politically close – Lord
Randolph Churchill, George Wyndham, Lord Lansdowne, even
his devoted secretary and henchman Jack Sandars – he sooner or
later separated himself and often when they most needed his support. His loyalty was not to persons, in politics at any rate, but
to the established values of Conservative England, and, it must

be said, to his own comfort. In any case it is doubtful whether he regarded Asquith, whose political talents were greater and whose influence is more continuing, as his equal in the league of gentlemen politicians; it is certain that he did not reciprocate the admiration Asquith felt for him.

He therefore had little difficulty in serving under the 'little Welsh attorney', and probably showed Lloyd George more loyalty than he showed anyone other than his uncle Salisbury. But, alas, the 'little Welsh attorney' was less dazzled by the old patrician than *vice versa*. His final judgement upon Balfour was that he was 'just like the scent on a pocket handkerchief'. Churchill on the other hand described him as 'a powerful graceful cat walking delicately and unsoiled across a rather muddy street'.

The feature common to both descriptions was fastidiousness of style. The substance is more difficult to appraise.

Tony Benn in the 1960s

Anthony Wedgwood Benn was born in 1925, educated at Westminster School and New College, Oxford and married Caroline de Camp of Cincinnati in 1949. He was Labour MP for Bristol South East from 1950 to 1960 when, as the elder surviving son of Viscount Stansgate (a former Liberal and Labour MP), he inherited the title on his father's death and was consequently excluded from the House of Commons, his two attempts (in 1955 and 1960) to renounce his succession having proved unsuccessful.

In 1961 he was re-elected for Bristol at a bye-election caused by his exclusion but was still prevented from taking his seat. He therefore instigated an Act to make a disclaimer to a title possible and in 1963 he, Lord Home and Lord Hailsham availed themselves of its provisions.

He was then re-elected for Bristol South East and represented that seat until the General Election of 1983. He is now MP for Chesterfield which he won in a bye-election in March 1984.

Tony Benn, as he came to wish to be called, served as Postmaster-General 1964–66, Minister of Technology 1966–70, Secretary of State for Trade and Industry 1974–75 and Secretary of State for Energy 1975–79.

In the 1960s Anthony Wedgwood Benn (as he was then happy to be called) was very much a figure of the soft rather than the hard left. He had just fought a brilliant, although slightly selfish, campaign to be the first man to free himself of a peerage. He had enlisted on his side a wide range of cross-party supporters, from Violet Bonham Carter to Tony Lambton to Dick Taverne, and in the course of it he had become somewhat impatient of the narrow proletarianism of some of his Bristol party. However, he

had never appreciated Gaitskell and was a naive Wilson enthusi-
ast, ignited by the 'white heat of the technological revolution'.
'David [Ennals] and I', he wrote in his diary, '. . . reflect[ed] on
the great change that has come about with Harold's leadership
and how awful Hugh had been', he wrote within six months
of Gaitskell's death. One of the themes of the next three years
was his gradual disillusionment with his hero of 1963. 'My
opinion of Harold was lower tonight than it has ever been
before', he wrote in February 1966. 'He really is a manipulator
who thinks he can get out of everything by fixing somebody
or something.'

Benn could show good sceptical judgement of others, notably
of Colonel Wigg, that half comic, half sinister figure of the
early Wilson period. But the Benn performance was flawed by
a combination of triviality and obsessiveness. He had practically
no sense of proportion. He treated his own battle to renounce
his peerage as a constitutional struggle comparable with the
great Reform Act or the Parliament Bill. He spent a remarkably
high proportion of his time at the Post Office dealing with the
Queen's head on stamps. He was indeed constantly obsessed
with what he regarded as the baleful influence of the Royal
Family. He was 'revolted' by having to confer BEMs on postal
workers, and found the feeling increased by the pleasure which
the medals aroused. He was wracked by whether or not to wear
a white tie at Lord Mayors' banquets (why did he have to go?
I didn't). And he regarded the BBC under Hugh Greene as a
right-wing conspiracy.

His description of his early period as Postmaster-General
is a manual on how not to be a minister. Maybe he had a
peculiarly isolated and rigid group of civil servants to deal with
at the Post Office, but even so it was hardly wise to treat them
as a monolithic hostile bloc. Even his private secretary, always
referred to as 'Tilling' or 'Mr Tilling', never by his Christian
name, had to be circumnavigated by papers he could not see
and a secret method of communication with 10 Downing Street.
Benn bombarded officials with peremptory written minutes which
rarely led to much, had meetings for long and inconvenient
hours, entertained trade union leaders and others to canteen
lunches (and was surprised they did not go better), filled his
office with his camp bed and his tea mugs, and behaved

altogether like a boy scout promoted to be an evangelical general.

For the portrait of the class warrior of the 1970s and early 1980s we have to wait for future volumes of the Benn diaries. From the 1963–67 volume he emerges as nice, honest, not very clever, but full of gimmicky talent.

Ernest Bevin

Ernest Bevin was born in 1881, the illegitimate son of an Exmoor midwife, who died when he was eight. He left school in Crediton at the age of 11 and was found work first as a farm boy and then as a drayman in Bristol. He married Florence Townley and had one daughter.

He was National Organiser of the Dockers' Union 1910–21, General Secretary of the Transport and General Workers Union 1921–40.. In Parliament he represented Central Wandsworth 1940–50 and East Woolwich 1950–51. He was Minister of Labour and National Service in the War Coalition 1940–45 and Secretary of State for Foreign Affairs 1945–51.

He died in 1951.

There have been 27 British Foreign Secretaries since the beginning of this century. Only two of them have imprinted their personalities on their officials with enough force to become Foreign Office legends. The one was Curzon and the other was Bevin.

To achieve this legendary status is not necessarily the mark of being a great minister. Curzon indeed was in many ways a weak Foreign Secretary who failed to defend his department against an earlier wave of Prime Ministerial depredations. But the grandeur of his appearance and the richly anecdotal nature of his personality give a vividness to his memory.

Bevin could match him in the latter quality. He also had the advantage from the point of view of memorability that it would have been impossible to imagine him in any Foreign Office position, unless it was that of a truculent liftman on the verge of retirement, other than that which he occupied. He could not have been an ambassador or permanent under-secretary, senior or junior official, Minister of State or parliamentary under-secretary. It was Secretary of State or nothing.

Furthermore, there was no question of Bevin allowing the prerogatives of the Foreign Office to be removed to the other side of Downing Street. Although no one now considers Attlee to have been weak, Bevin was if anything subject to too little Prime Ministerial criticism. He must therefore be rated a more dominant figure than Curzon.

How does he compare in influence and imprint with the other 25? Three seem to me to offer themselves for comparison. The first is Lansdowne, the second Grey and the third Eden. Lansdowne is included not because he was a dominant or colourful figure, but because he was the architect of the Anglo-French entente of 1903. As a result he set the course of British foreign and defence policy from then until 1940. He was therefore objectively of the first importance.

Bevin's central work – his part in launching the Marshall Plan, in creating NATO, in committing Britain to the United States - has now lasted nearly 40 years against the 37 years of Lansdowne's re-orientation. It is profoundly to be hoped that it will complete its fourth decade in better shape than did Lansdowne's work. Certainly it has so far done more for the peace of the world. Also, it was more consciously planned for the long term.

Grey and Eden must be considered on grounds of length of service, if no other. Grey was Foreign Secretary for 11 continuous years, Eden for a twice broken aggregate of nearly 10. Some significant deposits of influence and recollection must be left by a minister upon a great department of state after such long periods of office. But not on the Bevin scale. Grey immortalised the night prospect from the Foreign Office windows by one remark. For the rest he seems to me an overrated figure, insular and priggish, who disliked foreigners and led Britain into an eviscerating war with a policy which was at once stubborn and imprecise.

Eden is more difficult to evaluate. In the 1930s he was a figure of unfulfilled hope. In the war he was inevitably over-shadowed by Churchill. Between 1951 and 1955 he broadly pursued the lines of policy laid down by Bevin, although it is possible, but by no means certain, that he stuck to an exaggerated view of Britain's position in the world, and thereby vitiated our relations with the emerging European Community, longer than Bevin would have done. Certainly he compounded Bevin's worst misappraisal, and kept Britain away from the Messina Conference and out of the Treaty of Rome. Whether Bevin would have done the same is like trying to decide whether Kennedy would have got as deep into the quagmire of Vietnam as did Lyndon Johnson.

All in all, therefore, Bevin has a high claim on grounds both of personal impact and of long-term influence to be thought the most considerable Foreign Secretary of this century. This does not mean that he was always right or that he was a particularly amiable character. He was egotistical and conceited, although not vain. He was intolerant and personalised every dispute. He was ruthless when he judged it necessary and left a few, but not too many, badly mangled corpses on his road to power. Yet he was not self-seeking. He was one of the few men in modern British political history (Joseph Chamberlain, also ruthless, was another) who could have been Prime Minister, but did not think the place worth the effort. He preferred the power he was already exercising.

He was good with subordinates but bad at establishing equal partnerships of trust. I think he had only two in his life: with his wife and with Attlee. His relations with those with whom, in Acheson's phrase, he was 'present at the creation' of the spectacularly successful Western world of the 1950s and 1960s were those of respect more than of affection. This was true of Acheson himself, of Marshall, of Truman, of Robert Schuman. Yet he was a massive man, judged either by character or achievement.

George Brown

George Brown was born in 1914 in London and left school in 1928. In 1937 he married Sophie Levene and they had two daughters.

He was MP for the Belper division of Derbyshire 1945–70. He was Minister of Works 1950–51, First Secretary of State for Economic Affairs October 1964 to August 1966, Foreign Secretary 1966–68 and Deputy Leader of the Labour Party 1960–70. In 1970 he became Lord George-Brown. He joined the SDP in 1981. He died in 1986.

At the memorial service for George Brown the Speaker's Chaplain began by referring to him as 'one of the most dynamic, compassionate, courageous and mercurial politicians of our time'. The words were wholly appropriate, but were not complete.

George Brown had some but not all of the qualities of high statesmanship. Those that he had he possessed to an unusual degree. First among them was an instinctive sense of proportion – not in the details of life but in the issues of politics. He always knew what was a big issue and what was a small one. And he always preferred the risks and opportunities of dealing with big ones. And on these, in my view and experience, he nearly always showed wisdom, verve and foresight. On small matters he could be maddening, even foolish. Happily, when he was functioning at his best, he mostly chose to leave these to other people.

In addition he had an untutored mind of the highest speed and quality. It was an intellectual mind although without an intellectual's training. In this respect he was quite different from Ernest Bevin who was a hero of his. Bevin had a massive creative power but he wrote only with the greatest difficulty and his words came out viscously. I do not think he would have taken easily to formal education. George Brown would have. Just as I cannot imagine

Bevin writing flowingly in a neat classicist's script, so I have no difficulty in seeing George Brown, with different early opportunities, as a Fellow of All Souls of polemical temperament.

Perhaps for this reason he minded the missed opportunities more than did most of those - Bevin again, Arthur Henderson, even Lloyd George – who became major figures without it. But he need not have worried. In a Cabinet with an unusual and excessive Oxford predominance, he had at least as good a brain as anyone around the table.

Yet it is not primarily his cerebral qualities which will remain in the minds and the hearts of his friends, and of some part of the British public as well. He was generous and vivid. He was never dominated by his own interests. He cared about causes more than himself. He had vision. He was a good friend. He enhanced life.

R.A. Butler

Richard Austen (Rab) Butler was born in India in 1902, the elder son of Sir Montagu Butler, Indian Civil Servant and later Master of Pembroke College, Cambridge. He was educated at Marlborough and Pembroke College, Cambridge, where he was President of the Union. In 1926 he married Sydney Courtauld and they had three sons and one daughter. After the death of his first wife in 1954 he married Mollie Courtauld in 1959. She was the widow of Sydney Butler's first cousin, August.

Butler was MP for Saffron Walden 1929–65. He served as Minister of Education 1941–45, Minister of Labour June to July 1945, Chancellor of the Exchequer 1951–61, Lord Privy Seal 1955–59, Leader of the House of Commons 1955–61, Home Secretary 1957–62, First Secretary of State, Deputy Prime Minister and Minister in Charge of the Central African Office July 1962 to October 1963, Secretary of State for Foreign Affairs 1963–64.

In 1965 he was created Lord Butler of Saffron Walden. He was Master of Trinity College, Cambridge 1965–78. He died in 1982.

R.A. Butler is widely credited with having written the most distinguished volume of political memoirs of the past thirty years. They were of a quality which fully justified his position as President of the Royal Society of Literature. This was the more remarkable as we have subsequently learned that they were mostly ghosted by Peter Goldman, the victim of the Orpington débâcle of 1962 and then Director of the Consumers' Association.

However, they were totally infused with the spirit of Rab Butler's lapidary and idiosyncratic conversation. Rab, a designation of suitably indeterminate status between Christian name and acronym giving it the virtue of brevity without the fault of over-familiarity, was how he was almost universally known throughout his progress from young minister to Master of Trinity and slightly battered national monument.

He was under-secretary, first at the India Office and later at the Foreign Office for nine years, then President of the Board of Education, then Minister of Labour, then Chancellor of the Exchequer, then Leader of the House of Commons, then Home Secretary, then First Secretary of State and Deputy Prime Minister, then Foreign Secretary. With varying degrees of compliance, he served seven Prime Ministers. His personal choice is not altogether surprising. 'I had the most affection for Baldwin', he wrote. In outlook they were not dissimilar, although Butler was much cleverer, less effective as an orator, and enlivened by an agreeable streak of malicious irreverence which was lacking in Baldwin. They were drawn together over India, although Baldwin had never been there, while Butler was deeply influenced by his childhood experiences of the Central Provinces.

Butler much wanted to be Viceroy. He could think of 'no position in the world which so well combined administration, concentration, diplomacy and presence'. But he also believed in an early evolution towards self-government. He started his ministerial career defending the India Bill against the die-hards. He continued it, less felicitously, as Foreign Office spokesman in the Commons, defending appeasement against the opponents of Munich. He contrasts his pre-war experiences with those of Harold Macmillan:-

> I trod a different path, serving the establishment with patient if unglamorous tenacity. This is not a sure recipe for success in achieving the highest political rewards. As I invariably inform young men who now come and ask me about politics, the lives of leaders the world over have frequently been advanced by colourful rebellion or resignation . . . My own career, by contrast, exemplifies the advantages of the long haul, namely the steady influence one may exert by being at all times on the inside.

He was, however, aware also of the disadvantages involved in his chosen and consistent course of accommodation, at any rate in the last resort. Often he represented the cause of good sense, but sometimes pursued it with an ambivalent moderation which lost him the support of both sides. 'Whenever I moved in the weeks that followed', he wrote of the period after Suez, 'I felt the party knives sticking into my innocent back.' It was lack of cold steel which cost him the premiership first in 1953, when Churchill was incapacitated at Chartwell and Eden was in hospital in America, perhaps in 1957, certainly in 1963. He was aware of this, and, much though he wanted the highest office, did not in a sense regret what he regarded as having flowed almost inevitably from his temperament. 'The Chief Whip said to me later', he wrote about 1963, 'that it would have been possible to alter the whole decision in my favour, but that he thought I would never have been happy again if I had done so. With this diagnosis I agree . . . one cannot alter one's nature.'

Lord Butler considered which of his many posts – no man of this century other than Sir John Simon held so many of the highest below the premiership – he most enjoyed:-

> If I am to measure this by lasting achievement, the answer must be the Ministry of Education. If I am to measure it by contemporary and potential importance, the zenith was certainly reached at the Treasury.

Certainly his enjoyment of Education is reflected in the quality of his narrative dealing with this wartime period. The now remote waters of religious controversy in which he had to fish with such delicacy are made real and enthralling. And from this period comes some highly comic writing about Churchill. In March 1943 Rab was summoned for a working visit to Chequers. After an evening of extravagant conversation and semi-farce at a film show, he was sent to bed at one o'clock to work on part of a draft home policy speech which Churchill was planning:-

> I was up and about well before nine next morning, and was rather shaken to be told that it wasn't certain whether the Prime Minister would actually want to see me. However at a quarter to eleven my presence was demanded and I found him in bed, smoking a Corona with a black cat curled up on his feet. He began aggressively by complaining that the cat did more for the war effort than I did, since it provided him with a hot-water bottle and saved fuel and power. Didn't I agree? I said not really, but that it was a very beautiful cat. This seemed to please him. He then asked me if I had done anything overnight or whether I had been lulled to sleep. So

I produced my handiwork which was critically surveyed . . .
At this moment a rather flustered Private Secretary burst in
to say that there was a Private Notice question down that
afternoon from Aneurin Bevan; would he like to take it, or
should the War Office? 'Pray do not look so nervous and hotted
up,' replied the Prime Minister. 'You have no experience of
public affairs. I shall have to take the question, of course. But
it is very sad, very sad indeed, when I was just in the middle
of my majestic speech.' The Private Secretary fled and the
Prime Minister cheered up. After a few minutes he was happily declaiming his speech to the Minister of Education.

Throughout his memoirs Butler's descriptions of relations with
Churchill had an unmatched quality of detached, amused, semi-
affectionate observation, although I suspect that he once or twice
allowed his imagination to run away. Did he really find the 'liba-
tions of brandy so ample that I felt it prudent on more than one
occasion to tip the liquid into the side of my shoe?' It must have
been both uncomfortable and very bad for his shoes.

Another remarkable feature of Lord Butler's book was his ability
to portray naturally the movement of his life through his different
ages. When he wrote of himself as an under-secretary, he wrote as
a slim young man, anxious to make his way up the Tory hierarchy,
although without being unduly pressing. When he wrote of himself
as Minister of Education he wrote as a young minister, offered a particular opportunity and assuming just enough authority to exploit
it, although not to impose himself upon the central machinery
of government. In opposition and as the directing author of the
Conservative 'charters' he began to move into the centre of the
stage. When he wrote as Chancellor he had assumed authority,
although there was still a slight note of tentativeness about his
importance and success so early in his middle age. Then, with
Churchill gone, the note changed. As Home Secretary he was
almost an elder statesman, as Foreign Secretary undoubtedly so.
As Master of Trinity he saw the world with the hooded eyes,
slightly inclined head and rounded shoulders of one who has been
weathered by the experiences, achievements and disappointments
of 40 years of public service.

Sixteen years after *The Art of the Possible* there came the
authorised biography of Rab Butler. If in pursuit of his own

political interest he had displayed half the daring that he showed in the choice of his biographer, he would undoubtedly have been Prime Minister. Anthony Howard was a remarkable choice for the task, and the way in which it was made by Rab was characteristically diagonal. Two and a half years before his death Mr Howard asked if he could include Rab – with Gaitskell, Crossman and Macleod – in a gallery of political portraits which he was planning. A meeting was arranged at which Rab, in effect, said 'certainly not.' But on the way out he indicated that if Mr Howard cared to write a full-scale biography of him alone that would be a different matter, and that all the papers might be available.

It reminds me of a Welsh Nonconformist story I retain from my childhood. A revivalist preacher swept to his conclusion by asking all the congregation who wished to go to heaven to raise their hands. They all did, except for Deacon Evans, sitting in the front row. 'But Mr Evans,' the affronted shepherd said, 'surely you want to go to heaven.' 'Yes,' said Deacon Evans, 'but not by the excursion train.'

Rab let Anthony Howard loose among the 200 boxes of papers which he had taken to and left at Trinity College. This made him – along with Robert Rhodes James on Eden and Alastair Horne on Macmillan – one of the three musketeers of Conservative biographical subjects of the mid twentieth century.

Mr Howard's subject was, of course, the only one of the three who never climbed to the 'top of the greasy pole' (although Eden did so only to slide down it again with remarkable speed and discomfort). Rab was probably also the one who posed the most difficult and interesting problems for the biographer. There were sharp contrasts in the lives of the other two, in Eden's case between the young hope of liberal England of the 1930s and the affronter of the United Nations in 1956, in Macmillan's case between the rather boring politician of early middle age and the aged statesman, whose wit and style became still more appreciated as his eighties succeeded his seventies, and then gave way to his nineties.

With Butler the contrast between light and shade was less obvious. Both his character and his career evolved along a smoother curve. But the ambiguity and subtlety were much greater. Rab had a fine if slightly drooping style and an oblique wit with such a special tang that it had to be expressed with a syntax of his own which had some but not all of the characteristics of English.

He lived in quiet grandeur after he married into the Courtauld family, bestrode (without commanding) the Conservative Party for a generation, was rightly offered an earldom in 1964 (a revelation of Mr Howard), and yet was essentially a servant rather than a ruler of the state.

He lacked insolence, a quality possessed by Tory politicians from Canning through Disraeli, Joseph Chamberlain and F. E. Smith to Iain Macleod. This was despite the fact that he had a greater capacity for private irreverence than almost anyone I have ever known. I shall never forget his sudden exposition to me (whom he then hardly knew), *circa* 1958, of the splendours of being Home Secretary: 'If the Prime Minister were arrested in the park, it would come to me to deal with, you know.' But then the fantasy evaporated, for he saw the precipice ahead and said sadly: 'But I couldn't do anything. I would have to leave it to the law.'

His vanity was in no way exceptional for one of his occupation. What he required excessive quantities of was not praise but reassurance. After his second leadership defeat, Rab constantly interrupted Foreign Office meetings to say, half-interrogatively, 'I believe I was right not to split the party, don't you?'

Yet he had wonderful political antennae, was perhaps the most richly anecdotal figure since Curzon, and combined this with a gift for successful and constructive administration. He was not like Austen Chamberlain, who 'always played the game and always lost it'. He was not a games-playing man.

Nor was he a gambler. He never won the big game because he never really entered it. He was an intendant of politics, subtle, resourceful, dedicated, the best Prime Minister we never had, yet at the root more suited to be a great Cabinet officer under a presidential system – a Stimson or a Marshall or an Acheson – than a leader in his own right.

James Callaghan

James Callaghan was born in 1912, the son of a Chief Petty Officer in the Royal Navy. He was educated in Portsmouth and entered the Inland Revenue as a Tax Officer in 1929. In 1938 he married Audrey Moulton and has one son and two daughters. During the Second World War he served as a naval lieutenant. In 1945 he was elected MP for the southern part of Cardiff and represented this constituency, which occasionally modified its name, until 1987. He was a junior minister under Attlee, and prominent in opposition politics 1951–61. He unsuccessfully contested the leadership of the Labour Party against Harold Wilson and George Brown in 1963. He served in the Wilson Governments as Chancellor of the Exchequer 1964–67, Home Secretary 1969–70, and Secretary of State for Foreign and Commonwealth Affairs 1974–76. On Wilson's retirement in 1976 he was elected leader of the Labour Party and became Prime Minister until he was defeated at the General Election of 1979. He resigned the leadership in 1980. He bacame Lord Callaghan of Cardiff in 1987 and also a Knight of the Garter.

There is now a very considerable chance that James Callaghan will stand in history as the last Labour Prime Minister. MacDonald, Attlee, Wilson and Callaghan make an odd quartet of figures for the pantheon: MacDonald banished from his plinth; Wilson without (for the moment, at any rate) many floral tributes on his anniversaries; Callaghan allowed to remain but begged to be as silent as possible; and only Lord Attlee accorded a hero's retrospective respect.

Yet the achievements, both domestic and international, of Labour's 55 years as a party of office were very considerable, and it is not a small thing to stand second in esteem, as Lord Callaghan does, amongst those who headed the governments.

The accomplishment is made the more remarkable by two further considerations. He was the nearest approach to a Prime Minister of working-class birth and education (there were differing ambiguities about the origins of both Lloyd George and MacDonald) in the 250-year history of the office. And he has been the only politician to occupy all the other great offices of state, Chancellor, Home Secretary, Foreign Secretary, before becoming Prime Minister. Palmerston, his nearest rival in this respect, refused the Exchequer but became Home Secretary and (several times) Foreign Secretary.

Perhaps more significant than the roll-call of Lord Callaghan's offices was his ability to perform best in the highest of them. His premiership did not end well (not many do), but there was no question of his being another Eden who attained his goal only to disappoint his promise. There were few who thought that his personality or temperament were not up to 10 Downing Street.

On what has he done it all? No-one, including himself, would, I think, put it down primarily to intellect. But he is far from being alone amongst Prime Ministers or even great men (Roosevelt for example) in that respect. Nor is it to be explained by oratory, despite an avuncular persuasiveness, flavoured with a dash of menace, in his speech-making. Still less can he lay claim to an innovative cast of mind, not merely in the personal sense of having a darting quicksilver intelligence, but in the wider one of being anxious to seize upon the imaginations of others and harness them to his own purposes. No-one who knows him and reads his own assessment can doubt that it is conventional, even conservative values which exercise the strongest pull upon him.

As a result it is difficult to attribute to him a single great policy initiative in any of his offices. His short-term judgement has mostly been good, often very good, his strategic judgement less so. His nerve has rarely cracked. His ability to surmount a major setback, as with his retreat from the Treasury in 1967, and to do so holding his head high and not petitioning his way back to the front rank of politics, has been outstanding. He has always handled himself well in public, displaying a mixture of authority, dignity and calming common sense. He has cultivated his allies carefully, and time and chance (the words he chose for the title of his memoirs) have been kind to him.

In his memoirs published in 1987, he was good-tempered

and generous. There was practically no-one mentioned, except for Richard Crossman, who is dead, the Turkish Foreign Minister of 1974, who may well be so also, and the general secretary of NUPE in the 'winter of discontent', who did not get a tribute. The expression of such widespread goodwill is obviously a cousin to blandness. Yet he avoided by quite a wide margin that Panglossian wiping away of the wrinkles from the face of his own history which made Lord Wilson's account of the Government of 1964-70 more comforting than informative.

Lord Callaghan reserved his excessive kindness for others and not for himself. His general standpoint, I suppose, was one of an agreeably surprised satisfaction that he should have achieved so much starting from so little. An irreverent eye for the ridiculous aspect of any grand occasion or major international colleague was not one of his literary tools. He is an enthusiastic member of the club of former world statesmen, and there was nothing in his memoirs which endangered his future membership of it. Presidents Ford, Carter and Giscard, as well as Chancellor Schmidt and Secretary Kissinger, ought all to be well-satisfied readers.

But about his own setbacks and failures he wrote with a quiet honesty. When something did not go well he did not attempt to pretend it did, or to put the blame upon others. Sometimes he complained about circumstances when they were only predictably adverse, rather like a man who repeatedly organised January picnics, and was surprised when the weather did not allow them to be more successful. Thus the hopeless nature of his 1964-7 struggle to maintain the $2.80 rate for sterling emerged with cumulative clarity. There was practically no event in Britain or the world, from a strike, through a misjudgement in the *order* of his proposals in one Budget, an unkind word from a French minister, the resignation of Frank Cousins, to hesitancy by the U.S. about putting together yet another assistance package, which did not shake sterling. Surely if he had not been so addicted to 'this symbol of national pride', he might have decided earlier that it was not one circumstance after another but the nature of the task which he had set himself which was at fault.

It was his inherent conservatism (and vestigial imperialism) which condemned him to this honourable but perverse campaign. He has always instinctively been a Commonwealth man, and saw the integrity of sterling as essential cement. Next to the

Commonwealth he was a North Atlantic man. One of his favourite recollections of the '60s was of 'a rollicking afternoon in the Oval office' with President Johnson; there is indeed something of LBJ without the scatology about James Callaghan. This orientation set a strict limit to the effectiveness of his collaboration with Schmidt and Giscard, well though he handled his personal relations with them, particularly with Schmidt.

As an example there was a significant Callaghan/Schmidt encounter in March, 1978. Schmidt believed that he had given Callaghan an advance exposé of the European Monetary System, of which his mind was then full and which he was to launch on the European Council at Copenhagen two or three weeks later. But Callaghan did not take it in, for his mind was equally full of a new pound/dollar initiative within the framework of the IMF, of which he wished to give Schmidt prior notice before trying it on Carter. Schmidt's mind was equally impervious to this. On this occasion they were like two friendly ships which passed in the night without recognition. The difference was that Callaghan's monetary scheme came to nothing, Schmidt's to a great deal.

Inevitably, I fear, the Callaghan period in 10 Downing Street will be seen in history as a postscript to that of Harold Wilson. That is true of all short premierships almost independent of merit: Rosebery to Gladstone, Balfour to Salisbury, Home to Macmillan. But although there will be no age of Callaghan, the career of Callaghan will be one of the most intriguing of the second half of the twentieth century.

Henry Campbell-Bannerman

(Sir) Henry Campbell-Bannerman was born in 1836, the younger son of Sir James Campbell (the Bannerman came as the result of the will of a maternal uncle.) He was educated at the High School and University of Glasgow and Trinity College, Cambridge. He married Charlotte Bruce, a general's daughter, in 1860.

He was MP for Stirling Burghs from 1868 and leader of the Liberal Party in the House of Commons from 1899 until his death in 1908. He served as Financial Secretary to the War Office 1871–74 and 1880–82, Secretary to the Admiralty 1882–84, Chief Secretary for Ireland 1884–85, Secretary of State for War 1886 and 1892–95 and was Prime Minister from 1905 until his death in 1908.

Henry Campbell-Bannerman was not the greatest of Prime Ministers, or the most charismatic of the political figures among whom he lived. But he had an unusual character of considerable interest; he was a major political influence for a decade and a half; and when he died (only a few days out of office), he did so in a glow of respect and left a Liberal Government securely based and surprisingly united.

He was an unlikely man to have become a party leader. He enjoyed the House of Commons, in which he spent 40 of his 72 years of life, participating adequately but without either great brilliance or thrust in its work, and being fairly effortlessly re-elected each time for the sound Liberal constituency of Stirling Burghs. He became Secretary of State for War at the age of 50 in the third Gladstone Government, and returned to the same office when the G.O.M. formed his last Government six years later. He was a competent and tactful departmental minister much liked by the generals. His greatest feat was to dislodge the 76-year-old Duke of Cambridge from the post of Commander-in-Chief after decades of office, which led to his being rewarded by the Queen with the unusual honour for a politician of the GCB. His major though accidental failure was to provide the occasion for the defeat of the Government on the 'cordite' vote of 1895 – the last time a Government resigned after a defeat in the House of Commons. At no stage in this Government were his political ambitions high. When the Speakership fell vacant he tried very hard to get it, believing that it would provide him with a more agreeable retirement than life on the front benches, and he was offended with his colleagues when they ruled him out because he was a minister.

Liberalism then entered a 10-year shadow. The mood of the country was imperialist. Gladstone had gone, and Rosebery had proved an appalling successor. Campbell-Bannerman became leader by default. First Rosebery flounced out, and then Harcourt and Morley did the same. There were only four 'ex-Cabs', as they were then quaintly known, left in the Commons. Fowler and Bryce were clearly not possible. That left Asquith and Bannerman. Asquith was much the better parliamentarian but he was doubtfully acceptable to much of the party and unanxious to give up his lucrative Bar practice. Bannerman then accepted with moderate reluctance.

He found himself with one of the most thankless leadership roles which any politician of the past 100 years has had to face. The Liberal Party tore itself to pieces over the South African War. Not only was it divided into at least three factions, pursuing different voting courses in the House of Commons. In addition, the most talented figures paid no respect to Campbell-Bannerman's leadership and were constantly looking outside to the impossible Rosebery.

Once in the job, however, the new leader was determined to stay there. He survived the buffeting and the indignity, which continued right up to his accession to the premiership in 1905, when there was a concerted attempt to make him a half-superannuated Prime Minister in the Lords, and then emerged into a glow of evening sunlight. He exercised an easy command over the vast and heterogeneous Liberal majority, and was effectively in control of the House of Commons as a whole. Having been tormented for years by Balfour's dialectical skill, he suddenly discovered, with a majority behind him, that he could sweep him away as irrelevant and convoluted. He got on well with all his Cabinet colleagues, including his former detractors, and secured graceful admissions from Edward Grey and Haldane that they had been wrong.

Whether he could for long have been a good Prime Minister is another matter. He was always fairly idle, and after the death of his wife, followed by the decline of his own health, his grip on Government business became very tenuous. He developed a habit, engaging to those whom he pleased but maddening to his colleagues, of listening to odd snatches of debate in the House of Commons and then suddenly rising and announcing a switch of Government policy. When remonstrated with by King Edward VII for the jejuneness of his Cabinet letters, he in effect replied that the discussion had been fairly pointless and that he did not wish to bore the Sovereign with matters which he himself had found tedious. His essential role was to be a prologue to Asquith, and this would have been so even if his health had lasted longer. Two years of his benign and instinctive Liberalism, assuaging to party feelings after so many years of defeat and schism, made it easier for his more efficient but less popular successor to be accepted.

Campbell-Bannerman's style of life was odd. He always lived prosperously, but not at all fashionably. Apart from his Scottish baronial pile filled with French furniture, he had a succession of huge London houses. But he did not entertain greatly in them. He was in 29 Belgrave Square when he became Prime Minister. He went abroad a great deal, and probably spoke the best French of any Prime Minister this century. He was almost equally devoted to the food and novels of France. 'He could order a dinner with any man in Europe', Augustine Birrell recorded. His gastronomy however did not make him exclusively francophile. Apart from anything else, it had the effect of sending him regularly for five or six late summer weeks cure in Marienbad, where he spoke 'German with a smart Viennese accent' (Lord Acton) and hob-nobbed latterly with King Edward VII.

This *confort cossu* in no way affected his views or personality. He remained a rather pawky Scots radical whose *forte* was restoring self-confidence to his party. But it did put some strain on his considerable but not vast fortune, which came from Glasgow retail trade. In his last years he had to borrow to keep going. But it did not much matter as he had no children and his wife had already gone. Since Pitt he was the only Prime Minister to die in 10 Downing Street, and he timed it rather well.

Barbara Castle

Barbara Castle was born Barbara Betts in Yorkshire in 1910. She was educated at Bradford Grammar School and St. Hugh's College, Oxford. She became a Daily Mirror *journalist and she married a colleague, Ted Castle (later Lord Castle) who died in 1979. She was MP for Blackburn from 1945 to 1979.*

She was Minister for Overseas Development 1964–65, for Transport 1965–68, First Secretary and Secretary of State for Employment and Productivity 1968–70, Secretary of State for Social Services 1974–76. She has been a member of the European Parliament for Greater Manchester since 1979, and was leader of the British Labour group 1979–85.

Judged by the detail in which it has been recorded by its members, the first Wilson Government of 1964-70 is by far the greatest in our history. It now has three major chroniclers, all of whom are generous to a fault in their use of words.

There is the then Prime Minister himself, who quickly gave us a bland but not brief account of a Government which faced fearful odds but in which, in comradeship between brothers (and sisters), all pain was washed away and all tears were dried up.

Richard Crossman, the great destroyer of the veils of Cabinet secrecy, did not have the same preferences for the bedside manner over the X-ray machine. He saw his diaries, dictated in great retrospective chunks each Sunday morning, as providing the raw material for a more penetrating understanding of the reality of power in British Government than anything since Bagehot. And the rawer and bloodier the better it was for his rumbustious taste. The account was obviously written from the point of view of Crossman's somewhat fluctuating judgement, and was sometimes distorted, but more out of a desire to shock than to achieve self-justification. Yet, given his scant respect for facts in argument, his *Diaries* were in my view remarkably accurate in essentials. They were quite often boring about his own departmental affairs, but they were not particularly self-centred. It was the frailties of British politics not the greatness of Crossman the statesman that he wished to reveal.

Mrs Castle wishes to reveal Mrs Castle. She takes a long time doing so. It is an immense volume, a good half million words, or at least 25 hours' solid reading time. This was a little too much, even for me, who had the normally compelling incentive of finding my name on nearly every other page. From a readability point of view it ought clearly to have been substantially pruned. And yet it must also be said that it is by far the best account of the inner proceedings of that 1960s Government that has yet been published, and probably the best account that ever will be published.

As a source book it will be invaluable. I take one example. In January, 1968, following devaluation and my replacement of James Callaghan at the Exchequer, we had to carry through a major public expenditure reduction. It could not be done without policy changes and I was determined that we should hold firm to each point of a balanced quadrilateral. We should advance and thus bring within the control of a single Government the date of withdrawal from east of Suez. We should cancel our order for the expensive American F111 planes. We should impose prescription charges. And we should postpone the raising of the school leaving age. This exercise occupied the intolerable total of seven 3 or 4 hour Cabinets (for such was Harold Wilson's method) all concentrated into eleven days, as well as many preparatory meetings. The process had more than its fair share of tedium, but also some excitement, for Lord Wilson always 'counted noses' in Cabinet, and on none of the issues did we have more than a narrow majority, and that majority was each time made up of different people. So it was a close run thing. All this is meticulously chronicled by Mrs Castle, in more detail than I could now assemble, with more vividness than could be captured from any Cabinet records, and to the best of my recollection with almost complete accuracy.

Mrs Castle's *Diaries* are very honest. This is so in two senses. First she wrote what she thought and felt. She was immensely self-centred, and she could be maddeningly obsessive, vain and coy. But she did not dissimulate, she did not make up false facts, and her judgement about the performance (although often not the motivation) of individuals was mostly shrewd and fair. Her swans did not always have to be swans nor her geese geese.

Second, there seems to be strong evidence that her diaries – with a few, too few, excisions – are published as she wrote them. She has not gone back and smoothed out the inconsistencies. Thus for April 29th 1969 we read: 'Over dinner I felt my anger rising coldly and uncontrollably. "I'm through with Harold now", I told him (Crossman). "Henceforth I dedicate myself to his destruction." Yet five days later she was writing: 'Harold has had a triumph at the Festival Hall. His capacity for comebacks is remarkable and I'm relieved.'

Her capacity for criticism of others was formidable. Crossman (apart from the Prime Minister) was her great friend in the Cabinet. Diarists and ex-Bevanites together, they hunted like two animals of incongruous shape and doubtful loyalty who were nonetheless inseparable. She ran to him instinctively whenever she had a grievance or was in trouble. They even went on holiday together. But this was an 'eye opener on Dick's character . . . His boorishness astonishes me. I knew he was an intellectual bully, but I didn't know before that he was a social one as well which is far less excusable and makes the reliability of his judgement still more suspect.' James Callaghan, her chief enemy, comes off almost easily by comparison. 'I've merely registered another reason why I should despise him', she says lightly after some appalling sin on his part. I am also amazed at how lightly I escape. However, she redeems any weakness here in an epilogue which concludes by blaming the 1970 Budget (which in fact, for some reason I have never understood, achieved with one other the equal highest poll approval rating of any Budget since the war) for the loss of the subsequent General Election.

So 'the baddies' (ex-Gaitskellites) were wrong in the end and 'the goodies' (ex-Bevanites) were right. It was this tribal approach, as she engagingly confessed in November, 1969, despite her courage, flair and bursts of adventurous pragmatism, which determined her political fall-back position, and in particular enabled her, when *In Place of Strife* was frustrated, to turn round in a way that made a squirrel in a cage look consistent and hysterically denounce the rather similar legislation from the Heath Government. This was deeply damaging, not only to her own reputation, but to that of politics generally.

How did she get this vast diary written? I think it must have been dictated every night, a prodigious feat of determined stamina, on top of the crushing schedule, with every ounce of vigour and commitment given to nearly every engagement, to which she habitually subjected herself. She was always 'dragging' herself to an early meeting, 'crawling' with exhaustion out of Cabinet and finally 'creeping home' to a tired bed. She made exhaustion into a political virility symbol, and was foolishly critical of the diligence of those who did not believe that decisions were best taken in a state of prostration.

Yet her total commitment, combined with her warmth, spontaneity and fearlessness were the secrets of much of her success. And a very considerable success it was. These *Diaries* are not only the best account of the first Wilson Government; they are written by one of its best members.

Anthony Crosland

Anthony Crosland was born in 1918, the son of a senior War Office official. His mother was a lecturer in Old French at Westfield College in the University of London. His family were Plymouth Brethren. He was educated at Trinity College, Oxford where he was a classical scholar.

He was MP for South Gloucestershire 1950–55 and for Grimsby 1959–77. He was Secretary of State for Education, 1965–7, President of the Board of Trade, 1967–9, Secretary for Local Government 1969–70 and for the Environment 1974–6. He was Foreign Secretary 1976–7 and died in that office.

I first saw Tony Crosland in 1938 or early 1939. He was 20, and I was 18. The gap seemed bigger. He was a very impressive undergraduate, showing every sign of intellectual and social self-assurance. He was immensely good-looking, and even in those days rather elegant. He wore a long camel-hair overcoat, and drove a powerful low MG known as the Red Menace. I, like many of his near-contemporaries, admired him from afar, and was rather intimidated.

Then one winter's evening a few months after the outbreak of the war, he came to my rooms, probably on some minor point of Labour Club business, and having settled it, remained uncertainly on the threshold, talking, but neither sitting down nor departing for nearly two hours. His character was more ambivalent than I had thought, but also more engaging. Thereafter, I saw him nearly every day for the next six months until he left Oxford, and afterwards enjoyed a close friendship with him over nearly four decades.

He was educated at Highgate and at Trinity College, Oxford,

where he was a classical scholar. His university years were interrupted by the war and five years in the army. He was an officer in the Royal Welch Fusiliers, transferred to the Parachute Regiment in 1942, and subsequently served in North Africa, Italy, France and Austria. His most characteristic military exploit was to land by parachute on the casino at Cannes, during Operation 'Anvil' in the summer of 1944.

At Oxford he had a notable career, both academically and as an undergraduate politician. He lost interest in classics and got only a second in Honour Moderations in 1939. He then switched to Modern Greats, primarily economics, and, after his return to the University in 1946, got a clear first in Philosophy, Politics and Economics, and was elected a Fellow of Trinity in 1947. Before the war he was an active and orthodoxly Marxist member of the Labour Club. In the early months of the war, however, he found himself increasingly out of sympathy with its fellow-travelling and neutralist line, and in May 1940 he joined with others to lead the successful break-away of the Democratic Socialist Club, which was much closer to the national Labour Party position. He was elected Treasurer of the Union Society, but was defeated for the presidency. Six years later, however, on his return from the army, he redressed this setback and secured the higher office.

As a young don, with a few contemporaries, notably (Sir) Raymond Carr and (Professor) Ian Little, he formed something of a cult group, of which the distinguishing characteristic was the unusual combination of hard intellectual endeavour and undisciplined, even rather riotous, relaxation.

In 1950, at the age of 31, he was first elected a Member of Parliament, for the constituency of South Gloucestershire, which he was able to win for the Labour Party because it contained a good deal of Bristol suburb as well as of south Cotswold countryside. He gave up his Oxford fellowship a few months later, and never returned to professional academic life, although he remained very much an intellectual in politics. In the House of Commons he had a considerable, although not perhaps a remarkable, success. He was an economic specialist, and a close friend and assistant of Hugh Gaitskell, who for most of that period was shadow Chancellor of the Exchequer. In 1952 Crosland married Hilary Sarson, of the vinegar family, but the marriage was brief and was finally dissolved in 1957.

Before the 1955 general election the boundaries of South Gloucestershire were redrawn in a way unfavourable to Labour, and Crosland decided to seek another seat. This was a mistaken move, for the one which he found, Southampton Test, produced a larger Conservative majority than the one he had left. He was not, however, greatly disconcerted by his exclusion from Parliament, for although devoted to politics in a broader sense, he regarded the trappings and life of the House of Commons with some indifference.

He had other things to do. In 1953 he had already published his first book, *Britain's Economic Problem*. This was a lucid but fairly conventional analysis of the country's post-war trading difficulties. By 1955 he was already well into a much more original and substantial work, which he completed in the next year and published in the autumn of 1956. *The Future of Socialism* was well received at the time, but only gradually, over the next decade or so, achieved its position as the most important theoretical treatise to be written from the moderate left of British politics in the 25 post-war years. It assumed the triumph of Keynesianism, and with it a future of broadening abundance and the withering of the Marxist class struggle. It disputed the importance of nationalisation and challenged the bureaucratic socialism of the Webbs' Fabian tradition: 'Total abstinence and a good filing system are not now the right sign-posts to the socialist Utopia; or at least, if they are, some of us will fall by the wayside'. It was at once libertarian and strongly egalitarian. It saw no conflict which could not be resolved by the flowing tide of continuing economic growth. It was in the mainstream of the optimism, many would now say the complacency, of the English liberal tradition. It influenced a generation.

Political theory having been disposed of with imagination, even if not total prescience, Crosland showed his utilitarianism by devoting the next two years to acting as secretary (under Gaitskell's chairmanship) to the Independent Committee of Inquiry into the Cooperative Movement and writing a good report. Then he re-entered the House of Commons in 1959 as Member for Grimsby, the constituency which he represented for the remaining $17^1/_2$ years of his life. He was quickly involved in all the Labour Party disputes which followed that lost election, urging Gaitskell on in the argument over 'Clause Four' (the nationalisation clause in the Party's constitution), supporting him against unilateral disarmament, sharply disagreeing with him over his reticence towards Macmillan's initiative for British entry to the European Community.

Even apart from the European issue, however, he was in no way a client of his leader. He had too strong a personality and too critical a judgement for that. In some ways Gaitskell sought him more than he sought Gaitskell, and he was less thrown by Gaitskell's early death in 1963 than were some others in the circle. In the Harold Wilson election to the leadership which followed he showed his detachment by supporting Callaghan, who ran a bad third, rather than George Brown, who was the candidate of the majority of the 'Gaitskellites'.

In 1964 Crosland married again and also entered Government for the first time. His second marriage was to Susan Catling (née Watson) of Baltimore, Maryland, who under the name of Susan Barnes became a prolific writer of skill and perception, and later under her married name a columnist; unlike the first marriage it was a great and continuing success. His initial Government post was as Minister of State in the newly created Department of Economic Affairs, but after only three months he filled an unexpectedly early Cabinet vacancy and became Secretary of State for Education and Science.

He stayed at the Department of Education for $2^1/_2$ years and was then transferred to the Board of Trade in 1967, hoping that this would lead on to the Exchequer. When the vacancy in the Chancellorship occurred a few months later and this did not follow (I was in fact appointed) he was deeply disappointed. His relations with Harold Wilson were never close, and in the autumn of 1969 there was some doubt about his survival in the Government. But he was too able a man to lose and for the last few months of that Government occupied a coordinating role over unmerged departments as Secretary of State for Local Government and Regional Planning.

There followed nearly four years in opposition. He worked hard as a party spokesman, published another book, *Socialism Now*, in 1974 (which, like its 1962 predecessor, *The Conservative Enemy*, was a collection of political essays, but more circumscribed in scope by his housing and local government responsibilities), and surprised and disappointed many of his friends by failing to vote with 68 Labour MPs in favour of Britain's entry to the European Community in the decisive division of October 1971; he did not vote against, but abstained. This ambiguity probably accounted for his poor result in the deputy leadership election of 1972.

In the 1974 Wilson Government he was Secretary of State for the Environment, essentially the same job that he had occupied in 1969, but with a different name, tighter control over his subordinate ministers, and a more senior position at the Cabinet table. His experience as an upper middle rank departmental minister had become unrivalled, although the great offices of state continued to elude him. He responded by being increasingly effective in his department, and by exercising more authority in the Cabinet than in the previous Government, while moving consciously away from the right and towards the centre of the party. In March 1976, when Harold Wilson resigned as Prime Minister, Crosland was determined to contest the succession. He ran fifth of five candidates, securing only seventeen votes. Yet the contest did not damage him. He succeeded to the Foreign Office in the new Callaghan administration with an unimpaired authority, and had he lived might well have been a stronger rival to Michael Foot in 1980 than Denis Healey proved to be.

He was Foreign Secretary for only 10 months. Although he had always tried to think and write in an internationalist context, his experience was insular. He was unacquainted with the intricacies of the nuances of the foreign policy game. He knew foreign sociologists rather than foreign statesmen. Yet, after a hesitant start, he impressed most of his officials and his foreign colleagues by his authority, his wit and his intellect. His personality, if not his fame, was a match for that of his principal confrère, Henry Kissinger. He was no longer the glamorous *enfant terrible* of his Oxford days, or even the adventurous thinker of *The Future of Socialism*. He was not old, but he had become a little tired in body, heavy and hooded-eyed, yet mordant of phrase, contemptuous of pomposity, and capable of a still dazzling charm.

He was pleased to be Foreign Secretary, but he still wanted, as ten years before, to be Chancellor of the Exchequer, and devoted some of his overtaxed and waning energy to preparing for that office which he was never to hold. This was a last typical manifestation of the paradox of Anthony Crosland. His intellect was one of the strongest in post-war British politics, and he fortified it by exceptional powers of application. But it was weakened by some uncontrolled demon of discontent, which marred his satisfaction in his own particular roles of excellence. He died in office at the age of 58, six days after a massive cerebral haemorrhage, on 19th February 1977.

My friendship with Anthony Crosland fluctuated under the pressure of circumstances, of the separation of the war, of political commitment, and penultimately, alas, of political rivalry, but never died. I last saw him across the large table of the Council of Ministers in Brussels. He presided. I sat opposite. It was just over 37 years since his havering 'threshold' appearance in Oxford. As was his habit in public, he was much more decisive on the latter occasion. He was an excellent chairman, already after a few weeks putting a strong stamp of authority on his presidency of the Council and his relations with his fellow foreign ministers.

As a private person he was by no means an easy friend. He was immensely critical, both of himself and of others. Particularly during the years when he lived alone, he assumed – largely, I think, for reasons of self-discipline – an inflexibility about time which made making social arrangements into major diplomatic negotiations. He was a man of contradictions. He was a puritan with an inclination to self-indulgence. He was an immensely diligent worker of indolent physical habits. He wrote almost the whole of his great 500-page theoretical *Future of Socialism*, sitting in a peculiarly low and battered armchair.

He had a mind of high perspective, yet cared little, in a personal as opposed to an aesthetic sense, about the past. He had practically no sense of nostalgia. He believed in applying highly rational standards to decision-making (he always thought me hopelessly intuitive) but he was full of strong emotions. He was devoted to politics, but impatient of its trappings. I do not think he ever enjoyed the House of Commons. He was always antipathetic to most forms of social life, yet he had one of the strongest social personalities I have ever known. He could suffuse a room (and indeed a house) with either a glow of warmth or a gloom of disapproval. He *could* be one of the most enjoyable companions in the whole world but this was certainly not always the case.

To say that his tragic death was a cruel deprivation is the tritest of understatements. His loss in mid-career was comparable for post-war British politics only with the equally early deaths of Hugh Gaitskell and Iain Macleod.

Hugh Dalton

Hugh Dalton was born in 1887, the son of a canon of Windsor (J.N. Dalton) who had been tutor of King George V. He was educated at Eton and King's College, Cambridge and then acquired a doctorate at the London School of Economics 1911–13. In 1914 he married Ruth Hamilton-Fox and they had one daughter who died in 1922 aged four and a half. He served in the First World War as an artillery officer on the Italian Front.

He was MP for Peckham 1924–29, and for Bishop Auckland 1929–31 and 1935–59. He served as Minister of Economic Warfare 1940–42, President of the Board of Trade 1942–45, Chancellor of the Exchequer 1945–47, Chancellor of the Duchy of Lancaster 1948–51, Minister of Local Government and Planning 1951.

He became Lord Dalton in 1960 and died in 1962.

I knew Dalton well, liked him considerably (contrary to fashion) and regarded him until recently as being unjustly ill-considered or forgotten. Largely thanks to Dr Ben Pimlott's masterly biography *Hugh Dalton* and sensitive editorship of his diaries (*The Second World War Diary of Hugh Dalton 1940-1945* and *The Political Diary of Hugh Dalton 1918-40, 1945-60*), posterity can now know more about Dalton and his views than about any of his contemporaries with the possible exception of Churchill, works by and about whom are much more pasteurised. Of course, no-one in their right mind could regard Dalton as a figure of equivalent interest to Churchill. Dalton, for all his vanities (in spite of the booming voice he was not nearly self-confident enough for them to be conceits), would not have dreamt of thinking so. He was touchingly grateful when in 1953 he *thought* that the great man had called him by his Christian name – but he (Churchill) was 'pretty tight' and 'his speech was not quite clear', he sadly added. Even within the Labour Party it was other people rather than himself that he was always intriguing to make Prime Minister. He would not have refused the leadership had it been offered to him, but by some process of inverted snobbery he instinctively wanted to replace 'rabbit Attlee' and 'his little Victorian villa at Stanmore' (whom he consistently underestimated) with someone lower down rather than higher up the social scale. It was the cricket hierarchy upside down. Dalton thought he was a better performer than most if not all of the others, but precluded from captaining England because he was a gentleman, which, in spite of his many qualities, he very doubtfully was.

In writing about his subject and editing his diaries, Pimlott enjoyed the considerable advantage of not having to be circumspect for fear of offending Dalton's surviving relatives, because none remained. This freedom was not accidental. It stemmed from the cruel jejuneness of Dalton's family life. He was the son of a canon of Windsor who had been tutor to King George V, and who boomed his way around the cloisters of St George's Chapel until the age of 92. He was obviously much like his son, but they were separated by a wide generation gap of 48 years. His mother engaged neither his interest nor his affections. He had one sister, four years younger, who disliked him as a child and allowed political differences in later life to produce implacable personal hostility. Her children, his only surviving relations, never met their uncle.

Dalton's own marriage brought little compensation for the chill of his provenance. He married at 26 an intelligent, brisk Fabian of upper-middle-class origin and means, who was none the less as free of family affiliation as was her husband. They had one daughter, who died, searingly, at the age of four. At times in the 1920s and 1930s they achieved a successful political partnership. During the Second World War and over the period of his high political tide they separated completely. Ruth Dalton went to work first in Manchester and then in France. She returned and looked after him in his decline with an aseptic care. The great emotional involvements of his life were with Rupert Brooke in his twenties and with Tony Crosland in his sixties. Neither wholly reciprocated his feelings.

Dalton, except in that part of his own mind which was preoccupied with a sort of clamant Housmanism, with metaphors of the battlefield, of youthful strength and early death all a little too easily to hand, was not a romantic figure. He had panache but he did not have charisma, either public or private. He was too anxious to please - not everybody, but those he wanted to be his friends and supporters.

Furthermore, as Dr Pimlott noted, 'There was a clown-like element, later tragi-comic, which made those who admired him despise him at the same time . . . Physically he was becoming odder: his body ever more top-heavy and pear-shaped, with an increasing tendency to stoop, his bald dome more gleamingly polished, his voice more thunderous, his (rolling) eyes more disconcerting.' Although he was born 20 years too soon to have been a possible contributory model, there was a touch of Anthony Powell's Widmerpool about Dalton.

Yet he was a considerable political figure, who on the whole stood for sensible causes, and he had some remarkable and engaging personal qualities. His best period was the 1930s, when he did more than anyone else to drag the Labour Party back to sensible radicalism from the infantile extremism which even Attlee had half-embraced after the shock of 1931. He also fought hard and courageously to make the party see that there was a need for arms as well as for resolutions if Hitler was to be resisted.

In 1945, as a result of a sudden switch of Attlee's mind, which may well have been due to the son of King George V not wishing the son of Canon Dalton to become Foreign Secretary, he became Chancellor of the Exchequer. He had 18 splendid months, the most popular (among his own supporters) and apparently confident of the 'Big Five' of the Attlee Government. Then came nemesis.

It was only partly his own fault. He was not a particularly improvident financier. But he was so addicted to braggadocio as to make it appear that he was. Very cheap money might for instance have lasted a little longer had he not proclaimed that 'never before . . . have HM Government borrowed so much for so little for so long'. 1947, in contrast with 1946, he found 'a pig of a year'. In its eleventh month he was out of office, brought down by a most trifling budget indiscretion.

He lived another 14 years and, until he became physically devastated towards the end, appeared buoyant and content. He was not bitter about his setbacks and was not jealous about his successors. He thrust forward Gaitskell, who had been his private secretary during the war, with a selflessness which was nearly unique in politics. He was dedicated to trying to promote the

71

political careers of his young associates. The brutal side of his indiscreet and resonant tongue he reserved for his contemporaries, amongst whom he always had few friends.

Reading Pimlott I realised that Dalton's boisterousness concealed a life which was a hollow shell. I knew that his confidence was only skin-deep. He set himself up as an Etonian cheer-leader for the Labour Party, showing that he could shout louder and more patronisingly than any Tory. Yet he was socially extremely uneasy. He was very class-conscious. I remember once being rather shocked when he dismissed Herbert Morrison as 'a board-schooligan.' Dalton came from a somewhat indeterminate semi-courtier social delta. Having deliberately cast off from that soggy shore he never found firm alternative ground elsewhere. He was suspicious of the upper class, contemptuous of the middle class, and nervously patronising of the working class.

I vividly recall occasion, *circa* 1955, when Dalton and I were pacing the library corridor of the House of Commons, which for him was the equivalent of the Windsor cloisters for his father. He seized upon a passing Labour MP for a northern constituency. 'How are you, Bert?', he boomed. The encounter over, he turned on me and said: 'You will never get anywhere in politics until you call that man Bert.' I said: 'I don't think you're right, Hugh. Apart from anything else his name is Fred.' That was the figure of fun side of his personality, which made him highly enjoyable to be with. But beneath the ebullience his melancholy was deep.

On a less personal note, we are lucky that Dalton recorded so minutely the events both of the Second World War and the political events which both preceded and followed it. His diaries are purely political. They do not epitomise the psychological conflicts of an age as Gladstone's did. Despite Dalton's ecclesiastical provenance there is no religion in them. Nor is there any art, any acute social comment or any general London gossip. It is politics, politics all the way. But they are eminently readable, at any rate to a limited audience, because they take amateurs of recent history at a good pace through reasonably familiar countryside by a hitherto unfamiliar route. It is as though, having been used to pounding down the motorway to, say, Swindon (appropriate for Dalton who in 1930 scarred a particularly fine brow of downland seven miles south of it by building a sub-Bauhaus-style walking lodge) the journey were unusually done by train. Not only is an alternative general angle of view presented, but occasional quite unsuspected clusters of trees or buildings are discovered.

Thus, to take scattered examples, I had no idea that there were rumours in December, 1930, taken quite seriously by Arthur Henderson as well as by Dalton, that MacDonald was about to become Viceroy of India; or of the extent to which the alleged machinations of a Labour MPs' lodge of Freemasons (entitled New Welcome and centred around Arthur Greenwood) was agitating Dalton and some others in the late Thirties; or that, just before the 1950 election, Stafford Cripps had the greatest difficulty in getting re-adopted for his Bristol constituency, which had unanimously backed him when he was thrown out of the Labour Party in 1939, but was less enthusiastic about his Iron Chancellorship and the local neglect which went with it (eventually he turned the corner by promising to visit them once a quarter).

Nor was I by any means wholly aware, even from a very close vantage point, of the full hilarity of Dalton's 1955 efforts to get Phillips Price, an ex-Communist Gloucestershire fox-hunting squire, made a peer in order to provide a safer seat for Anthony Crosland. He roamed around the House of Commons, pestering Eden and Attlee and priming Price to an extent which made Dalton himself recognise that elements of French farce were creeping in.

The enterprise ended in total failure. Price did not get his peerage and returned as a shop-soiled candidate to his constituency. Crosland eventually fought a seat which produced a worse result than the one he had abandoned. And Dalton made an ass of himself with both the Prime Minister and the leader of his own party. Yet he records the whole *dégringolade* with almost loving care.

This is part of the quality of the Dalton diary. It is often prejudiced, but transparently so. It is never squeamish, and very rarely dissimulates. Dalton's occasional crashing misjudgements stand unerased: his 1918 belief that John Simon would be the most desirable Liberal recruit to the Labour Party; his 1930 view that Nevile Henderson was amongst the brightest and the best of British diplomats; and his 1940 support for Halifax rather than Churchill as Prime Minister. For most of its span it is also unique. Dalton was the only parliamentarian of the left keeping a diary of significance in the 1920s, '30s and '40s. (Beatrice Webb looked at politics from outside, and Richard Crossman only began in the Fifties.)

A dominant imprint left on my mind is the extent to which the post-1931 Labour Party, in sharp contrast with the quarter century when I was a Labour MP, was outside the arena of government and diplomacy. Dalton was the main emissary to the outside world, but even for him cross-party contacts meant Boothby and very few others. Journalistic contacts meant mostly the *Daily Herald*. And diplomatic contacts meant mostly the Soviet Embassy, with the Poles and the Roumanians thrown in as a special Dalton interest. America (and its politicians) was *terra incognita*.

The great claim to interest in the war-time diaries is that they are the only day-to-day record of the politics of wartime London kept by a participant almost of the first rank. There are plenty of memoirs: Churchill, Eden, Lyttelton, Woolton, Butler. There are notable biographies: Churchill again, Attlee, Bevin, Morrison. There are diaries of quality from those on the fringes of power: Harold Nicolson, Chips Channon, Alexander Cadogan, and, most recently, Jock Colville. But Dalton is the only 'No. 1 Minister', the category into which he frequently and engagingly put himself, who had the combination of literary fluency, surplus energy and self-curiosity to pour out an average of 500 words for every day of the war.

I have long believed that major participants in important events are not good diarists. Either they are too exhausted or too concerned with self-justification. Dalton makes me hesitate over this theory. He shows that one can be self-obsessed without being self-deceived. He could not however quite see to the core of his own weakness (or, if he could, to correct it), which was the loneliness which made him constantly seek company (always 'got Attlee to dinner', never 'Attlee asked me to dinner') and the incontinence not so much of ambition as of temperament which made him use such occasions for the unsubtle pursuit of alliance and counter-alliance.

But he always knew when he was doing well and when he was doing badly. Nor was he a bad judge of the characters of others. His prejudices were on the surface. He could write a good phrase. And he did not bother to clothe his own actions in hypocrisy.

The hero of this part of the diary is Lord Gladwyn. Having been Dalton's Foreign Office private secretary as a young man in 1929-31, he became a sort of *chef de cabinet* to him at Economic Warfare in 1940. Gaitskell was then the principal private secretary, but Gladwyn shines through the diary much more vividly than does that great man of the future. His self-confident energy, muscular intelligence, inability to suffer fools gladly, and indifference to most criticism made him an excellent hunting companion for Dalton in the Whitehall jungle. Dalton greatly appreciated his quality and retained a fairly close contact after his own translation to the Board of Trade and Gladwyn's return to the Foreign Office.

The picture of that jungle which emerges is, superficially at least, a fairly squalid one. It is difficult at times to remember that this was our 'finest hour', when Britain was led by a Government of all the talents, presided over by one of her greatest Prime Ministers, assisted by three of his successors and at least two or three others with high claim to be statesmen. Yet, curiously, behind the in-fighting and the ambition and the jealousies there is a sense of a higher and common purpose and Dalton was very much part of it. He *liked* young men, booming conversation, showing off, and dreams of the great offices of state he might occupy. But he *believed* in Britain, victory and Churchill. And his commitment to these causes illustrates some of the forces which held the nation and the Government together throughout the war.

Anthony Eden

Anthony Eden was born in 1897, the only surviving son of Sir William Eden, 7th and 5th Baronet. He was educated at Eton and Christ Church. He served on the Western Front in the Rifle Brigade in the First World War. In 1923 he married Beatrice Beckett, of grand Yorkshire squirarchical provenance. They were divorced in 1950. They had two sons, the elder of whom was killed in Burma in 1945. In 1952 he married Clarissa Churchill, the daughter of Winston Churchill's younger brother.

Eden was MP for Warwick and Leamington 1923–57. He served as Secretary of State for Foreign Affairs 1935–38, 1940–45 and 1951–55, for Dominion Affairs 1939–40, for War 1940, and was Prime Minister 1955–57.

He was created first Earl of Avon in 1961 and died in 1977.

Why does Anthony Eden present such a formidable biographical challenge? Superficially it might be attributed to the prevalence of paradox in his character and career. There are of course elements of this in the make-up of most politicians, or of most grocers or most clergymen for that matter. But Eden had a quadruple ration. He was a creature of politics, hardly even thinking of, let alone following, any other significant occupation. But he disliked many aspects of political life: men's clubs, the purlieus of the House of the Commons, and the Conservative Party. He liked private life punctuated by bursts of public adulation.

For public life he was fortified by a capacity for very hard work and by a natural charisma. The first was, however, unaccompanied by the exceptional physical resilience of most politicians; even before the disastrous 1953 slip of the surgeon's knife his health obtruded too often at critical moments. The charisma was sometimes unfriendlily attributed only to his looks and elegance. But there was more to it than that. He was an attractive and persuasive speaker, who could sway the opposition benches in the House of Commons and draw great audiences in the country - and mostly send them away satisfied. Yet he never coined a memorable phrase in his life, and re-wrote Foreign Office draft speeches so as to make them more cliché-ridden.

Eden was a 'silver spoon' politician, born with almost every advantage except that of money, who was nonetheless forced by Churchill's political longevity to wait on the threshold of full power for a longer time than anybody who has ever eventually become Prime Minister. (It was a considerable feat to maintain an unchallenged second position during these 12 or 13 years of waiting.) He was a consensus politician, who was the heir to Baldwin's emollience at home without his indolence abroad, but whose final crisis created greater scenes of partisan bitterness in the House of Commons than had been seen for a third of a century. He was a man of exceptional good manners who could fly into the most appalling rages. He had a sure and sensitive aesthetic taste but little concern with ideas, philosophical, political or economic. 'The trouble with Anthony', Rab Butler felinely but memorably said to be in a *wagon restaurant* pulling north out of Milan station on a January evening in 1949, 'is that he has no intellectual interests'. It was half true.

The paradoxes could be multiplied almost indefinitely. They are striking and they illuminate his high talent and engaging but elusive personality. They are not, however, the essence of the problem which his career sets for a biographer. This arises from the apparent contradiction between his dazzling and idealistic early career, when in Churchill's phrase he was the 'life-hope of the British nation', and the stark tragedy of his political end, when he seemed to many of those he had previously inspired to be battling for wrong causes in a miasma of deceit. Put less ideologically, there can be little doubt that in 1937 he was the politician whom, more than any other, most people would have wished to emulate, but that in 1957 he left office in circumstances more disagreeable than was the fate of any other Prime Minister this century, with the possible exception of Neville Chamberlain.

The literary difficulty of handling this dichotomy is that there is a strong temptation for a biographer to portray one period with too much of an eye upon the other: if he is anti-Suez to look for feet of clay in the pre-1945 Eden; if he is pro-Suez to seek over-strenuously, as did Eden himself, for continuity between Mussolini and Nasser.

The method of transcending the problem chosen by Robert Rhodes James in his 1986 biography was to treat Eden's life as a three-act opera (one of the few art forms to which his subject was completely indifferent) in which the greater the contrast between the acts, the better it is. He epitomised this with a not wholly apposite quotation from Churchill on Curzon: 'The morning had been golden; the noontide was bronze; and the evening lead'. But the method has the advantage of freeing him from any false pressure to interpret Suez in terms of Abyssinia or *vice versa*.

Suez apart (if that is not too much like asking Mrs Lincoln how she enjoyed the play apart from the incident), how should Eden stand? It is difficult to elevate his premiership. He won an election, but beyond that he did not have much touch or luck, even before Nasser erupted. In any event twenty-one months is too short a period on which to establish a prime ministerial reputation. That is one of the most unvarying rules of British politics. There is only Campbell-Bannerman, at least since 1800, who has much enhanced his reputation with less than four years in Downing Street, and he hardly left a major imprint.

We therefore have to judge Eden as the three-times Foreign Secretary who spent a total of nine years looking out from Gilbert Scott's building at the park over which Sir Edward Grey's lights went out. His virtues emerge as being very considerable. He was a diplomatic technician of exceptional skill. His apogee in this respect was reached at the Geneva Conference in the late spring of 1954, which brought the French war in Indo-China to an end. His wartime record was also more formidable than is widely recognised. He had wise judgement and he constantly stood up to Churchill's prejudices and aberrations with courage and tenacity.

Yet his imprint on the broad direction of British foreign policy, mainly because he was not 'present at the creation' in 1947–49, was less than that of Ernest Bevin, whose illusions about Britain's continuing great power rôle he more than shared. As a result, Eden more than anyone else was responsible for our allowing Europe to be made without us in the crucial years from 1951 to 1957.

I do not think he was a great man, and he was too fastidious and elusive to be a great poster (although he had immense and continuing popularity). But the golden promise turning into failure and tragedy makes him a great subject for a portrait.

Dwight D. Eisenhower

Dwight David Eisenhower was born in 1890 in Texas, the third son of a mechanic. He was educated at the US Military Academy at West Point and served as an army officer from 1915. In 1916 he married Mamie Geneva Doud and they had one son. During the Second World War he was Assistant Chief of Staff in charge of Operations Division of the War Department until 1942. He was Commander-in-Chief of the Allied Forces in North Africa November 1942–44, Supreme Commander Allied Expeditionary Force in Western Europe 1944–45, and Chief of Staff, US Army 1945–48. In 1948 he became President of Columbia University, New York for one year. In 1949 he returned to Europe as Supreme Commander of the newly established NATO forces.

In 1952 he was nominated Republican candidate for the presidency and resigned from the army. He was President of the United States from January 1953 to January 1961. He died in 1969.

Thirty years after the mid-point of his presidency Eisenhower's rating on those fairly bogus scales of history flickers around like a speedometer needle gone wrong. He has not enjoyed Truman's steady and early post–White House ascent. Nor has he been sucked down into the whirlpool of an unwinnable and unstoppable war like Lyndon Johnson, or buried beneath a patronising view that the wrong farm manager had been engaged like Jimmy Carter.

On the whole the Eisenhower direction has been upward. This has been true both about his presidency and his abilities. 1953-61 now look pretty good years in the United States. McCarthyism (against which Eisenhower was less than valiant) disfigured the first one and a half of them, but that bubble then burst. Thereafter the period has in retrospect become suffused with an almost golden glow of traditional values, secure living and dreamy music. John

Foster Dulles practised brinkmanship abroad, but he never went over the brink or seriously upset Eisenhower's calm captaincy of the West. It was Britain and France who went to war in 1956, and had to be brought back into line by the wiser head boy.

Views about Eisenhower's personal quality have gone through something approaching a double metamorphosis. The view of him as the general with the smile who exuded confidence and good will and could solve all problems with these attributes, which was what got him the presidency, had worn fairly thin by 1960. Was there anything behind that smile, except an intellectual vacuum, an unusually bad temper, and a high degree of self-interest?

More recently, however, there has grown a third tendency: the belief that Eisenhower, if not a particularly nice man, was an extremely effective one. Arthur Schlesinger, for example, who had written as many anti-Eisenhower tracts as Dulles dropped bricks, decided in 1979 that the ex-president was much abler than he had previously thought. Murray Kempton earlier recorded that he had 'a marvellous intelligence'.

No amount of revisionism could turn Eisenhower into an intellectual, nor would he have wanted it. Telegraph Cottage, his pre-D-Day Kingston-upon-Thames retreat (or *nid d'amour* as his English driver, Mrs Summersby, portrayed it) 'was a sanctuary, and serious books were banned', according to David Eisenhower (the President's grandson, who has published the first volume of a massive filial study), 'only the Sunday London newspapers and Eisenhower's bedtime Westerns were allowed'. Or, as Piers Brendon puts it in his 1986 biography, 'he spent 16 years as a major, much of the time engaged in coaching football teams'.

Mr Brendon found Eisenhower a man exceptionally riddled by bewildering paradoxes. Amongst the ones he cites are: Eisenhower's background of intense piety, against which he reacted not by revolt but by a combination of appropriating God for the Republican Party in public and almost complete religious indifference in private; Eisenhower's campaigning warmth accompanied by the impression of a 'terribly cold man' which he left on President Kennedy, whom some considered no mean expert; his 'jabberwockery' (Adlai Stevenson) and extreme superficiality (David Lilienthal), existing alongside his occasional 'intellectual ascendancy' (George Kennan) and the objective fact that he exercised, in succession, a greater combination of military and political responsibility than any man since Wellington, and did so, to put it at its very lowest, without failure. Mr Brendon also saw him as concealing a massive concern for his own popularity behind a facade of modesty and devotion to duty, and an inadequate sense of humour behind the most famous smile in the world.

The cumulative picture is not frankly an attractive one. Nor is it made much better by Mr Brendon unearthing a remarkable tribute by Richard Nixon to Eisenhower's deviousness, which is the equivalent to being complimented on escapalogy by Houdini. All in all, the net effect of the new wave of Eisenhower studies is to increase respect for his achievements and diminish respect for his character. This may not be good news for the Sir Henry Newbolt school of generalship, but it does not detract from the appropriateness of some gratitude to Eisenhower for winning a war in the fearsome Forties and keeping us out of one in the dangerous Fifties.

Hugh Gaitskell

Hugh Gaitskell was born in 1906, son of Arthur Gaitskell of the Indian Civil Service. He was educated at Winchester and New College, Oxford. He then taught economics at University College, London and was a temporary wartime civil servant. In 1937 he married Anna Dora Creditor and they had two daughters.

He was MP for South Leeds from 1945 to 1963. He served as Minister of Fuel and Power 1947–50, Minister of State for Economic Affairs February–October 1950, and Chancellor of the Exchequer 1950–51.

He was Leader of the Labour Party from 1955 until his death in 1963.

(i) Seen in the Year of His Death, 1963

My friendship with Hugh Gaitskell, although it arose out of politics, was not primarily a political one. To a substantial extent it could, I think, have survived prolonged political disagreement or even complete separation. Yet the Gaitskell I knew was always a leading politician. When I first saw him he was already a departmental minister. I have no clear recollection of speaking to him before he was Chancellor of the Exchequer. And during the years when I knew him best and saw him most frequently he was a highly dominant leader of the opposition, living under the constant pressure of public events.

Unlike many of his friends, therefore, who knew him in much earlier days, I did not see Gaitskell develop from obscurity to fame. When I knew him he was always in the centre of events, and most of his triumphs and failures were political ones. But not all of them. At times he dominated politics. But he was rarely dominated by them. This was not primarily because of the range of his interests, although that was considerable, and not at all because he had any peculiar quality of unconcern; on the contrary he was easily emotionally involved. The true reason was the immensely high priority which he always gave to matters of personal relationship. He cared desperately about his friends, and the small change of social intercourse assumed an unusual importance in his life. In the midst of a period of high success he could be temporarily but deeply cast down by the unexpected failure of some small private event to which he had been looking forward. As a result, he conspicuously lacked that quality of cool, tough, detachment from individual affections which is often considered essential for a leading politician. He could be blind to the faults of those whom he liked and equally blind to the virtues of those he did not - and in neither case was he in the least influenced by a calculation of who could be useful to him. He would sometimes throw away political allies with an extraordinary recklessness, yet he clung to personal friendship with a persistent loyalty.

All this sounds like a recipe for careless and attractive failure in politics. Yet Gaitskell was cheated of the highest achievement only by the tragedy of his illness and death. Even without its natural fulfilment, however, his life in politics was one of outstanding success. At forty-nine he achieved the leadership of a major party, and did so at a time when formidable rivals were thicker on the ground than they have since been. During the seven years for which he held this office he consistently opted for strong leadership. This was not a question of the force of his personality, or of any desire to dominate. It was simply that he believed it was his duty to make up his mind before rather than after his followers. He always pointed the way and asked them to follow. The result was that the Gaitskell era was an adventurous one in Labour Party history. The leader engaged in a continuous dialogue with a party of which he was the head. But this, while it does not make for a calm life, is the essence of strong democratic leadership. It is only then that great changes in the outlook of a party or a nation can be carried through. It is only then that a leader in opposition, without the prospect of immediate office (and this was Gaitskell's position during most of his seven-year tenure) can make as great an impact as any minister upon opinion and events. This latter effect Gaitskell undoubtedly achieved. Mild-mannered ex-don though he may have appeared at the date of election, he became better known to the general public than any former leader of the opposition who had never been Prime Minister.

Both at the higher level of influencing events and at the lower one of household fame, therefore, Gaitskell, in spite of his lack of professionalism and his privately rather than publicly, orientated personality, was a successful, even a memorable leader. What were the qualities which made him this, and how did they develop during the last decade of his life?

His first break-through to fame was when he became Chancellor of the Exchequer at the age of forty-four. This promotion came unexpectedly, almost casually. Previously he had been a quietly competent departmental minister and assistant to Cripps at the Treasury. His sudden elevation to one of the first three positions in the Government owed everything to the confidence of those with whom he had worked closely and almost nothing to his public standing. Even as Chancellor his public fame was limited. It was during the summer of 1951 that an incident, which he subsequently liked to relate, occurred in a London restaurant. Gaitskell was lunching with friends when a woman came across and asked if he would give her his autograph for her schoolboy son. By no means displeased, he smilingly obliged. 'Thank you very much,' she said. 'My son will be so pleased. You see, he has always wanted to be a lawyer, and he admires you, Sir Hartley Snowcross, more than almost anyone else.'

While he was at the Exchequer luck ran steadily against him. The Government as a whole was tired. Its majority was tiny. The Korean War and the rearmament programme which followed from it brought vast economic difficulties. Aneurin Bevan, the most popular minister with the Labour Party activists, was restless and looking to the years of opposition which seemed to lie inevitably ahead. In these circumstances a young Chancellor, without any particular following of his own, might have been expected to play for safety. Instead, Gaitskell showed a determination verging on recklessness. He emerged as the one strong man of the Labour Government's last year. He made enemies, but a public reputation as well.

When the Government went out, however, it looked as though his position might not hold. Nearly all the other leading figures in the Labour Party had experience in opposition. Gaitskell had

none. Before the war he had been a don and during the war a civil
servant. As a minister he might be very good, but surely he, more
than most, worked best with the smooth support of the Whitehall
machine and would be lost without it. This prognosis proved to be
the reverse of the truth. In office everything came easily to him and
he was a moderate success. In opposition he had to fight a long,
often disagreeable battle to establish his position, but he eventually
stood out as the dominant politician of his generation.

First, he had to take the decision to compete. In Parliament this
was easy enough. For a time, at any rate, his rôle there was secure.
But it needed to be buttressed by a position in the party outside
which he did not at that stage possess. That meant that he had to
make a place for himself as a Labour Party conference figure. The
temptation not to try for this – at any rate for a time – would for
many people have been overwhelming. In 1952, the first year of
opposition, with Bevanism firmly in the constituency saddle, the
conference was much more a demonstration against the right of
the party than a deliberative assembly. In theory, Gaitskell could
easily have stood aside. There have frequently been Labour ministers almost but not quite of the first rank, who have been active
in Parliament, but have steered clear of the rougher arena of the
party conference.

Gaitskell, however, was prevented from following this course
by two factors. First, he could never bear to contract out of conflict. Perhaps surprisingly for a man of gentle manners and quiet
charm, he was fascinated by it. He did not positively like rough
interchanges and political in-fighting, as Ernest Bevin or Aneurin
Bevan appeared to do, but he could not keep away from them.
Morally, he was in the bravest of all categories: he flinched, but
he always went on. He disliked the noise, but he never kept away
from the place where the guns were firing loudest.

Second, he had a shrewd sense of power and realised that,
without establishing a position in the conference, he could never
achieve the commanding rôle in the Labour Party to which his
other talents seemed to entitle him. Accordingly, in 1952, in the
dismal resort of Morecambe and at the most bitter and snarling
of all such assemblies, there began the curious love-hate relationship between Gaitskell and the Labour conference which was to
dominate much of the rest of his life.

That year he was heavily defeated for the National Executive

Committee. He followed this up by the challenge of his Stalybridge speech. This was delivered on his way back from Morecambe and seemed at the time to be an act of almost foolhardy defiance. Many were muttering that the Labour Party was slipping into an irresponsible extremism which would condemn it to a long period of sterility, and that Communist infiltration was doing much to stir up this mood. Gaitskell said in public things which others were merely whispering. By so doing he made himself the most exposed man in the party, who looked for the moment as though he could never again be acceptable to the bulk of its opinion. Exposed, as prominences always are, he had certainly become, but he had also taken a big step towards becoming the recognised leader of that moderate section of the party, which, particularly as elections approach, almost always triumphs. Henceforward, there could be no question of his being thought of as merely a 'technocratic' minister, a sort of substitute civil servant who had been pushed up quickly because he was good at running a department. He had become a political power in his own right.

In the meantime, Gaitskell was rapidly increasing his parliamentary stature. R.A. Butler was at the Exchequer and he was Shadow Chancellor. Although they were both accused of the besetting party sin of 'Butskellism', economic debates during this period were conducted at a higher level and with more interest on both sides than in any other period since the war. Gaitskell's annual reply to the Budget became a regular parliamentary *tour de force*, listened to with rapt attention by a packed House. For the first time in these speeches there was shown to the full those qualities which became characteristic of his parliamentary oratory at its best: a very full knowledge of the subject, presented with a relentless logic, which avoided aridity because of the emotional force, never shrill or bitter, which lay behind it. In addition, I think that, at this time, he had a more successful and more frequently applied lighter touch than in later years.

During this first period of opposition it was also possible to discern Gaitskell's quality of leadership, exercised at first on a fairly intimate stage. Still very much an economic specialist, he worked closely with a group of four or five lieutenants, one or two of whom had distinctly uncompromising personalities. Private relations were very close amongst the group, and Gaitskell could be treated with as much mocking but friendly disrespect as anyone else. But in the matters of work his authority was effortless. Everyone would undertake tasks because he wanted them done, and enjoyed doing them under his direction. He could build up loyalty by the imposition of burdens.

Outside Parliament, Gaitskell's position remained uncertain until the autumn of 1954. In 1953 he was again defeated for the party executive. It began to look as though he and Aneurin Bevan had settled down to the boring attrition of trench warfare. From his emplacement with the constituency parties Bevan kept up a fairly constant bombardment of Gaitskell's equally well dug-in position with the parliamentary party, and *vice versa*. But it was not an exchange which seemed likely to produce a decisive result. Then the treasurership of the Labour Party fell vacant. For this post, unimportant in itself, the whole conference, trades unions as well as constituency parties, was the electoral college. Both contestants were given an opportunity to get out of their trenches and they both responded with alacrity. The result was a clear victory for Gaitskell. The majority of the big trade union leaders had decided that Gaitskell, despite his utterly dissimilar background from their own, was a man with whom they could work, and that Bevan was not. The decision came at an important stage in his career.

After this result there was a gradual ebbing of the ideological conflict within the party. The General Election of 1955 contributed towards this, but even when it had been lost, there was no return to the full bitterness of the preceding years. 'Bevanism' was on the wane, and several of its most intelligent adherents were beginning to seek other rôles. At the 1955 conference the old lines of dispute were much less in evidence, and Gaitskell surprised his audience, many of whom had been conditioned to think of him as 'a desiccated calculating machine', with a strong declaration of his basic political beliefs:

I would like to tell you, if I may, why I am a Socialist and have been for some 30 years. I became a Socialist quite candidly not so much because I was a passionate advocate of public ownership but because at a very early age I came to hate and loathe social injustice, because I disliked the class structure of our society, because I could not tolerate the indefensible differences of status and income which disfigure our society. I hated the insecurity that affected such a large part of our

community while others led lives of security and comfort. I
became a Socialist because I hated poverty and squalor.

We in the Labour movement can be proud of what we have
done in these 50 years to remedy these ills, but do not let us
make the mistake of supposing that all is over. I want to see
- and I am a Socialist because I want to see - a society of equal
men and women. . . . Nationalisation . . . to me at any rate
is a means and not an end in itself. It is a vital means, but it is
only one of the means by which we achieve these objects.

Curiously the speech foreshadowed many of the things he was
to say in the Clause 4 dispute four years later. But this did not
prevent it making a profound impression on the delegates. For
the first time Gaitskell began to acquire a hold on the emotions
of the party.

That year Attlee was clearly near to relinquishing his twenty-
year-old leadership. Gaitskell came only gradually and reluctantly
to accept the view that he ought to be a candidate. This was not
out of mock modesty. I do not think he doubted, at that stage, that
he would one day be party leader. But, at forty-nine, he believed
that Herbert Morrison, with whom he had worked closely over
the preceding five years, should have a turn first. In June, 1955,
he argued most determinedly in favour of this course. Over the
summer, however, he was persuaded that the desire of the Labour
MPs was for a much younger leader than Morrison. If he allowed
him to be the only 'moderate' candidate, Bevan might conceivably
still snatch a victory; and even if this was not so, a short Morrison
tenure might lead to a subsequent reaction in favour of the Left.

Once he was convinced of the force of these arguments
Gaitskell went forward unhesitatingly. He told Morrison of his
decision at the earliest possible moment in October, choosing a
luncheon with no-one else present - not perhaps the easiest occasion - for breaking the news. He certainly did not look forward to
doing so, and when it was over he was greatly relieved. Morrison
had taken the information remarkably well. Perhaps at this stage
it was natural tolerance. Perhaps he underestimated the force of
Gaitskell's challenge. If the latter was the case, he was greatly
mistaken. When the contest came, in December, Gaitskell swept
the field. He was elected on the first ballot, with nearly twice as
many votes as the combined total of Morrison and Bevan. He was

the youngest leader of any party for sixty years, although, such is the shift in fashion, his record in this respect has since been surpassed both by Harold Wilson and Edward Heath.

Suez was Gaitskell's first crisis in his new position. To begin with he seemed to hesitate, but as soon as he saw that Eden intended to seek a solution through force, Gaitskell mounted an impassioned denunciation of his actions. He carried most of the Labour Party - and many others - enthusiastically with him on his course. But there were a few Labour MPs who stood more or less quietly aside, and it was noticeable - a piquant situation - that Aneurin Bevan was much less wholehearted in his condemnation of the Government's adventure.

Superficially Gaitskell's reaction may have been surprising. He was not particularly sympathetic to Colonel Nasser's régime, and he had been opposed to the method by which it had taken over the Canal. Nor was he, as the chief supporter of the 1951 rearmament programme, in any way sympathetic to pacifism or backward in the legitimate defence of British interests. But his outlook at that stage, and for all but a very brief period of his life, was instinctively internationalist. He believed deeply in the Western Alliance and in friendship with the United States. He was naturally a mid-Atlantic man, almost as much at home in New York as in London. The rôle which he sought for Britain was that of a loyal ally, not of a maverick power chasing off irresponsibly on her own. He cared greatly too about our standing in the United Nations. He had a high respect for the institution and for world public opinion. He had always been willing to stand against Soviet aggression, and he was revolted by the thought that we had reduced ourselves to their level. Equally, he was inclined to favour a bi-partisan foreign policy, and was the more resentful of Eden for, as he saw it, shattering the basis of this than were others who, always believing the Tories were wrong, had no store of surplus indignation to use against them.

Gaitskell's vehemence on this issue, widely criticised though it was, even by some who were themselves opposed to the Government's action, probably did him no harm in the country. It helped to imprint his personality upon the public, and it began a period in which the Labour Party bounded ahead of the Conservatives in the public opinion polls. Where it did do him some harm was in the House of Commons. For some months afterwards he had difficulty in getting a good hearing from the Government benches. Their occupants paid him back with mocking noise for his part in the destruction of Eden. It was an experience to which he was unused and which was peculiarly upsetting to his style of oratory. It caused him great concern, which I remember him expressing to me in May, 1957. When would this derision end, and if it did not, could he continue to be an effective leader of the opposition?

In fact it ended very soon, and Gaitskell never again had the least difficulty in exercising a full command over the House. What was perhaps a more permanent legacy of Suez was that this naturally moderate statesman was never afterwards on really good terms with the leader of the Conservative Party. With Eden until Suez he got on well enough. But their easy relationship did not survive the clash. And with Macmillan he was always on terms of armed hostility. It seems unlikely that either understood or respected the other. What Macmillan thought of Gaitskell I do not know, but what Gaitskell thought of Macmillan, above all, was that he cheated at politics. His own reckless honesty, accompanied by a compulsive desire to set out every argument in terms which were logically convincing (but sometimes emotionally provocative), made him disdainful of Macmillan's fondness for doing everything behind a smoke-screen. Only, perhaps, in the last weeks before his illness did Gaitskell begin to develop a somewhat warmer feeling for the then Prime Minister.

With his principal rivals within the Labour Party, however, Gaitskell's relations improved rapidly in the period after Suez. Harold Wilson had already succeeded him as shadow Chancellor. Aneurin Bevin was at first a little more recalcitrant. But at the Brighton conference of 1957 his 'naked into the conference chamber' speech led both to a rupture with his old friends of the unilateralist Left and to a reconciliation with Gaitskell. Shortly afterwards Gaitskell asked him to become shadow Foreign Secretary and the relationship between the two men became amicable and moderately close. It reached its high-water mark during their joint visit to Russia immediately preceding the 1959 General Election. Power seemed near, and Bevan appeared satisfied with his prospective rôle as Foreign Secretary. Gaitskell was happy to see him fill it in a big way. Not the least of his achievements of leadership was that, for a time, he acquired the knack of working closely with Bevan's rumbustious but magnetic personality, and of

91

harnessing its force without hiding himself beneath its shadow.

This important partnership was first made less relevant by the election defeat, and then destroyed by Bevan's sudden illness and subsequent death. The election campaign, on the whole skilfully fought by Gaitskell (although he was subsequently critical of himself for one major mistake), was hard throughout and at the end cruelly disappointing. Before it began he had been cautious about victory. Until the last six months or so of the Parliament it had looked as though the Government could hardly hope to recover. Then the public opinion polls had begun to swing and Gaitskell had half reconciled himself to this new outlook. Throughout the campaign itself, however, he was consistently buoyant. He generated confidence by effort and swept others along with him. His confidence was not a facade. Twelve days before polling he told me that he was sure of a Labour victory, and remained so, I believe, until the returns began to come in. The disappointment was therefore as sudden as it was heavy.

His hopes died in the Leeds City Hall, with the television cameras frequently upon him. As the Conservative gains mounted previously dammed-up waves of tiredness rolled over him, and as they did so he faced the prospect, not of the period of constructive power for which he was perfectly poised at the time, but of the unavoidable bickering of a three times defeated party. One was inevitably reminded of Adlai Stevenson's 'It hurts too much to laugh, and I'm too old to cry'. Yet if he did not laugh, Gaitskell at least managed to smile, slowly and a little sadly, as he so often did, when with a quiet grace he conceded defeat.

Looking back, this defeat was unavoidable. No radical leader could have carried the country in its 1959 mood. Gaitskell did at least as well as anyone else would have done. But the inevitability was not so obvious at the time. The whole Labour Party began to cast about for the causes of the setback. From the moment of his return to London, Gaitskell was active in the search. Perhaps mistakenly, he allowed himself no period of recuperation. Without doubt, he and those of us who were close to him, made serious tactical mistakes during the ensuing weeks. We overestimated the rationality of political movements. Equally without doubt, however, the battle which then began and continued in different phases, for two years, had to be fought. Broadly the Labour Party was divided into two camps. On the one side stood those who wished to react to defeat by giving the party a more modern appearance and a stronger appeal to the uncommitted voter. They saw its essential rôle as that of providing an effective alternative government to the Conservatives. It must therefore appeal to the marginal members of the leftward-thinking half of the country.

On the other side stood those whose primary concern was to defend the ideological citadel. If the citadel became increasingly cut off from the surrounding countryside and unpopular with the inhabitants that could not be helped. Elections were not of primary importance. One prominent socialist thinker wrote cheerfully of another ten years of Conservative government.

Some members of the party stood a little apart from both the camps, and it would have been theoretically possible for Gaitskell to have joined them. But it would have been utterly out of keeping with both his character and his convictions. He was incapable of equating a leader's rôle with that of a chairman.

The first phase of the battle - that over Clause 4* - was far from an immediate success. Gaitskell and those who were with him tried to move an injured party into a more comfortable position, and were rewarded for their efforts with some sharp and angry cries. Even so they got it a little way, before the attempt had to be abandoned. Yet, after this abandonment and the shifting of attention away from the issue, the party began quietly and almost imperceptibly to move itself in the direction indicated. No-one looking at the programme, outlook, and assumptions of the Labour Party in 1963 could doubt that Gaitskell, in a long-term sense, had won his battle. The party is incomparably closer to what he wanted than to what his opponents wanted. It would not go the whole way at his bidding. But it would not have gone at all had he not taken the risk of pointing the way.

After the Clause 4 stalemate came the counter-attack. It was on another front, that of unilateralism and neutralism *versus* the commitment to the Atlantic Alliance and the defence policy which

---

*Clause 4 of the Labour Party Constitution, which dates from 1918, commits the Party to 'secure for the workers by hand or by brain the full fruits of their industry and the most equitable distribution thereof that may be possible, upon the basis of the common ownership of the means of production, distribution and exchange, and the best obtainable system of popular administration and control of each industry and service'. Gaitskell did not put forward an alternative draft, but suggested that this clause was inadequate and misleading.

this entailed. But basically it was the same issue - whether the Labour Party's rôle was to be primarily that of a party of power or a party of protest. During the spring and summer of 1960 the unilateralist forces built up with frightening speed. Trade union after union toppled almost casually into their camp. Gaitskell's position became more exposed than that of any party leader since Baldwin in 1930.

At the Scarborough conference that autumn the almost unthinkable happened. On the central policy issue of that year the leadership was defeated. It had nearly - but not quite - occurred over German rearmament in 1954, and everyone had then assumed that an adverse vote would be an intolerable humiliation for Attlee, rendering his continuance in office almost impossible. Yet he was less committed on that issue than his successor was on unilateralism.

What, then, would Scarborough mean for Gaitskell? Would it force his resignation, or would it leave him with the possibility of carrying on only as the prisoner of a section of his 'followers', a figure shown to be so weak that he could not hope to command respect in the House or in the country? In fact, by one of the odd quirks of history, Gaitskell avoided both these alternatives by the widest possible margin. Even the conference itself was far from being a humiliation for him, although it was a great emotional strain. A majority of the delegates were committed to vote against him, but by the time the crucial debate took place many of them were regretting their mandates.

Gaitskell, in his own speech, had both to capitalise this mood and to raise a banner around which men would fight, if necessary risking their political positions in the process. Typically, he chose to do this in the least equivocal way possible. There was no doubt about his banner; the doubt was whether the men with uneasy minds would follow it.

This last doubt was soon removed. His old bastion of the Parliamentary Labour Party remained reasonably secure. When Harold Wilson hesitantly decided to run against him for the leadership Gaitskell's majority was more than two-to-one. And as the contest was fought on the clear understanding that Gaitskell, if successful, would lead against the Scarborough decision, the result struck a great blow, not only against the decision, but against the whole principle of conference authority. Yet he could not rest on this victory. Throughout that winter of 1960–61, Gaitskell 'fought,

fought, and fought again' on innumerable platforms up and down the country. Nearly every weekend he would make three or four full-length speeches. His physical resilience appeared as high as ever, and he would often fortify himself with a late evening of relaxed conversation before setting out on these grinding expeditions; but, in fact, he was near the margin of his strength.

Sometimes at these meetings the reception would be hostile and even noisy. In these circumstances one of Gaitskell's greatest strengths was his stubborn faith in the power of reasoned argument. What he prided himself upon being was a rational man. The superiority of the multilateralist case was to him so obvious that intelligent people of goodwill must surely see it. He would go on patiently explaining what he believed until others believed it too. And this approach, combined with his immense agreeableness of manner in friendly intercourse, succeeded in shifting a good deal of opinion within the party. But was it shifting fast enough? As the Easter union conferences approached this looked extremely uncertain. Gaitskell suddenly began to foresee the prospect of a second defeat, and to recognise that this might be fatal. For a party leader to defy a single conference aberration was one thing. For him to attempt to ignore a series of adverse decisions, amounting to the expression of a settled point of view, was something quite different.

At this stage, more I think than at Scarborough, Gaitskell faced in his own mind the distinct likelihood that in six months' time he might have to go - probably to retire completely from politics. It was a discouraging prospect. It would mean that his period as a party leader, which had begun under such bright auspices just over five years before, would end in complete failure. He would be remembered only as the man who led his party to its third successive electoral defeat and was then rejected by his own followers. Once he had assimilated this possibility in his mind, he faced it with equanimity.

Then, with bewildering rapidity, the outlook changed. When it was least expected an avalanche movement began. The unions followed each other back into the Gaitskell camp as quickly as, the year before, they had moved the other way. Many of the constituency parties did the same. All the hard persuasive work of the winter began to bear simultaneous fruit.

The victory which this made certain was ratified at Blackpool in October, 1961. It left Gaitskell in a far stronger position than he had been before Scarborough. He was dominant in the Labour Party, and he had impressed the public outside as a leader of force, wisdom, and courage. No-one foresaw that he had only fifteen months of leadership ahead. By his efforts he seemed to have secured for himself a long tenure on conditions of tolerable authority. But what in fact he had done was to bequeath this ease-ment to his succcessor, and to give Harold Wilson the elbow-room which helped him, in opposition, to look like a Prime Minister. If Gaitskell had lost, not only he himself but any other Labour leader for years to come would have paid part of the price.

The use to which Gaitskell himself put the new room for manoeuvre was, ironically, a most unwelcome one to many of his closest supporters on previous issues. He swung the Labour Party into a posture of general hostility towards Britain joining the Common Market. The merit of this issue need not be argued here. I would merely record that while his attitude seemed to me not wholly consistent with his previous general outlook on world affairs, it was in no way the result of a sudden lurch, taken with electoral considerations heavily in mind. I had seen his opposition growing for a year or more before it finally revealed its full force to the public. Like all his political positions it was fixed partly by logic and partly by emotion. And once fixed, he held to it with great tenacity.

I then had the opportunity (although it was a small consolation at the time) to see his political qualities and defects through, as it were, the other end of the telescope. Broadly, they looked much the same as I had previously thought them to be, although I inevitably felt more sympathy with those who had differed from him in the past. Courage could be interpreted as inflexibility and an aggressive respect for rationality as a tendency to equate little points and big ones. Yet, by and large, he appeared just as impres-sive as a temporary opponent as he had so long done as an ally and leader. The warm persuasiveness of his manner and the absolute honesty of his purpose were formidable weapons, on whichever side of them one stood.

Nor did this difference make close personal relations with him impossible. At first I thought it would, but that was under the shock of a sudden break in a long habit of agreement. But then he made it clear that he was still faithful to his old rule of the primacy of private relations. For the last few weeks of his active life we were back on terms of the closest friendship.

What did he leave to English politics? First, the promise of being a great Prime Minister, not because he could necessarily have avoided mistakes, but because he would have infused the whole Government with a sense of loyalty and purpose, and made men of widely differing gifts and character proud to serve under him. Second, a Labour Party with both the will and the capacity for victory, two qualities of which, without him, it might only too easily have deprived itself. And third, a memory which is a standing contradiction to those who wish to believe that only men with cold hearts and twisted tongues can succeed in politics.

(ii) Seen as a Diarist Twenty Years Later

From Hugh Gaitskell's diaries (1945-56 published in 1983) there emerges, surprisingly for those of us who knew him best in the last seven years of his life, the picture of a man obsessed by politics, or perhaps more precisely the business of government. This is strikingly true of the years 1945-51. During this period he moved up not exactly with ease but with momentum and confidence from being a newly-elected back-bench MP, through a brief period as a parliamentary secretary, two years as a full minister but outside the Cabinet, and eight months as deputy to a sick Cripps at the Treasury, to a testing and controversial year as Chancellor of the Exchequer in his own right. He did this without achieving great public fame, but it was a remarkable political achievement.

For this he paid the price of leading a much narrower life than he subsequently achieved, and than he perhaps really ever would have wished. Apart from a few remnants of his pre-war academic life, he saw very few people who were not engaged in politics or administration. He hardly travelled, except on official business, although he greatly relished the occasional escapes from Britain which this provided. He read few books, although his writing style, when not weighed down by the technicality of the subject, was vivid and literate. He had remarkably few windows on to the outside world, and those which existed were somewhat artificial, as through the film industry, with which he had old wartime Board of Trade connections.

Within his restricted circle, however, he already set great store by friendship. In 1950 he was complaining about Harold Wilson: 'What is depressing really is . . . that he is such a very impersonal person. You don't feel that really you could be close friends with him, or in fact that he would ever have any close friends . . . How different he is, for example, from John Strachey with whom one may often disagree, but . . . with whom one can have that emotional and intelligent intercourse which is really the stuff of friendship . . .'

Gaitskell was also, until the latter part of the period, instinctively insular. When he mentioned foreigners, it was mostly to complain that they tried to prevent Britain running things in its own way, as they ought to have been run in the rest of the world. But a big change began to occur in 1950, when he began to become closely involved with the affairs of the Organisation for European Economic Co-operation and in other international economic dealings. He became strongly pro-American, not uncritically, nor to the exclusion of some tough bargaining with them, but deeply because multi-dimensionally so, liking the country, the life, the intellectual style. He always, I am afraid, much preferred Americans to continental Europeans.

During the first half of the 1950s which was the period during which I came to know Gaitskell well and to support him enthusiastically, he was greatly preoccupied with the long-running Bevanite dispute. The political differences between Gaitskell and Bevan were certainly not vast when compared with the chasms in the recent Labour Party. There were differences of temperament and style, and each of these very considerable figures was remarkably inept at containing them. Bevan was much the vainer and more petulant of the two. This made him incapable of respecting Gaitskell's quality. Gaitskell's approach was shot through with occasional shafts of respect for Bevan and, given a little encouragement, these could have become less intermittent, as indeed they later did. Bevan was also the more jealous, but he had more to be jealous about, for Gaitskell always walked away with the prizes. Bevan had to be content (and was not) with the applause.

On the other hand Gaitskell's method of dealing with this sulky but important bear was remarkably unskilful. He frequently prodded him with a stick, and then believed that he could control the enraged animal by tying him up with manifestly ineffective strips of disciplinary paper. They were made out of fluctuating and unstable majorities, and always came apart. The result was an unnecessarily ineffective Labour Party. Gaitskell occasionally saw the futility, but he thought that he had to go on in order not to show the weakness of which he accused the declining Attlee. It was not glorious and it was not far-sighted. A less obsessive political life (which was certainly not Bevan's weakness) might have produced greater perspective.

Nevertheless Gaitskell's inherent qualities of warmth, courage, integrity and intelligence were such that at the end of this phase he achieved the leadership of the Labour Party by a massive majority. The end of the diary covers the first eighteen months of this leadership, up to and over the Suez war. Here we see the long-delayed broadening of his life, with the accompanying removal of some, though not all, of the previous deficiences. There is no known diary for the remaining four years of his life.

Edward Grey

(Sir) Edward Grey was born in 1862, the elder son of a North-umberland kinsman of the Lord Grey of the Reform Bill. He was educated at Winchester and Balliol College, Oxford. In 1885 he married Dorothy Windrington who died in 1906. He then married, in 1922, Pamela Glenconner (née Wyndham) who died in 1928. He had no children.

He was MP for Berwick-on-Tweed 1885–1916. He was under-secretary at the Foreign Office 1892–95 and Foreign Secretary 1905–16. He became Viscount Grey of Falloden in 1916. In 1919 he was appointed temporary Ambassador to the USA. He was elected Chancellor of Oxford University in 1929. He died in 1933.

Sir Edward Grey was British Foreign Secretary at the outbreak of the First World War. He had then held the office for nearly nine years, and was to hold it, with declining application, for more than another two. It was the longest continuous Foreign Office reign since 1832.

Its distinction did not match its length. Grey was a man of 'character' rather than of intellect. But as he carefully maintained a withdrawn position, both in public and in private, communing little with others beyond his wife and his birds, it was difficult to know exactly to what this amounted. He was always fairly awkward. The politician he most admired was Rosebery, whose favourite political posture was that of withdrawal. Asquith, with whom he was most closely associated over decades but whom Grey did not wholly respect and who in turn did not much enjoy Grey's company, accepted a description of him as 'a man rather to see difficulties than to help people over them'.

Grey was also a man of most remarkable insularity. When he went to the Foreign Office he had been abroad only twice, once to the West Indies and once to India. He passed his first eight years as Foreign Secretary without ever leaving these shores. Then, in the spring of 1914, he went to Paris on a state visit with King George V. Reasonably, in the circumstances, he was reluctant to go to the races, because he wished to do some sight-seeing instead. In that summer he planned a visit to a German clinic because his eyesight was failing. But other events intervened. In 1919 he went for a short time to Washington as a special ambassador. That was the extent of his visits abroad.

He was also a man who by deliberate choice made himself older than he was. In fact, he did everything very young. He became a Member of Parliament at 24, a junior minister at 30, and Foreign Secretary at 43. Even when he left the Foreign Office, clearly an elder statesman, half-blind and bowed down with the 11-year burden of office, he was only 54. His contemporaries were never quite of his generation. Asquith was ten years older, Haldane six. This was not accidental. After the death of his first wife in 1906 he decided that he felt like a man of 70, and proceeded to behave as though he was, until he eventually reached that age, 26 years later, and then died.

He was not a man of books. When he had been elected Chancellor of the University of Oxford in 1929, an honour for which Asquith, better qualified and more anxious, had been defeated three years before, the following interchange took place amongst his friends:-

> It was generally agreed that 'character' was required. Haldane thought that 'intellectual character' was desirable, and Grey never read a book. The little circle was aghast at this remark, which was then repeated for emphasis. Archbishop Lang then intervened to state that Grey was known to have read Wordsworth: to which Haldane replied that Wordsworth was not a book. The remark was greeted with general stupefaction and the company pressed Haldane to admit that Grey did have intellectual interests. 'Oh, yes', came the answer, 'among birds and fishes'.

Nor was he a memorable phrase-maker. He only achieved one in his life. 'The lights are going out all over Europe . . .' has lived and will continue to do so, although sometimes a little confused with Pitt's 'Roll up that map . . .' But nothing else has survived, which is indeed not surprising for most of Grey's oratory suffered from a good deal of fuzziness at the edges. But he was a man whose imprecise phrases were listened to.

His diplomacy also suffered from some imprecision. He saw the importance of Anglo-American friendship much earlier than most. But in Europe, the unvisited theatre to which the overwhelming part of his attention was devoted, he operated on little beyond a vague conviction that we ought to stand by the French. Yet because he was a man who was listened to, and had a wide cross-party following, he played a crucial role in carrying an almost wholly united nation into its 1914 declaration of war. Having done so, he had little further power of leadership left. He hated the war into which he had felt it his duty to take the country. He had little idea how it should be waged. He gravitated to the 'civilian' side in the Cabinet. He went when Lloyd George took over, and although he accepted the 1916 palace revolution almost with relief, he became increasingly dominated by the view that Lloyd George was corrupting everything that he liked in English life. But he did little to resist it. 'As to politics', he wrote at the age of 59, 'I am not the sort of person that is wanted now: Lloyd George is the modern type, suited to an age of telephones and moving pictures and modern journalism. . .'

Yet, although (or because) he was so pessimistic and elusive he was constantly sought after in the 1920s – by Oxford, by some who wanted a centre party – in a way that Asquith, with his far more massive achievements, was not.

David Harlech

David Ormsby Gore, 5th Lord Harlech, was born in 1918 and killed in a car accident in 1985. Hew was educated at Eton and New College, Oxford, served in the Berkshire Yeomanry 1939–45, was Conservative MP for Oswestry 1950–61, a Foreign Office junior minister 1956–61, British Ambassador to Washington 1961–65 and deputy leader of the opposition in the House of Lords 1966–67. He married Silvia Lloyd Thomas in 1940, who was herself killed in a car accident in 1967, and Pamela Colin in 1969.

In November 1960 John F. Kennedy was elected President of the United States. David Ormsby Gore, two years his junior, had been a close friend since Kennedy's pre-war years in London during his father's embassy. In the interval David Gore had spent ten years in the House of Commons, the last four of them as a Foreign Office minister, dealing mainly with disarmament negotiations, partly in Geneva and partly in New York during successive UN General Assembly sessions. Harold Macmillan, anxious to achieve the closest relations with the new President, who was a brother-in-law of his late nephew by marriage, Lord Hartington, decided to send as British Ambassador to Washington another nephew by marriage. David Gore resigned from the House of Commons and arrived in Washington in May 1961 to begin his brilliant four-year mission.

Until that point the new ambassador's career could be fairly described as remarkably nepotic. The success which he then made of his embassy, however, sprang from qualities which could not be bestowed by family connection. David Gore was almost perfectly attuned to the new United States administration. His friendship with the President strengthened rather than wilted under the strains of office and official intercourse. It was buttressed by the fact that he was also on close terms with Jacqueline Kennedy, as were the Kennedys with his first wife, Sissy, whom he had married young in 1940, whose shy but elegant charm made her as easily at home in the White House of those years as was her husband. Jack Kennedy much liked to have small dinner parties organised at short notice. The Gores were probably more frequently invited on this basis than anyone else, including even Robert Kennedy. Jack Kennedy sometimes found his brother and Attorney-General too insistantly his conscience to be wholly relaxing at dinner.

It was a wholly exceptional position for any ambassador to be in. It made him almost as much an unofficial adviser to the President as an envoy of the British Government - although there was never any suggestion that British interests were not well represented in Washington during these years. His position was particularly influential during the Cuban missile crisis in October 1962.

Gore's special relationship may have caused some jealousy amongst other ambassadors but it in no way weakened his position in official Washington outside the White House. Other members of the administration – McNamara, Robert Kennedy, McGeorge Bundy, Arthur Schlesinger - became his close and continuing friends, and he was even able to be a more than averagely effective ambassador after Kennedy's assassination for the first 17 months of Lyndon Johnson's presidency. But the *raison d'être* of his embassy had gone.

In early 1964 his father died and he became Lord Harlech. Later that year the Conservative Government which had sent him as a political appointment to Washington was replaced by a Labour one. The new Government was in no hurry to remove him. Nor should it have been. Apart from his effectiveness on the spot, his Kennedy years had shifted Harlech to the centre or even the left-centre of politics. After his return to England (in the spring of 1965) he was briefly deputy Conservative leader in the House of Lords, but he had lost any taste which he ever possessed for political partisanship and resigned after a year. This apart, all his subsequent semi-political activities were firmly centrist: the presidency of Shelter, the chairmanship of the European Movement and of the National Committee for Electoral Reform. He was also twice concerned in a semi-official capacity with trying to find a multi-racial solution to the Rhodesian problem. In addition he was President of the British Board of Film Censors from 1968, the initiator and chairman of Harlech Television and a director of a few other companies, although never centrally occupied with business. He was chairman of the Pilgrim Trust for five years and of the British branch of the Pilgrims (a quite separate organisation) for twelve. He was also the leading British figure in all Kennedy commemorative activities.

Sadly his own life then came to be almost as marked by tragedy and violent death as was that of the Kennedy family itself. In 1967 Sissy Harlech was killed in a car crash just beyond the gates of their North Wales house. In 1974 his eldest son committed suicide. He surmounted these vicissitudes with fortitude and buoyancy, greatly assisted by his 1969 second marriage. Pamela Colin, New Yorker, Vogue editor and talented compiler of books, had the gift of keeping her husband young. David Harlech at 66 looked no different from the way he had looked at 56, and little different from his appearance as a young ambassador at 46. He had no mountains left to climb, but he lived a life of style and grace, in which pleasure played a large part, although tempered by high public spirit, good judgement, and unselfish instincts on all the main issues of the day.

His principal period of achievement had been twenty years earlier but he was peculiarly unscarred by frustrated ambition. He had many qualities but his unique one lay in a blending of devotion to liberal values and causes of sense and purpose with an unusual capacity to give and enjoy pleasure. As a result his good works were always free of portentousness and his hedonism was not indulgent.

There seemed little reason why he should not continue for many years as an easy-going public figure of sound sense and high repute. But tragedy struck again. On the evening of 25 January 1985, driving from London to Harlech, he was involved in a car crash (the third major one of his life) near to his constituency of the 1950s and the Shropshire homes of his earlier life. He died in hospital in Shrewsbury early the next morning.

Although he was in his sixties there was no twilight in his life. It went from the full splendour of late afternoon to darkness with an appalling suddenness. It was like a young life being cut off and was a peculiar deprivation for his friends.

Lyndon B. Johnson

Lyndon Baines Johnson was born in 1908. He was educated at Southwest Texas State Teachers College and Georgetown Law School. In 1934 he married Claudia Alta (Lady Bird) Taylor and they had two daughters. He was elected to Congress for the 10th District of Texas in 1937, was a Congressman until 1948 when he became a U.S. Senator. In 1960 he sought the Democratic nomination to the presidency but was beaten by John F. Kennedy, on whose narrowly winning ticket he accepted the vice-presidential nomination. He acceded to the presidency on the death of President Kennedy in November 1963. He was elected President in 1964 and served until January 1969. He was not a candidate in 1968. He died in 1973.

Of the seven Presidents of the United States I have encountered, five while they were in office, two outside it, I liked Lyndon Johnson the least. I respected some of the things which he had done but I did not enjoy his conversation or think him an agreeable man. After reading his 1971 presidential memoirs (*The Vantage Point*) however, I liked him rather more. And this is not an effect which volumes of memoirs necessarily produce.

Its great virtue was that it was an honest book. By this I do not mean that it was an objective account of those five years of American history. It did not seek to be that. It was consciously and defiantly subjective. Facts were often selectively presented. But it was honest in the more fundamental sense that in the course of it we were made fully, if not explicitly, aware of the change in Lydon Johnson's character and outlook over the different phases of his presidency. At first he is awed by the magnitude of the task and the nature of his accession. He is humbly anxious to do everything in the most proper way so as to ease the shock of Dallas and carry on in the mould of President Kennedy. It was not primarily that he felt a sense of inferiority *vis à vis* the Kennedy family. That has always been much too brittle an explanation. It was much more due to his scepticism that a man of his geographical origin could lead the United States:-

> The burden of national unity rests heaviest on one man, the President. And I did not believe, any more than I ever had, that the nation would unite indefinitely behind any Southerner. One reason . . . was that the metropolitan press of the Eastern seaboard would never permit it. I was not thinking just of the derisive articles about my style, my clothes, my manner, my accent, and my family - although I admit I received enough of that kind of treatment in my first few months as President to last a lifetime. I was also thinking of a more deep-seated and far-reaching attitude - a disdain for the South that seems to have been woven into the fabric of Northern experience.

He would, I believe, have been even more self-defensive about following a Roosevelt than following a Kennedy.

Gradually, however, in spite of this ingrained belief, he began to gain confidence. This happened even before the 1964 election, largely as a result of legislative successes which had eluded President Kennedy. But the process was greatly accelerated by the campaign and even more by the result. President Johnson genuinely hesi-tated, although perhaps with just a touch of self-dramatisation, as to whether to run at all. But once he was in the campaign his self-confidence soared. He was even acclaimed by unprecedented crowds in New England. The result was a still greater triumph. 'The American people knew what they were voting for in 1964', he writes with a touch of savage self-satisfaction. 'They knew Lyndon Johnson was not going to pull up stakes and run.' He was even able to feel that he had given Robert Kennedy a necessary tug upon his coat-tails in the New York senatorial contest.

He then began the high period of his presidency. He was firmly progressive at home, and continued to land a great legis-lative haul. He defied his own background on Civil Rights. And he symbolised his sense of achievement by choosing the most dramatic and attention-attracting places in which to sign the more important Bills: the Elementary and Secondary Education Bill in the schoolroom in Texas where he had first been taught; Medicare with ex-President Truman in Independence, Missouri, because it was Truman who had tried to start it. In foreign affairs generally he flexed his muscles as leader of the West. In Vietnam he continued doggedly with the legacy which he convinced himself President Kennedy had left him. But in the White House he increasingly - and rightly - ran his own system of government with his own men.

After about two years the mood began to change, and so does the tone of the book. In Vietnam disappointment succeeded disappointment, greater and greater numbers of troops were poured in, and the fissure at home became steadily deeper. President Johnson did not lose his nerve, but he lost his zest. He again became highly self-defensive, but this time his self-defence was not against the Eastern establishment but against a large segment of the whole American nation. He no longer sought acclaim. He began to show himself less and less in public. 'Security' became the great bugbear. And with it came a sense of beleaguerment and isolated determination. Dogs might howl or whimper, but he at least was going to keep the caravan on its route. And as he settled more deeply into this rôle, so both his self-righteousness and his sentimentally grew. So, too, did his sense of mutual but exclusive loyalty with those who were still willing to go along with him. His decision not to run in 1968, widely but falsely interpreted as a ploy, was in fact a logical outcome both of the mood which he had created for himself and the political situation which he had created for the nation. A weary Titan could not spare the time for electioneering, particularly if he might lose.

The nervous morning of his presidency, having unexpectedly cleared into a glorious midday, settled back into the most oppressive of evenings. And for the Democratic Party, which he had led to so great a triumph in 1964, a full and confident dawn has never by mid-1988 yet come.

John. F. Kennedy*

John Fitzgerald Kennedy was born in 1917, second son of Joseph Patrick Kennedy, later U.S.Ambassador to London and Rose Fitzgerald. He was educated at Choate School and Harvard University, and served with the U.S. Navy 1941–45. In 1953 he married Jacqueline Bouvier and they had one son and one daughter (and a son who died).

He was a member of the House of Representatives 1947–53 from a Boston district and Senator from Massachusetts 1953–60. He took office as President of the United States in January 1961 and was assassinated in November 1963.

Kennedy's tenure of the White House was the shortest since the United States became a world Power. The youngest President to come, he was the quickest to go. There can be no Age of Kennedy, with a gradual fulfilment of policies and a descriptive meaning for a whole epoch of American life. The most that he was able to do was to open doors through which others, if they have the will and the capacity, may be able to walk.

Compared with the greatest Presidents of American history therefore he inevitably leaves more promise and less achievement behind him. Yet, aided perhaps by the manner of his death, it is difficult to believe that his name will not live with theirs. He will be the great 'might-have-been', the symbol of fate in its most vicious and retaliatory mood.

Yet his achievement was by no means all still to come. He had revitalised Washington and, still more important, he had led the world with almost faultless skill and precision through the Cuban missile crisis in 1962, the nearest it has yet come to self-destruction.

*This tribute was written within twenty-four hours of Kennedy's assassination.

The hackneyed criticism of John Kennedy is that he was a cold and calculating man, unwilling to take politcal risks, unable to infuse great issues with the warmth of human sympathy. This criticism is at once exaggerated and irrelevant.

Of course he was capable of political calculation. No-one who has read the story first of his fight for the nomination, then for the Presidency, can doubt that he was a political planner of the most careful and determined kind. I am very glad that he was. Otherwise Richard Nixon would have been in the White House for the past three years.

To suggest, however, that he habitually subordinated vital policy decisions to narrow political considerations is nonsense. In and after the Cuban crisis he did precisely the reverse. So anxious was he not to damage the future world prospect by any humiliation of Khrushchev that he completely failed to bring home to the American people the magnitude of the victory which he had won.

His decisions were, admittedly, not emotional ones. But who would have wished that they were? To cite the Cuban crisis once again, the essence of his strength was his ability to watch the cases for and against the different courses of action being built up or destroyed, without rushing into a prior commitment to one or another; and then, when all of the relevant information and arguments were available, to make a clear decision in favour of the one that seemed best. He himself attributed the wisdom of the choice to the time that was available for the process; at least equal credit should be given to his own capacity to evaluate the evidence objectively.

No doubt the reverse side of the coin was a certain hardness of presentation. As a speaker he had force and clarity, and at times a touch of eloquence. When I first heard him at the height of his presidential campaign on Columbus Day, 1960, I listened to him making five New York speeches on that one day. All of them were invigorating, one or two of them were moving. His command of widely contrasting audiences was complete.

He was not, perhaps, an orator in the fullest sense. The play and interplay between himself and the audience was not sufficient for that. Despite his Massachusetts-Irish background, he could never have made a vast audience in the Boston Garden chant back slogans at him as Roosevelt did in 1940. Nor could he pick out with inspired timing the one moment for a launching of an idea and the one simple phrase in which to do it, so that millions of stolid minds might be shifted.

But this is a rare gift indeed, and liable to be perverted even when it exists. For most practical purposes Kennedy's eloquence was a worthy and persuasive vehicle for his clear and cogent thoughts.

His private personality was far removed from that of a man who lived a life of narrow political calculation. That he had gaiety and charm goes without saying. But he also had sustained intellectual interest and zest. As any President must do, he saw an almost unending stream of visitors. But he chose them on the basis of who would interest him just as much as who would be useful to him. And he gave enough time and contributed enough energy to these interviews to make them an exchange of ideas and not merely an empty formality.

I saw him in this way one evening in January 1963. When I came into the room he was standing talking to Sorensen, Salinger and a naval aide. In a moment they left and he settled down in his rocking chair; there were no further interruptions for 40 minutes.

Three features of the conversation remain imprinted on my mind. The first is that he talked about half the time and encouraged me to do the same. Almost any other Head of Government would have struck a different balance. Either he would merely have answered questions or he would merely have asked them – perhaps resting his mind during the answers. Kennedy chose the much more stimulating and exhausting middle course. He asked a series of rapid-fire questions about all sorts of subjects – economic growth, Europe and de Gaulle, the Labour Party. He interrupted the answers, he gave his own views, he followed up a weak or unconvincing reply by forcing one hard against the ropes.

My second memory of this conversation, therefore, is that it was peculiarly intellectually testing. My third memory is that the President, during these interchanges, contributed two pieces of original, rather unconventional, analysis. That, again, was unexpected from any Head of State.

Yet the inexorable intellectual vigour was only one facet of Kennedy's personality. He could turn his mind in much more frivolous directions. He could switch away from the highest affairs of State and back again with the greatest speed. He had the self-confidence to feel that he could always get his eye back on the ball at the right moment.

This self-confidence was indeed one of the great changes which the New Frontier brought to Washington. It stemmed directly from the President. He gathered around himself a team of outstanding intellectual quality. They were not strikingly experienced in affairs of government. They were not strongly politically connected in any traditional sense. They came from Harvard and the Ford Motor Company and from private law practice. But together – McNamara, Robert Kennedy, Bundy, Schlesinger, Gilpatric, Sorensen – they amounted to a most formidable group.

Kennedy's great gift was that he could use them effortlessly. He trusted them. They respected him. He could give them very free rope without ever endangering his own command. Whether the same system can work equally well under another President remains to be seen.

Under Kennedy, however, it performed the great service of increasing the respect of the American people for their own system of government. He was elected by the narrowest of majorities after a bitterly fought campaign. He replaced the most widely popular President in American history. He was young and relatively inexperienced. His politics were disliked by most of America's more prosperous citizens. Yet there was hardly ever a whisper that he was not up to the job.

He was frustrated by the conservative majority (partly Republican and partly Democratic) in the Congress. He provoked disagreement and criticism and satire. But he and his Administration were never sneered at or patronised. They greatly increased the prestige not only of the executive branch of American government but of democratic leadership throughout the world.

John Maynard Keynes*

John Maynard Keynes was born in 1883, the elder son of John Neville Keynes, Registrar of the University of Cambridge. He was educated at Eton and King's College, Cambridge at both of which he was a scholar. He became a Fellow of King's and sometime Bursar and spent much of his time there for the rest of his life. In 1925 he married the Russian dancer Lydia Lopokova; there were no children.

He worked as a civil servant first at the India Office, 1906–08 and then at the Treasury 1915–19. He represented the Treasury at the Paris Peace Conference in 1919 and wrote his famous polemic The Economic Consequences of the Peace *as a result of his experiences there. He published* A Treatise on Money *in 1930 and* The General Theory of Employment, Interest and Money *in 1936.*

He was Editor of the Economic Journal *1911–44. In the Second World War he was again in the Treasury and played a key role in negotiating both the Bretton Woods monetary system in 1943–44 and the American loan to Britain in 1945. He was chairman of C.E.M.A., the forerunner of the Arts Council. He became Lord Keynes of Tilton in 1942 and died in 1946.*

I never knew Keynes. I do not believe that I ever saw him, unlike, say, Lloyd George, Baldwin or Léon Blum, whom I saw and heard in public but never met in private. If, however, I could nominate two men whom it might have been possible, without the

*In December 1983 I delivered this lecture in the Guildhall, Cambridge to an audience assembled by the Alliance in the centenary year of Keynes's birth and presided over by Provost Bernard Williams of King's College. Professor John Kenneth Galbraith also addressed the gathering.

benefit of a time machine, for me to have encountered, I would choose Keynes and Roosevelt.

This is partly but not wholly on account of their fame. And it is not because they were a pair, the one the theorist and the other the exponent, or 'the sorcerer and the sorcerer's apprentice' - but which could possibly be the apprentice? - as is sometimes superficially thought. Roosevelt certainly never read a word of Keynes's main works (although of course some of those around him did), and their one pre-war meeting was not a success. Keynes was disappointed with Roosevelt's hands, a human feature to which he always attached great importance. They were 'firm and fairly strong, but not clever or with finesse'. Roosevelt on the other hand found Keynes too clever, or at any rate too mathematical and abstruse. He referred to him afterwards as 'the gent', not a very obvious term of approval.

So it is not a question of their going automatically together. It is more that of all the near contemporaries about whom I have read a lot and written a little they are the two the physical impact of those personality I find it most difficult to imagine and for which I would therefore most like to be able to fall back upon direct memory. In the absence of this I must confess that the most vivid 'stills', in the old cinema sense, from Keynes's life have been imprinted upon my mind by Roy Harrod, bowdlerizing though his biography has been shown to be, rather than by Robert Skidelsky. But perhaps that is merely due to the fact that Skidelsky has so far written only about the first part of Keynes's life. And while his life and achievements, being many sided, can be separated into different strands, they are not in my view very suitable for chopping up into neat little parcels of time.

There are three obvious strands. There is Keynes the semi, but not very, private man, the Keynes of the Apostles and of the philosophy of G. E. Moore, of Bloomsbury and the South Downs and to some extent the Keynes of Cambridge, the Bursar of King's, the Founder of the Arts Theatre, the bibliophile and picture-buyer, the coruscating conversationalist and controversialist, a man of strong, original and mostly iconoclastic views, an unmatched polemicist. Had this been all, had he negotiated no loans or monetary systems and written no word of lasting note, it would still have been enough to make him a figure of continuing, if minor, interest. He would have been the twentieth century equivalent of such

nineteenth century figures as Abraham Hayward, who talked so
well that, if he were present at dinner, Gladstone, too hurried to
wait for the correction of posterity, was said to sulk because he
could not compete with him.

Then there is Keynes the state official, neither a political
minister nor exactly a servant of ministers, occupying a position
almost without parallel in Britain, but a little more familiar in a
French or American context: a Jean Monnet or a General Marshall.
In this role he was advisor, initiator, negotiator, the man of the
Paris Peace Conference at 35 and of Bretton Woods 25 years
later, the begetter of Britain's necessary but unpopular post-war
American loan. All this would have put him into a substantially
higher category of renown. It would have fully justified his
Westminster Abbey memorial service, almost unique I think for
being attended by both his parents. But it would not have made
him (with Churchill and Bertrand Russell) one of the three most
world-famous Englishmen of this century – or perhaps four if
Charlie Chaplin is counted as an Englishman. Keynes is put into
this category only by his economic writing, and pre-eminently,
by the *General Theory* which struck such a balance between theoretical elegance and practical application that, being also lucky in
its timing, it profoundly influenced a generation of world policy
making, extending in its impact to many who, despite the lucidity
of his style, never read a single paragraph of his original words.
It put him as a major station on the line of great economists,
which started with Adam Smith, and extends through Ricardo,
Mill and Marshall to himself, but not yet, perhaps never, to any
further point of comparable importance. It is about this aspect of
his life, together with his political activities and views, that I have
been asked to speak.

Professor Galbraith is to deal with his impact on America and
the world. We were both urged to deal with him in a practical
and political, rather than an abstract and theoretical, context. That
was an instruction of supererogation, certainly for me but also,
if 30 years of warm friendship have taught me anything, for the
Professor. It would be rather like asking Talleyrand on one of his
rare visits to the seat of his bishopric at Autun, not to make his
sermon too spiritual.

I begin with the politics, and will then turn to the economics.
Keynes's Liberalism, it must be said, was not that of a dependable

militant. He was a cool Liberal. His first burst of fame came from the denunciation of Lloyd George's policy at the Paris Peace Conference, which was particularly remarkable for the fact that it was a famous polemic with its most polemical passage cut out and only published 14 years later. However, he was a friend of the Asquiths (more of Margot than of Henry) and infuriated Bloomsbury by saying that he thought that the former Prime Minister was more intelligent than Lytton Strachey. His feeling for Asquith was considerable but was expressed in typical terms which might have commended themselves more to Asquith himself than to some of his more enthusiastic followers. He referred to his quality 'of a certain coolness of temper' which 'seems to me at the same time peculiarly *Liberal* in flavour, and also a much bolder and more desirable and valuable political possession and endowment than sentimental ardours'. Asquith's ardour for Keynes was certainly under control. 'Not much juice to him', he was reported to have said on one occasion. But this may have been after an incident several years earlier when the Prime Minister and Keynes arrived together at Garsington (the scene of the famous Keynes, Strachey, Bertrand Russell photograph) and were announced by the butler as 'Mr Keynes and another gentleman'.

What is more certain is that Keynes, while firmly Asquithian in the days of the Coalition and always more akin to Asquith than to Lloyd George both temperamentally and on grounds of international policy, nonetheless moved back into full communion with Lloyd George (on domestic policy at least) under the stimulus of the writing of the Yellow Book and the run-up to the 1929 election. In 1926, just before this period, he came nearest to a precise definition of his political bearings in the Britain of the Twenties. He did so with a deadliness of criticism rather than a gush of enthusiasm:

'How could I bring myself to be a Conservative?' he began. 'They offer me neither food nor drink - neither intellectual nor spiritual consolation. I should not be amused or excited or edified. That which is common to the atmosphere, the mentality, the view of life, of - well, I will not mention names - promotes neither my self-interest nor the public good. It leads nowhere; it satisfies no ideal; it conforms to no intellectual standard; it is not even safe, or calculated to preserve from spoilers that degree of civilization which we have already attained.'

He looked at the Labour Party a shade more charitably but then stated his objections with his habitual eschewal of euphemism:

'Ought I, then, to join the Labour Party? Superficially that is more attractive. But looked at closer, there are great difficulties. To begin with it is a class party and the class is not my class. If I am going to pursue sectional interests at all, I shall pursue my own . . . I can be influenced by what seems to me Justice and good sense, but the Class war will find me on the side of the educated bourgeoisie'.

He decided that he was therefore a Liberal, even if by elimination, his main doubt stemming from a lack of confidence in the ability of the Liberal Party, on its own, to regain its pre-war power. He did not want to fight the class war from the other side either. Those who believed 'that the coming struggle was Capitalism versus Socialism and that their duty was to fight for Capitalism, ought to get out of the Liberal Party'. He moved on to a still more heartfelt cry: 'I do not wish to live under a Conservative Government for the next 20 years'. The only recipe that he could see as he surveyed the bleak landscape, but one which he propounded without his usual degree of certainty, was Lib-Lab cooperation, with a rejuvenated Liberalism providing most of the ideas.

I think it can be claimed on this evidence, without too much affront to the rule that views on unforeseen events should be only cautiously attributed to the dead, that Keynes would have welcomed the Alliance. Over 50 years ago he wanted to defeat Conservatism, without the Labour Party winning. He saw that the Liberal Party could not do this on its own. It needed a partner. But the only avoidable choice brought one back to the Labour Party, the second of the (for him) unloved ugly sisters. Cinderella hadn't been created. He would surely have rejoiced in her birth. The Alliance was made for him. I wish he were here to help make it.

The only qualification which must be considered in the interests of the astringent fairness and accuracy which is a characteristic of all (or at least most) Alliance pronouncements is that, like some but not all others, Keynes took a slight lurch to the right in the last years of his life. In 1938 he had supported Stafford Cripps's Popular Front campaign, but in October 1939 he wrote to the *New Statesman*, which he had done much to create but which he found an ungracious child:

'The intelligentsia of the Left were loudest in demanding that the Nazi aggression should be resisted at all costs. When it comes to a showdown scarce four weeks have passed before they remember that they are pacifists and write defeatist letters to your columns, leaving the defence of freedom and of civilisation to Colonel Blimp and the Old School Tie for whom Three Cheers.'

The perhaps deliberately odd grammar (rather reminiscent of Queen Victoria's famous 'these news are dreadful' telegram to Gladstone after the fall of Khartoum) suggests that he was writing with emotion, and justifiably so in my view.

There were, however, a few signs of a retreat from radicalism in his remaining $6^1/_2$ years. I suppose that one could have imagined him as a Macmillan Tory in the late 1950s at the age of 76. But, whatever had happened in the meantime, and even at the age of 96, post-1979 policies would assuredly have brought him coruscatingly back into the anti-Conservative fold. A waste of resources greater even than in the 1930s would have been a most powerful twitch upon the thread. The intellectually slipshod nature of the monetarist case, accompanied by the complacent Panglossian belief that there is no alternative must have aroused his mocking contempt. But above all he would certainly have been repelled by the sheer irrationalism of judging economic policies not by material results but as though it were a religious practice in which the purification of the spirit could be achieved by the mortification of the flesh. There may be some fields of human endeavour in which this is so, but the management of the economy is certainly not one of them.

So much for trying to predict on the basis of Keynes's known but not unchanging views what would have been his developing political orientation. My next task is to try to appraise with the benefit of 48 years of hindsight what has been the economic and indeed political impact of his main theoretical work.

The General Theory of Employment Interest and Money was published in January 1936. It did not arrive unheralded, for Keynes had been writing and talking a good deal around the subject of demand deficiency and the under-use of resources in the preceding several years. He had developed at least one of the major ideas – the absence of any causal connection between savings and investment – in *A Treatise on Money* (published in 1930) and he also made substantial use of tools fashioned and announced by others, most notably of R. F. Kahn's 'multiplier', which dates publicly from June 1931. But the *General Theory* was certainly not derivative. Keynes was more open to the charge that he had been too busy to read enough of the works of others. He had been eager to get it out. It was an elegant work of theory but it was also urgent, in the sense that it was a direct response to the major economic problem of the time. This accounted for much of its impact.

In addition it was complete, although not perfectly finished, it was new, and it fully justified its title of *general*. It was complete because it was not merely a torpedo fired at the hull of neo-classical economics. Keynes and others had let off a lot of these in the past. But this was a new model ship to set alongside the old. It incorporated some traditional features, and some of the new ones were not wholly watertight. But it was recognisably different: a full-scale re-shaping of the doctrines of macro-economics in terms directly relevant to the major problems of the time.

It was new because previous general theoretical works had assumed that supply created its own demand. The unspoken premise, except in special studies of the trade cycle, was full employment. If it did not exist, it was because wages were too high or some other rigidity had tiresomely but temporarily intervened. The real issue of economics was the most effective allocation of resources, not the danger that they might never be created.

Keynes changed the angle of view. To an excessive extent he regarded the allocation of resources as a resolved issue, and he was prepared to leave the problems of supply to businessmen, which meant that he regarded them as very minor. He was concerned with demand, which, contrary to accepted doctrine, had no natural tendency to settle at full employment level.

The classical theory held that the rate of interest combined with the wage level would perform any necessary corrections. Keynes argued that neither of these mechanisms would work. He dismissed the traditional view of the rate of interest as not merely inadequate but as nonsense. There might well be decisions to save without subsequent decisions to invest. No manipulation of the rate of interest or the money supply alone could deal with this. There would be no increase in the 'propensity to invest' to offset the decreased level of consumption. The economy would simply settle down at a lower level of activity.

A lowering of wages might be equally ineffective as a route to full employment. It was dangerously easy to draw a false analogy between an individual firm and the economy as a whole. (He would no doubt have found Mrs Thatcher's economic equation of a family with a State still more intellectually derisible.) If, with total demand remaining constant, one firm could get its wages down, it would tend to employ more people. But in the economy as a whole the decline in total demand was much more likely to cancel out any beneficial employment tendency.

The key was investment. It was the element of demand which fluctuated most and was in the greatest need of stimulus from government. This led Keynes on both to advocating an active role for the State in investment policy ('When the capital development of a country becomes a by-product of the activities of a casino the job is likely to be ill-done') and to deficit financing in certain circumstances. Balanced budgets when resources were under-used was a mark not of virtue but of stupidity. As a result he became pinned with an inflationary tag. But this was economic primitivism. *How To Pay For The War*, which he published four years later, was written within the assumptions of the *General Theory* but offered a prescription for war-time finance which, had it been followed by Lyndon Johnson 25 years later, might have done more to avoid the great world inflation of the 1970s than all the words of Milton Friedman.

What Keynes rejected with contumely was that it was sensible to prescribe the same remedy in totally different circumstances. As he had rebutted a charge of inconsistency in 1931: 'I seem to see the elder parrots sitting round and saying: "You can *rely* on us. Every day for 30 years, we have said 'What a lovely morning!'"' But this is a bad bird. He says one thing one day and something else the next.'

Another quality of the *General Theory* was that it endeavoured to re-unify economics. Previously the study of demand and the factors of production had become sharply divorced from the study of banking and monetary policy. As Keynes put it: 'We have all of us become used to finding ourselves sometimes on one side of the moon and sometimes on the other, without knowing what route or journey connects them . . .' He provided the connection. It was indeed a *general* theory.

Keynes did not underrate the importance of his book. He wrote to Bernard Shaw a year before publication saying: 'To understand my state of mind . . you have to know that I believe myself to be writing a book on economic theory which will largely revolutionize . . . the way the world thinks about economic problems'. 'I can't predict what the final upshot will be in its effect on actions and affairs', he added. 'But the Ricardian foundations of Marxism will be knocked away.' This was both a bold and an odd claim. It is not the 'Ricardian foundations of Marxism' which have been the main victim. It is rather the framework of traditional 'capitalist' economics which was first sundered and then put together in another mould. Keynes thought it 'moderately conservative in its implications'. In other words, as Professor Seymour Harris, perhaps his most devoted American exponent of his own generation, wrote: 'Keynes's mission . . . was to save capitalism not to destroy it.'

A number of his Cambridge peers, including Pigou, his old teacher, and Robertson, his old collaborator, hadn't greatly liked it. This was partly because he had not gone out of his way to be gracious and had attacked Pigou in typically astringent terms. Pigou, after an interval of ten years and Keynes's death, was notably gracious in return: 'We were pedestrian, perhaps a little complacent. . . (He) broke resoundingly that dogmatic slumber. . . Economics and economists came alive. The period of tranquility was ended. A period of active and . . . creative thought was born. For this the credit was almost wholly due to Keynes.' So much for the academic response to the political effect.

So far as the effect upon policy making was concerned there was no significant influence in Britain before the war. The position in America is more arguable. What is certain is that the main practical impact throughout the world came after and not before the war. By then Keynes's central doctrine had achieved most powerful practical vindication. The principal economy which was stimulated but not ravaged by war was that of the United States. The increase of national output was there so great that it made possible not only a vast outpouring of war material but a substantial increase in private consumption as well. Munitions production proved a good substitute for his old mocking recipe of getting the Treasury to fill old bottles with bank notes, burying them in disused coalmines and leaving it to private enterprise to dig them up again.

Thereafter there was a quarter century and more with no return, either in the U.S. or, after post-war recovery took off, in the other principal industrial countries, to the massive debilitating unemployment of the inter-war years. There was also in the countries of the European Community and in Japan the greatest surge to wealth that has ever been seen in the recorded history of the world. How far this was due to Keynes's writings and their ripple effect is difficult to judge. What is undoubtedly true is that his analytical methods combined with the greatly improved pro-vision of national income statistics, which he had done a lot to prod along in Britain, affected the whole post-war economic practice and discussion of demand management in the finance ministries and the central banks of the world. No-one in 1951 or 1961 or even 1971 - 1981 is a different matter - could have spoken in the terms used by Montagu Norman in 1931 and escaped public ridicule. 'Crude Keynesianism', as it has for some time been fashionable to describe some applications of his doctrine, may have some limitations, but it was an immense advance on crude pre-Keynesianism, and is in any event not where Keynes's thought would have stopped had he been alive today.

As in addition he did a great deal to fashion the sun of the Bretton Woods system - although by no means in the exact form he would have wished - which warmed world trade over the same period, his contribution to this generation-long period of economic success must be regarded as remarkable and unique.

This success cracked gradually but not evenly over the 1970s. First, in 1971 the strain of being the pivot of the world monetary system became too great even for the dollar. And it should be said in passing that had Keynes's own Clearing Union scheme prevailed at Bretton Woods itself the strain would have been more evenly spread, and the system might have lasted longer. But it did not so prevail and the world moved into a disruptive era of violent and often irrational currency fluctuations. Trade and investment both suffered. Then in 1973 came the first wave of oil price increases with its inflationary effect on prices and its deflationary effect on the levels of economic activity in the West. By 1978 some attempt at concerted recovery was underway. But within six months of that year's Bonn Economic Summit, at which this was planned, a second wave had a still more devastating effect upon both Western and Third World economies, and was fortified by the growth of the doctrine that the way to deal with a slump was to make it deeper. As a result we have been back, so far as wasted output and wasted lives even if not absolute poverty are concerned, in the conditions of the 1930s from which Keynes helped to rescue us. And approximately there, unless new policies are pursued, we show every sign of staying.

How, in view of this history, it can be rationally contended that Keynsianism has been the road to disaster and its monetarist rejection the key to success, I cannot begin to understand.

What, on the contrary, is needed now both nationally and internationally is an injection into Downing Street, the White House and other chancelleries of the world of some of the rational panache which Maynard Keynes showed nearly 50 years ago. We may not see his like again, but let us at least hope that the world economy is not ruined by his denigrators.

Harold Macmillan

Harold Macmillan was born in 1894, the son of Maurice Macmillan, publisher. He was a scholar at Eton and an exhibitioner at Balliol College, Oxford. He was ADC to the 9th Duke of Devonshire as Governor-General of Canada 1919–20. He married his daughter, Lady Dorothy Cavendish, and had one son (later Maurice Macmillan MP who died in 1984) and three daughters. During the First World War he served in the Grenadier Guards and was wounded three times.

He was MP for Stockton-on-Tees 1924–29 and 1931–45 and for Bromley 1945–64. In 1942–45 he was Minister Resident in the Mediterranean. In 1954 and 1955 he served briefly both as Minister of Defence and then Secretary of State for Foreign Affairs. He was Chancellor of the Exchequer from December 1955 to January 1957 when he succeeded Eden as Prime Minister and held that office for 6³/₄ years until 1963.

Until his death in 1986 he was President of the Macmillan publishing group (Chairman 1964–74) and Chancellor of Oxford University (from 1960).

He became 1st Earl of Stockton in 1984.

(i) As Statesman and Sage

Harold Macmillan was the longest-lived of all the forty-nine Prime Ministers in the series which began with Walpole. Yet in a remarkably durable occupational group (79 has been the average age of Prime Ministers dying this century) he wins by only a short head from Churchill, who had Gladstone only a nose behind him.

What is remarkable about Macmillan's very long life is that nearly the whole of it was required to make his reputation. Churchill's fame would have lost nothing by having ten years cut off, and might even have gained by losing twenty. Gladstone's could have done without the last twelve years, Lloyd George's the last twenty, Asquith's and Baldwin's the last ten, Eden's at least the last twenty, and Rosebery's (a rather extreme example) the last thirty-six. But Macmillan required nearly all the long years of his retirement for the development of the patina of his reputation. Had he died in 1963, when illness drove him out of office, his place in public esteem would no doubt have recovered somewhat from the low point which it then occupied, but would have lacked the essential appurtenances of venerable sagacity and elderly wit. Attlee is in this respect the most comparable figure. His reputation also rose strongly in retirement. But I think his own presence was less necessary to the process.

An important factor in the brilliance of Macmillan's afterglow was that he gave every sign of greatly enjoying being an old man. I do not think that Churchill did, and Gladstone referred with distaste to 'the gradual closing of the doors of the senses'. But Macmillan, while no doubt he felt acutely the deprivation of being unable to read in his last years, found compensation in the aura of age: in, for example, the suspense inevitably created by audiences waiting to see whether he could mount very slowly to his rostrum (particularly in the Sheldonian Theatre in Oxford for one of his virtuoso performances as Chancellor of the University), and whether he could remember or improvise his lines when he got there. His hooded eyes added to the mordancy of his wit, his shuffling gait (which he had adopted many decades ago, almost before it was necessary) to the authority of his experience.

In his earlier years, by contrast, he was probably under-esteemed. The friends of his youth, he frequently stated, were nearly all killed in the First World War. 'It was a city of ghosts', I remember him dramatically saying about 1919 Oxford. Amongst those who survived, he was rather friendless. He was an MP at thirty and as a young and early middle-aged politician he behaved with outstanding political bravery, renouncing the whip and speaking for anti-government candidates at Munich-time bye-elections. But he was certainly not a nodal figure amongst anti-appeasement Conservatives, and even more certainly was not regarded as a witty and sparkling companion. 'Harold can be counted on, but don't let's have him to dinner because he is rather a bore', was what one Edenite MP later told me about Macmillan's reputation in the late 1930s.

Not surprisingly, his political career did not prosper. At the age of 45 in 1939, with a briefly broken 15 years in the House of Commons behind him, he was miles from the most junior of offices. Even when the balance of power in the Conservative Party shifted a year later, he was far from bounding forward. His years as Minister Resident first in North Africa and then in Italy amounted to a considerable public service (despite recent calumnies) and produced his best book, but they hardly made him central to the political process. By the last years of the war he was no more important a politician than Duff Cooper (four years his senior) and incomparably less so than Anthony Eden (three years his junior).

Losing his seat in 1945 might have been expected to bring a middle-rank political career to a middle-aged end. In fact however it galvanized his party political commitment in a way electoral success had never done. Stockton, the scene of his defeat, was to retain its place in his nostalgia and (much later) achieve a new one on his escutcheon, but Bromley, its antithesis in almost every respect, was his realistic base for the future. Macmillan threw himself into opposition to the Attlee Government with an apparent display of partisan relish. As a result he was a fairly automatic choice for the Cabinet when Churchill came back in 1951, but not in one of the highest offices. He had however a job which was temporarily in a very active sector of the political battlefield, and he made the most of it. As Minister of Housing he built a lot of houses (and the first of the high-rise flats as well), and he exploited this success with a flamboyant showmanship which had not hitherto been seen to be part of his character.

Nonetheless his political advancement was relatively slow-moving. He is the only Prime Minister of the past 100 years who reached the age of 60 (and after 30 years in the House of Commons) without occupying one of the great offices of state. That came only in 1955 when he became Foreign Secretary and then, eight months later, Chancellor of the Exchequer, but again for months (13) rather than years. He was in both the Foreign Office and the Treasury for too short a time to make much mark upon them. Had the Government (and not just the Prime Minister) collapsed at the time of Suez and Macmillan gone into retirement at the age of 62, he would have left less imprint than most politicians who have recently got near to the top without wearing the crown, Bevin or Cripps, Butler or Macleod. This illustrates again his need for a long career.

However, far from Suez destroying him it appeared to make him. This was strange, for his part in the events of those months was neither wise nor glorious, less so probably than his record in any other major conjuncture of his life. He was rash before the battle and all for quick retreat when the guns (of Wall Street) started firing. Harold Wilson's jibe that he was 'first in and first out' was fully justified. Yet when Eden resigned in January 1957 Macmillan romped into 10 Downing Street with the overwhelming support of his Cabinet colleagues, who had all been in the best position to observe these tergiversations.

Paradoxically this destroys the view that Macmillan just slipped in at a lucky moment and would not have succeeded otherwise. Even without the Suez debacle it is unlikely that Eden would have survived long enough as Prime Minister to enable a plausible successor other than Macmillan or Butler to emerge. And after the end of 1955 Macmillan would always have been preferred to Butler by the Conservative Party.

So Macmillan achieved his premiership, and with the clearance of the high but by no means impossible hurdle of the 1959 election, became one of the longest serving and more significant Prime Ministers of the century. As a peace-time head of government he is in a group with Asquith, Baldwin, Attlee, and, of those whose term is complete, no-one else. How he should be rated amongst this quartet is difficult at present to appraise, but it would not in my view be top. His Government did not leave the imprint on the nation's affairs of those of Asquith or Attlee, nor could it match them for strength of personnel. For much of the time his principal ministers were Selwyn Lloyd and Heathcote Amory.

Nevertheless the Macmillan Government was not without its achievements: it picked Anglo-American relations up off the Suez floor and brought them to a high pitch of intimacy during the Kennedy presidency. It took the first belated steps towards Britain's membership of the European Community. It carried through the major second phase of the ending of empire. It played a useful role on the world stage, giving fully adequate support to the United States at the time of the Berlin Wall and the Cuban missile crises, while constantly urging dialogue with Moscow, and helping to secure the Test Ban treaty. And it maintained full employment and low inflation at home, even if it missed the full European surge to prosperity.

Macmillan himself was very much the animator of all these different but consistently moderate policies, which he often executed behind a partisan facade and with an exhibitionist flourish. This dissimulation was more admired by Harold Wilson than by Hugh Gaitskell, who were his two principal opponents. The latter thought him tricky to the verge of dishonesty. In retrospect I think this was a superficial judgement. Macmillan often finessed, but underneath he was broadly and steadily true to a loose doctrine of expansionary economics, social emollience and liberal internationalism. There are many worse combinations.

(ii) As Memoir Writer

Although a great publisher by inheritance and a great reader by election, Harold Macmillan will be much better remembered for what he did rather than for what he wrote; as an author he was prolific rather than distinguished. His memoirs (six long volumes plus a substantial and more vivid war diary) were on a scale which no Prime Minister other than Churchill has approached. Surprisingly, however, for all his classical training he never had a feeling for the use of words comparable with his feeling for the handling of issues or management of men. This applied to his speech as well as to his writing. The result is that several of the phrases for which he is remembered – 'there ain't gonna be no war', 'you have never had it so good' - match his character about as comfortably and appropriately as a Christmas cracker paper hat on the head of a bishop. The memorable words of most great men of politics ('Roll up that map. . .' 'It was a damned close-run thing,' 'blood, toil, sweat and tears . . .' 'You have nothing to fear but fear itself', 'My mission is to pacify Ireland') are exceptionally forceful and succinct expressions of their style and outlook. Macmillan's were something apart from himself, not a promontory but a ship moored off-shore. He believed the best way to reach the public mind was consciously to play-act, and to watch himself doing it, with detachment but without discrimination.

Of course, several of those quoted above were great actors, notably Roosevelt and Gladstone. Indeed, when asked in later life what was the most sympathetic audience to which he had ever spoken, Gladstone replied without hesitation that it was a gathering of actors to which he had once lectured. They were the group who best understood what he was trying to do, he added. But both he and Roosevelt threw themselves wholeheartedly into their parts. Macmillan never quite did this. He always cared what he did, but he cared less what he said and in *Riding the Storm 1956-59* (1971) he did not seem to have cared much what he wrote, either at the time or recalling it later. How else can one explain some of the letters and documents which he picks out from the past, and quotes as though he were peculiarly proud of them. The following is a minute written when Chancellor of the Exchequer to his second most important civil servant, about the conference which created the European Community:-

MESSINA
1 We have spoken about this.
2 I think our approach is too negative.
3 I would like to propose a joint Treasury/FO study by officials of possible alternatives.
4 These might be based
(a) on OEEC
(b) on NATO.
5. How do I arrange this?

This might, I suppose, be regarded as magisterially succinct. To me it appears a document which was jejune when it was written, and which has gained neither penetration nor prescience with the passage of time.

Again and quite different, except that it is an example of slipping almost into a style in just the way that he slipped into a *Finnish* white fur hat for his visit to Russia six months later, there is a letter which Macmillan wrote to Dulles. He did not much admire Dulles. But he thought he had to get on with him. That was obviously desirable. But was there any need to write to him in a sort of parody of what Macmillan himself called Eisenhower's 'lack of elegance of expression'? 'It was grand to see you in London', Macmillan's letter ran, 'and to have a good talk about all our

129

problems. They do not look like decreasing but it is fine to feel that we can face them together.' Might not Dulles have been more impressed had he not been written to in pidgin-Eisenhower?

As a political thinker and strategist his thought, and even more importantly, his actions were dominated by the need to defeat the class appeal of the Labour Party, and he succeeded brilliantly, in 1959 at least. Failure on the part of the Conservative Party to cling on to at least a segment of its industrial working class support he recognised as disaster. He was always sceptical of suburban Toryism and never, I suspect, in spite of his later triumphs, wholly reconciled himself to his rejection in 1945 as member for Stockton-on-Tees and his retreat to Bromley.

This view is obviously very good party political sense, but some of the analysis upon which he based it seems to me more questionable. He saw the Asquith/Lloyd George split in the Liberal Party as crucial to the rise of the Labour Party. I think he was 30 years out, and that the Gladstone/Joseph Chamberlain quarrel was far more seminal. The consequent inability of the Liberal Party to deliver social reform and its concentration upon the Irish issue were much more fundamental. This created the weakness. Asquith and Lloyd George merely tore along the ready-made perforation. Equally I found unilluminating his view expressed in *The Past Masters* (1975) that in the Labour Party at that time 'the moderate section is still largely composed of men of industrial experience. The more extreme position has been occupied by the intellectuals.' This was at best a piece of Baldwinesque romanticism.

In the later volumes of his memoirs his comments on individual statesmen of his time could be acerbic. (This was in sharp contrast with the earlier ones; perhaps he was getting bored with urbanity.) Thus in *Pointing the Way* (1972), he describes how Adenauer 'has become - like very many old men - vain, suspicious and grasping . . . carrying on a great campaign of vilification of Her Majesty's Government and especially of me'. To Adlai Stevenson is attributed 'incredible folly and weakness (mixed with vanity)' for his attitude to the Congo, and a little later he is described as one of the 'half-baked "liberals" whom [the United States Government] commonly employ (for internal political reasons) at the United Nations'. Nor were the American strictures confined to Democrats. 'Under a strong President, Foster Dulles might have been a good Secretary of State; under Eisenhower he was a disaster.'

Compared with these acerbities British ministers and officials are still treated very gently. But we are at least told, in relation to early 1960, that the Chancellor and the Governor of the Bank of England 'do each other harm - for there is a sudden mood of despondency and alarm . . . I am worried not so much about the boom but about the loss of nerve . . .' These asperities are at least more interesting than the reference to the resourceful Chancellor fortified by the indomitable Governor which were the style of the previous volume; and it leads on to a notable portrait of de Gaulle, written after the General's visit to Macmillan's Sussex house in November 1961:-

The Emperor of the French (for he is now an almost complete autocrat, taking no notice of any advice and indeed receiving little of independent value) is older, more isolated, more sententious and far more *royal* . . . He is well-informed, yet remote. His hatred of the 'Anglo-Americans' is as great as ever. While he has extraordinary dignity and charm, 'unbends' delightfully, is nice to servants and children and so forth, he does not apparently listen to argument. I mean this almost literally. Not only is he not convinced, he actually does not listen. He merely repeats over and over again what he has said before. And the doctrine - almost dogma - is based on intuition, not ratiocination. He talks of Europe, and means France.

De Gaulle aroused Macmillan's interest more than any of the other world figures with whom he had close contact. This interest illuminates his writing about the General. Yet I find it difficult to believe that he dealt with him well. He was too inclined to try to emulate the General's style; to talk and indeed to negotiate with him in French, which was a strain, well though Macmillan spoke it; to seek to rival de Gaulle's own mordant historical generalisations; to play constantly upon the French ground rather than his own.

How naturally Macmillan thought in terms of the sweep of history I find it difficult to judge. He was a great writer of minutes to his colleagues, a habit in which I believe him to have been followed by none of his successors. In these minutes he consciously adopted a standing-back, ruminative style, raising fundamental questions in a simple form. 'I have been reading a good deal lately about the beginning of the 1914 war', he began a

Berlin memorandum to the Foreign Secretary in June 1959. 'The more I think about our conversation yesterday the more depressed I am', he encouragingly told the Chancellor of the Exchequer in February, 1960. 'Max Beerbohm once said that history does not repeat itself. It is the historians who repeat one another. This is certainly true of the economists and professors.'

The value of minutes beginning in this form and continuing in a style which ignored the minutiae of departmental policy-making was that they made ministers look at the landscape for a moment through the other end of the telescope. The disadvantage was that they did not give them much guidance as to what to do in their ministries. But such minutes were an improvement on Eden's petulant ones and perhaps sometimes on Churchill's grandiloquent ones.

Jean Monnet

Jean Monnet was born in 1888 in Cognac, the son of a brandy producer and merchant. He was educated locally and went to no university. He got to know the world as a brandy salesman.

He was deputy Secretary-General of the League of Nations in 1919, reorganised the Chinese railways in 1932 and was a member of the British Supply Council in Washington, 1940–43. He created the Monnet Plan for France in 1946 and was president of the preparatory conference of the Schuman Coal and Steel Plan in 1950. He was President of the European Coal and Steel Community 1952–55, and chairman of the Action Committee for a United States of Europe 1956–75.

He died in 1979.

Jean Monnet's funeral mass on a March afternoon in 1979 in the little Ile de France town of Montfort l'Amaury, captured to a remarkable extent the paradoxes and achievements of his life and character. It was obviously a French service in a characteristic French parish church, and he was very much a child of the land of France, where his forbears (and he himself for a time) engaged with one of its most renowned products. But it began with a choral recording of the Battle Hymn of the Republic, sung in English, and the leading official mourners, the Chancellor of the Federal Republic of Germany, and then the President of the French Republic, arrived to the hammering out of its transatlantic words and notes. So France was firmly set in an international context.

Thereafter the simplicity of the service, with family, neighbours, faithful collaborators and the leaders of nations intermingled in a small and intimate framework, symbolised his unofficial status and his modesty of life and manner on the one hand, combined with his inner self-confidence and his vast public influence on the other.

Jean Monnet was the most central of the founding fathers of modern European unity. During the period of post-war creation, he worked with and through others of greater public force: Adenauer of Germany, Schuman of France, de Gasperi of Italy, Spaak of Belgium. They provided the oratory and the political power. But Monnet provided the determination and the detail.

When I last spoke to him, a year before his death and when he was 89 years old, he no longer had his old strength but he retained his lucidity and conviction. He was not a utopian, although he had an impregnable long-term optimism. He never doubted the rightness of his own views. He believed that logic, of course, but, more important, history, was on his side. In this sense he was not modest. Had he been so, had he been afflicted by self-doubt, he would never have played the part he did in changing the face of Europe.

Jean Monnet was born into a family of Cognac merchants in the West of France. At the age of 18 - in 1906 - he began his international life by travelling to Winnipeg to sell brandy. By the time of the First World War he was deeply involved in inter-allied purchasing missions, spending much of his time in London, some of it in Washington. He became almost completely at home, administratively and linguistically, in the Anglo-Saxon world. Although he did so much to create the Europe of the Six, he had never been an inward-looking European. His experience at this time also gave him the simple conviction, from which he never subsequently varied, that international cooperation rather than national rivalry was the key to solving most of the problems of the world.

At the age of 30 he was sufficiently well-known to be pressed into becoming the deputy Secretary-General of the new League of Nations. After four years in Geneva he had to go home to Cognac and pull together his faltering family business. He did so successfully and quickly. He was always a practical and not a starry-eyed idealist. For the most part of the rest of the inter-war period he was an international banker – in San Francisco, in Warsaw, in Shanghai, in Paris.

The outbreak of the Second World War brought him back into unobtrusive but influential public service; back indeed into his former work of coordinating inter-allied purchasing missions. He played a major rôle in 1940 in the attempt to create an Anglo-French union out of the disaster of that time. From 1940 to 1943 he was in Washington as a friend and '*interlocuteur valable*' of the Roosevelt Administration. Between 1943 and the liberation of France he was in Algiers. There, and thereafter, his relations with General de Gaulle were those of mutual respect and *politesse*, but no closer. Although there was never a common philosophical commitment, there was from time to time an identity of purpose and always an identity of determination.

From the beginning of 1946 he was head of the French *Commissariat du Plan*. This was an important and influential rôle but he was nevertheless able to devote a large part of his energy and imagination to the future organisation of Europe, and in particular to working out the basis for the Coal and Steel Community. When that Treaty was at last signed it was natural that the presidency of the High Authority should fall to him. Then, in his own words, 'on the morning of August 10, 1952, Europe came to Luxembourg'. For three years from 1952 to 1955 he built up the first institution of the European Community. In 1955 he gave up his last official position, but not his commitment to public action. He invested a great deal of energy in the plan for a European Defence Community, but he was not deterred by the failure to realise it and concentrated on another route to European unity. His Action Committee for a United States of Europe was first a driving force towards and then an underpinning of the Rome Treaty. It fostered the embryonic European Commission; it advanced the cause of Britain in Europe; and, on a wider front, it promoted his central purpose of European union.

This purpose was, for Jean Monnet, both a symbol and a rallying point for his life's work. But unlike many of those who have had a central ideal which they have sought to achieve, he never allowed his to distort his judgement. The declaration of purpose never became a substitute for action. He always showed himself to be adaptable to changing political reality and was never a prisoner of his own ideology.

His own *Memoirs*, published a year before his death, is a worthy monument to these qualities of imagination and practicality. It is a book which combines a considerable modesty of presentation with complete assurance of belief. For those in Britain who remain sceptical and sometimes even hostile to a committed rôle for Britain in Europe, it is an object lesson on the way in which myths about the conception of Europe can and must be avoided.

It is a book not about theology but about political reality. It is also a book about the achievement of objectives rather than personal success. Jean Monnet often recalled as one of the most significant observations he ever heard a statement of Dwight Morrow that 'there are two kinds of people: those who want to *be someone* and those who want to *do something*'. There is no doubt about the category to which Jean Monnet belonged.

Herbert Morrison

Herbert Morrison was born in 1888, the son of a London policeman. He was educated at elementary schools and then became an errand-boy, shop assistant, telephone operator and deputy newspaper circulation manager. In 1919 he married Margaret Kent who died in 1953 and with whom he had one daughter. In 1955 he married Edith Meadowcroft. He was Labour MP for South Hackney 1923–24, 1929–31 and 1935–45 and for Lewisham 1945–59.

He was Minister of Transport 1929–31, Minister of Supply 1940, Home Secretary and Minister of Home Security 1940–45, Deputy Prime Minister, Lord President of the Council, Leader of the House of Commons 1945–51, Foreign Secretary March-October 1951. He was deputy leader of the Labour Party 1951–55 and several times an unsuccessful candidate for the leadership. He became Lord Morrison of Lambeth in 1959 and died in 1965.

Lord Morrison of Lambeth shares with Lord Butler of Saffron Walden the distinction of being the greatest success-failure of British politics of this century. Perhaps Austen Chamberlain, Lord Curzon and Hugh Gaitskell all came at least equally near to the premiership without actually achieving it. But Chamberlain had so much practice at playing the game and losing it that he did not greatly mind; Curzon's near miss was a once-only approach, nearer in his own mind than in reality; and early death (Gaitskell) is different from continuing frustration. Only Morrison and Butler achieved a regular disappointment accompanied by remarkable careers of long-standing service in the highest subordinate offices.

Butler's reputation now stands much higher than Morrison's, and the comparison cannot be pushed any further beyond recalling that they both wrote autobiographies. Lord Butler's was one of the best of the period, Lord Morrison's one of the worst. It was as uninformative as that of his old chief rival, Lord Attlee, while achieving a special note of 'we was cheated' sourness which was all its own. Yet Morrison was an unusual man and a politician of note and achievement, the final droop of whose career was allowed to obliterate, partly because of his own obsession with it, too much of his earlier almost soaring success.

The central question is whether Morrison was a machine politician of very limited horizons, lacking any political philosophy beyond the desire to win votes, who was lucky to be able to use the base of his successful leadership of the London County Council to get as far as he did, and whose disappointment at not getting any further was not only ill-concealed but verging on the ludicrous; or whether he was a statesman whose performance, like that of many, was admittedly uneven, but who stood for something distinct and important in British politics, for a moderate Labour Party with a broad appeal across classes and a strong sense of efficient administration, and who might, had the cards fallen differently, have been a great leader.

The truth, almost inevitably, lies somewhere between the two. At times, as a minister in 1929-31, as a pillar of good sense in the foolish days of 1932-34, as a politician capable in the last year or so of the war of casting his mind into the future, he was better than almost anyone else. Yet in all his activities there was some built-in cut-off point, quite high up but always there, which restricted his oratory, his sympathy, his policies. He had to deal with Attlee, with Bevin, with Cripps, with Bevan. He thought he was better than all of them, and in one sense he was right. They each had bigger (although differing) deficiencies than he had. But they each also had greater qualities.

Morrison was a very good second man. His tragedy was that, baulked at the top, he could get very little satisfaction or pleasure out of a substantial but limited achievement.

Emile Noël*

Emile Noël was born in Turkey in 1922. He was educated at the Ecole Normale Supérieure in Paris. In 1946 he married Lise Durand who died in 1985. He has two daughters.

He was chef de cabinet to Guy Mollet when the latter was Prime Minister of France, 1956–57, the time of the Suez crisis. He was Secretary-General of the Commission of the European Communities from 1958 to 1987.

He is now Rector of the European University Institute in Florence.

My first clearly remembered meeting with Emile Noël was as recent as July 20th, 1976. I had just become President-elect of the Commission and invited him to lunch with me in London.

I approached him with a mixture of respect and caution. I remember that I selected the restaurant with some care. He was already in his 18th year as Secretary-General, a legend in the history of the Community barely behind Monnet or Hallstein. I suppose that I expected to find him a repository at once of the wisdom and of the traditionalism of the Commission.

I, although wholly committed to the cause of European unity, was in 1976 almost totally inexperienced in the ways of the Community. I liked to say that I had kept my European faith burning brightly by hardly ever visiting Brussels. On the other hand, I was fairly well-trained in the ways of government of a member state with a strong but insular tradition of public administration. Many of the most notable British civil servants of the previous 20 years - Philip Allen, William Armstrong, Douglas Allen, Robert

*This tribute is based on a speech in Brussels on the occasion of his retirement in September 1987

Armstrong (none of them brothers) – had served me, as Permanent Secretaries, in very roughly the role that Emile Noël was about to occupy.

The scene might therefore have been set for a bruising cultural clash: a confrontation between a brash Anglo-Saxon who believed he understood government but was untutored in the subtleties of the Community, and a Gallic *haut fonctionnaire* who knew every strand in the history and practice of the institutions of Europe as a spider knows every filament of its web.

The clash did not occur. Why not? First, I think, because these obvious superficial differences were modified by strong subterranean counterflows. In 1976, perhaps to a greater extent than in 1987, I had a strong disposition to believe, to paraphrase Lawrence Sterne, that 'they order these things better' on the Continent. And Noël's Cartesian habit of mind cloaked a deep interest in, and respect for, Britannic methods and tradition.

His knowledge of English is more deceptively great than that of anyone I have ever known. Linguistically he is the exact opposite of the present Pope. Hear him speak a few English sentences and you think his command is very halting. Discuss a complex subject with him the in the language and you realise that he has a profound understanding of both syntax and the exact meaning of difficult words.

Beyond these 'underwater' affinities, however, Emile displayed other qualities which made working with him rewarding and even easy. In method of thought and style of expression he could not be other than a Frenchman. Yet he is totally free of the sin of national self-seeking. In the Commission and in its *services* we all try, with varying degrees of vigour, to set aside narrow nationalism and serve only the wider European interest. Emile Noël, in my experience, is the only one who has *completely* achieved this goal.

He also has an instinctive sense of the appropriateness of relationships, which would have made him very loath, even when he disagreed, to serve me or any other President with other than complete loyalty.

He was therefore a pleasure to work with, and I shall always retain towards him a deep sense of respect and affection. Yet I would not be so foolish as to believe that I understand him perfectly. He is far too delicate, ironical and complex a character for that. No-one who did not have these qualities could have written his inimitable minutes, where *mots justes* jostled with subjunctives in almost every sentence. These qualities gave him the occasional ability to produce a formula which had eluded everyone else, but which once produced commanded universal support because everyone wished they had thought of it themselves.

Such attributes also imply a certain reserve and attachment to ambiguity. Perhaps my most vivid pictorial recollection of Emile Noël from my presidency is of a day early on, in 1977, when, meeting him on a platform of the Paris Gare du Nord to return together to Brussels, I asked him on which side was our train. He crossed his wrists in front of his body, assuming a posture worthy of an El Greco painting. Only by looking carefully could I see that one hand extended further than the other. On that side was our train. The sign was clear. But it required attention to interpret it. This was typical of Noël's style as Secretary-General. He never obtruded his opinion or advice, but it was always there, unprejudiced and wise, when asked for.

If I look back at the main contentious issues of my presidency on which I was the beneficiary of this considerable wisdom, I see them under five main headings:

First, in order of time, although not of importance, was the issue of Community presence at Western Economic Summits. Its significance stemmed from the fact that it became a battle for the legitimacy and effectiveness of Community supranational power. Broadly the small countries, although loyally supported by Italy, were on one side, and the big countries, although with Germany uncomfortably semi-neutral, were on the other. Surprisingly in the circumstances, the small countries and the Commission won. As a result, and at the cost of some mild social embarrassment, I moved over a few years from being the man who did not come to dinner into the more-or-less invited guest. Emile Noël's sense of proportion was invaluable throughout these delicate manoeuvres. The ambiguity of too many member governments about giving the Community and the Commission enough power and prestige to do its job properly remains a continuing problem.

Second, there was the renewed drive for monetary union, which I launched in the autumn of 1977, and which achieved the limited but substantial prize of the European Monetary System, which was in place by the spring of 1979. It took us perhaps 30% of the way towards the goal of my Florence speech (in which I had advocated full monetary union). But to achieve that over 18 months was by European Community standards remarkably quick progress.

As a third main issue, there was the almost perennial problem of enlargement. The commitment to Greece, already made, had to be made reality. And, more important, the attitude to Spain and Portugal had to be determined. I had no doubt that, to keep out these Iberian and European democracies eager to join would involve the Community betraying its purposes. I also thought that they could bring some special strength. But I had no illusions, nor I am sure did Emile Noël, about the additional strain which increased numbers would put on an already creaking decision-making process.

Fourth, there was the problem of coming to terms with the new directly-elected Parliament. We had all been enthusiasts for direct elections. But when their product first assembled in Strasbourg in July 1979, we greeted it with a mixture of pride and apprehension. It was good to see the puppy of the cosy old nominated Parliament grow into such a fine mastiff, but would it bite our head off, particularly if it grew frustrated through being unable to get its teeth into the Council of Ministers? Emile, who was an experienced Parliament-watcher, took up a position which I would describe as calm but wary. And, with a few crises, the Parliament settled down and went on much as before, perhaps a little too much so.

Fifth, damagingly dominating the last 15 months of my Commission, there was the British budgetary dispute. And it was not only those 15 months that it dominated. It went on deep into the Thorn Commission. It was all a dreadful diversion of energies. If the Commission could have imposed a solution which would have enabled it to be dealt with in the bud, I am convinced that Europe could have escaped slipping so far behind both the United States and Japan, from the technological, growth and employment points of view, as it did in the early 1980s.

However that was not to be, and endless European Councils had to be endured and endless formulae devised. Noël was by far the most ingenious deviser of such formulae, and so we survived, intact if not for that period inspiring.

From these experiences there are a number of lessons to

be learnt for the future. Some of them I have mentioned as I went along. I shall not attempt to draw out the rest. I can only express my profound thanks to Emile Noël and my sympathy to Jacques Delors and future Presidents who will have to live without him.

Edwin Plowden

Edwin Plowden was born in 1907. He was educated at school in Switzerland and then at Pembroke College, Cambridge. In 1933 he married Bridget Richmond (Chairman of the Independent Broadcasting Authority, 1975–80) and has two sons and two daughters.

He joined the Civil Service in a temporary post in 1939 at the Ministry of Economic Warfare. He then moved to the Ministry of Aircraft Production, 1940–46, and was Chief Executive and a Member of the Aircraft Supply Council 1945–46. He joined the Cabinet Office in 1947. From 1947 to 1953 he was Chief Planning Officer at the Treasury. He was adviser to the Atomic Energy Organization, 1953–54 and Chairman of the Atomic Energy Authority 1954–59. Over the next 25 years he has been chairman of numerous committees of enquiry. He has been a member of the Top Salaries Review Body since 1977 and its chairman since 1981.

He became Lord Plowden in 1959.

At the time when Britain was governed by the Butskellite consensus, and was the key to the creation of the institutions of the Western world, Edwin Plowden's position, while not spotlighted in the centre of the stage, was more involved than that of an occupant of even the most overhanging box. He was more like a trusted second in a boxing ring. All three of his Chancellors whom he served as Chief Planner at the Treasury, Cripps, Gaitskell and Butler, were substantially dependent on him and his relationship with each of them was based on an affection which, while it was impartial, was in no way impersonal.

What has been the particular quality of Edwin Plowden which made him so sought-after by three very different and considerable Chancellors, and at the same so well-regarded by the Treasury officials alongside whom he worked, but compared with whom he was paid much more, given a rank much more than commensurate with his age (then barely 40) and whose advice he sometimes controverted? This last point is important, for in theory I suppose he could have acquired his cancellarian popularity by being a sort of teacher's pet or trusty familiar of the Chancellor who could speak to him in a more relaxed manner than more hierarchical officials. Lord Plowden tells us in his memoirs that he did perform something of this function, although as in my experience the Treasury was, within the confines of its own éliteness, an irreverent and even equal society, it was less necessary than in many other Departments.

But there was a great deal more to his rôle than this. When I became a minister for the first time in 1964 one of the first things I did was to get Edwin Plowden to chair a small but major enquiry into the future of the aircraft industry. At the end of my second period as Home Secretary, twelve years later, one of my last acts as a minister was to get him to undertake the chairmanship of the newly established Police Complaints Board. Apart from the fact that he was a natural chairman in both cases, the tasks could hardly have been more disparate.

Why did I want him to perform two such different rôles? In the first case my primary interest was that he should shine a searchlight of sceptical judgement upon a somewhat cushioned industry. In the second case as well I wanted his judgement, but I also wanted the authority of his reputation and experience to launch a necessary but controversial scheme. This retrospective analysis of motives brings one close to an appreciation of Edwin Plowden's peculiar qualities, although to the two that I have stressed there has to be added a devotion to public duty and a faith that rational discussion *could* solve nearly all problems – but not an equal faith that it *will*, owing to the inherent irrationality of others, politicians certainly included, but not exclusively so.

These qualities of mind and outlook made a strong appeal to his three Chancellors, as they subsequently did to me, although they are perhaps less fashionable today. This is despite the fact that Edwin Plowden liked to stress that he was a businessman in Whitehall. There was an element of throwaway conceit about this, rather in the way that Ralph Partridge, although perfectly at home in the bosom of Bloomsbury, would have described himself as a farmer, or that Joseph Alsop, when writing the most successful column in Washington, always referred to himself in print as 'this reporter'. But there was also truth. Plowden had worked most of the pre-war decade for C. Tennant Sons and Co., in the slightly improbable rôle of selling Dead Sea potash all over Europe at undercutting prices in order to secure an invitation to join the cartel which they were undercutting. I do not think that he had anything to do with MI6 but it sounds an almost perfect cover.

Then he had six wartime Whitehall years and 12 months back with Tennants' before his six years as Chief Planner which were followed by another six as chairman of the Atomic Energy Authority. In 1963 he started his major private sector spell, which was thirteen years as chairman (and after that as president) of the engineering conglomerate Tube Investments. During this period he ranked as one of the seven or eight most princely of the captains of British Industry.

But he was never my idea of a British – or even an American – businessman in public life, bringing the urgent but limited perspectives of the boardroom to government. It is as impossible to imagine him paraphrasing Secretary of Defense Charles E. Wilson of General Motors and saying 'what is good for Tube Investments is good for Britain' as it is to think of him floundering around like Lord Ryder when he was mistakenly made head of the National Enterprise Board in 1974.

What Edwin Plowden is more like is a great French administrator, a product in the old days of one or other of the *Grandes Ecoles,* more recently almost inevitably of the *Ecole Nationale d'Administration*, who can turn his hand with versatility but without amateurism from the private to the public sector, from high policy to the profit and loss account. The greatest of them of this century was Jean Monnet, whose pre-1939 career was not entirely unlike Plowden's. Monnet however had an *idée fixe,* which is not something to which Plowden either could or would wish to lay claim, and as a result played a major part in casting half a continent in a new mould. So the comparison does not wholly run. Robert Marjolin or even André Giraud, the recent Defence Minister, are other French figures who come to mind.

Yet when Edwin Plowden found himself in the autumn of 1951, at the age of 44 and partly by accident, with Monnet and Averell Harriman, as one of the three 'Wise Men' of the Western world who were to soothe away the strains of re-armament by the fairness of the burden-sharing, there was no bathos about his participation even if there was not complete success in the enterprise.

Plowden was a major figure during the period of what Dean Acheson half self-mockingly called 'the creation' and he has been a major public servant ever since.

Eleanor Roosevelt

Eleanor Roosevelt was born in 1884, the daughter of Elliott Roosevelt, younger brother of President Theodore Roosevelt and Anna Hall. She was educated privately. In 1901 she married Franklin Delano Roosevelt, President of the United States from 1933 until his death in 1945 and they had four sons and one daughter.

She was a US representative at the UN General Assembly 1945–52. She remained active in American Democratic politics and world good causes until she died in 1962.

There is little doubt that Eleanor Roosevelt, by any standard, was a remarkable woman in her own right. How was she remarkable? On a public level the answer is that she was unique among Presidents' wives in establishing a distinct political personality for herself; and that she compounded the feat, in a rather breathtaking way, by just, but only just, keeping her independence within the bounds of a partnership which was on the whole helpful to FDR. Throughout the longest and most controversial presidency in American history there was always the added piquancy of watching to see whether she would fall off the tightrope of constant direct communication with the public into the sawdust of embarrassing indiscretion.

There have, of course, been other First Ladies, from Dolley Madison to Mrs Onassis, who have left a distinct imprint upon the White House. But all the others did so in a way that was traditionally feminine. Eleanor Roosevelt was not much concerned with the furnishings, still less with the food and drink, and hardly with the form of the entertainment, except when she insisted on introducing people whom her husband did not want to see but whom she felt he ought to.

Nor is it possible to think of a British Prime Minister's wife who performed anything like her role. The nearest example, I suppose, was Margot Asquith. She was certainly a public personality, with strong views upon politics as upon everything else. But that fact apart, the contrasts are far greater than the similarities. Mrs Asquith encouraged the social and frivolous side of her husband. Mrs Roosevelt did the reverse. Mrs Asquith saw politics almost exclusively in terms of personalities. Mrs Roosevelt saw them in terms of moral endeavour. And Mrs Asquith, at least until her autobiography was published, five years after the departure from Downing Street, confined her indiscretions to semi-private, even if much repeated, conversation.

Mrs Roosevelt did no such thing. Throughout most of her White House years she wrote her 'My Day' column, which appeared in 60 or so newspapers across the nation. She lectured for very high fees, and gave sponsored radio talks for even higher ones. She graduated from a mattress company to Pond's Cream, who paid her 3,000 1930s dollars each for a series of 13 short talks. The money went to various social service projects, but this did not entirely still the criticism. In 1936 she published a fairly frank volume of interim autobiography. Still more hazardously, she operated within the sprawling and ill-coordinated American government machine, promoting her own pet projects, forging alliances with Cabinet officers and other officials, fostering her protégés, even testifying before a Congressional Committee.

She was not seeking power for its own sake, but was endeavouring to keep the President, who often preferred a crab-like method of advance, on a more direct progressive axis. On almost every domestic issue she was significantly to the left of him. She was strongly egalitarian, she was anti-segregationist at a time when the Democratic Party had hardly woken up to the problem of the blacks. In foreign affairs, too, although a little muddled between pacifism and anti-fascism, her pressure was persistent. 'We should have pushed *him* harder', she said to Leon Henderson, in the President's presence, when the Spanish Government had been finally defeated. Roosevelt allowed the criticism to pass, without either response or resentment. He accepted this side of her character as part of the political furniture. It fitted in well enough with his methods of competing tensions and fluctuating personal alliances. And on the whole she won him votes.

How satisfactory a marriage partner she was is another matter. She had surmounted too many difficulties to be a relaxing and sympathetic companion to a hard-pressed, kaleidoscopic President who disliked being bored. Although born in the heart of New York's most privileged society, she had had a difficult life. Her mother was a beauty, her father an elegant but hopeless drunk. She disliked her and adored him. They were both dead before she was eleven. There were plenty of family left to look after her, but they considered her dull. She was an ugly duckling in a gilded cage.

Her only success was to marry Franklin Roosevelt, even though he was not considered much of a catch by her smarter cousins. 'He was the kind of boy whom you invited to the dance but not the dinner', her cousin Alice Longworth, Theodore Roosevelt's daughter, said, 'a good little mother's boy whose friends were dull, who belonged to the minor clubs and who was never at the really gay parties.' But Eleanor wanted him very much indeed, even though Mrs Longworth's always astringent criticism was correct at least to the extent that she got his mother, Sarah Roosevelt, with him. Much of Eleanor's life was a running battle with that formidable old châtelaine of Hyde Park, who lived until 1941.

After 13 years, when she had achieved some sort of stabilisation of the lines in that battle, she discovered her husband's now well-known affair with Lucy Mercer. Then three years later, when she had re-adjusted with difficulty to this, came his polio attack. The effort of nursing his mind and body back to active life and politics was immense. It gave her, with the other struggles, a new and formidable personality. It made her the best-known and most influential American woman of the three decades between 1930 and 1960. But it did not make her the perfect companion for FDR. She surveyed their later relationship with admirable objectivity in the second instalment of her autobiography, published in 1960: 'He might have been happier with a wife who was completely uncritical. That I was never able to be, and he had to find it in some other people. Nevertheless, I think I sometimes acted as a spur, even though the spurring was not always wanted or welcome. I was one of those who served his purposes.'

Franklin D. Roosevelt

And His Relations with Churchill

Franklin Delano Roosevelt was born in 1881, the son of James Roosevelt and Sara Delano. He was educated at Groton School, Harvard College and Columbia Law School and was admitted to the New York Bar in 1907. In 1905 he married Eleanor Roosevelt, a distant cousin, and they had four sons and one daughter. He was Assistant Secretary to the Navy, 1913–20 and unsuccessful Democratic candidate for the vice-presidency 1920. He was stricken by poliomyelitis in 1921. He was Governor of New York State 1929–33. He was elected President of the United States in November 1932 and three times re-elected until his death in 1945.

Franklin Roosevelt was, and remains, a hero to the British. During his rise to power we were detached from and ignorant of American internal politics to an extent that is not easily imaginable today. The Atlantic in the Twenties and Thirties was still very wide. The majority, even of the politically involved and informed, never crossed it. Very few did so frequently. Of our leading politicians of the period, Asquith never once set foot in the United States, Baldwin refrained from a visit between his hazardous debt settlement in 1923 and his retirement in 1937, and even Eden, a young, vigorous and peripatetic Foreign Secretary in the second half of the Thirties, spent $2^1/_4$ years in that office without ever once thinking of including Washington in his diplomatic tours. Churchill, after a nasty accident with a taxi on Fifth Avenue in 1931, did not go again for ten years.

The bitter internal controversies of Roosevelt's first term and a half therefore passed largely over British heads. There was little awareness of the enmity which he aroused amongst his moneyed opponents, or of the fluctuations of policy and uncertainties of delegation which flowed from his prismatic character. He appeared as a strong, attractive and accepted leader of an united people, almost above the politics at which he was in fact such a determined and skilful player. The result of the 1936 election, mostly for the wrong reasons, would have been more accurately guessed in Britain than by many in America.

And it mostly gave pleasure and reassurance. At a time when the war shadows were again beginning to lengthen over Europe it seemed better that the first President since Wilson whose name at least was a household word, should be confirmed in office. The fact that his first term had been almost entirely lacking in any internationalist initiatives was largely passed over. He was there, he had a great name, and he seemed to be handling the post-depression economy with more success than his British contemporaries.

The most temporarily powerful of these - Neville Chamberlain, Chancellor of the Exchequer for six years until he became Prime Minister in 1937 – did not share this view. He did not know Roosevelt personally - again an indication of the vast difference between the Western world of 50 years ago and that of today, when every European leader expects to be in Washington within three months of a new President taking office - but what he knew about him he was against. With a certain consistency he looked upon him with the same distrust which the restless, innovating, erratic genius of Lloyd George had long aroused in his mind.

Yet Chamberlain was an exception. For the moderate left Roosevelt was a beacon of successful liberalism at a time when any comparable feature was sadly lacking in Europe. For the anti-appeasement right he represented a reserve of strength, perhaps a little problematical, but already of immense potential importance in the mounting world power struggle. Both strands of opinion hardly noticed the major failures of the first half of his second term. Neither the *dégringolade* of his attempt to change the composition of the Supreme Court nor the recession of 1937–38 significantly weakened his position abroad.

This was partly because these dramatic issues were not greatly studied in Britain, and partly because, with each six months which went by, with each advance of Hitler and with each faltering of the Governments of Britain and France, the need for America, symbolised by Roosevelt, became greater. And as the need became greater, so there increased the determination to believe, sometimes against the evidence, that he would eventually save the democracies.

When, in 1941, Churchill quoted the lines of Arthur Hugh Clough, familiar to many as a Victorian hymn, he was merely expressing, in a peculiarly evocative form, a thought which had been strongly present in many minds for several years past:

And not through eastern windows only
When daylight comes, comes in the light,
In front the sun climbs slow, how slowly,
But westward, look, the land is bright.

Such was the resolve to believe that the many hesitations on the other side of the Atlantic and Roosevelt's slow progress towards involvement were, if not exactly unnoticed, received with a remarkable lack of impatience. It was the favourable statements which were remembered and the unfavourable ones which were quickly forgotten. Thus, in the run up to the 1940 election, Roosevelt's Charlottesville speech as France moved towards collapse was seen as a ray of substantial light in an otherwise dreadful world, while his dampening and doubtfully wise or honest Boston assurance to the 'mothers of America' four months later, that 'your boys are not going to be sent into any foreign wars', was passed over as an aberration on the path to his overwhelmingly desirable third victory. Poor Wilkie's resolutely pro-allied campaign carried no resonance across the Atlantic. There was faith in America because the alternative was too awful to contemplate, and that faith was concentrated on Roosevelt.

Yet, looking back, it is clear that Roosevelt's path to full involvement in 1939–41 was a much slower and more twisted one that had been Wilson's approach to 1917. It is amazing how quickly the United States slipped into that first war. The threat of the Kaiser to America was much less than that of Hitler. Wilhelm II would not have obliterated the democracies or even the sovereignties of Britain and France: he would merely have clipped the wings of their trade and power. Furthermore, while the second war would have been a worse one to lose, the first was a worse one to fight. No conditions of Western campaign in 1939–45 approached the squalor and the slaughter of the trenches of 1914–18. In addition, the strength and cohesion of the American German community was much greater in Wilson's time than it was in Roosevelt's; and the United States was much further away from the natural acceptance of world leadership. Perhaps Wilson anticipated that responsibility too precipitately, and reaped the harvest of an inevitable reaction in 1919. Perhaps Roosevelt's greater caution showed not merely the wiles of a superior politician, but also the skill of a wider sweep of statesmanship, and that it was no accident that he was able to hand on the legacy of the American imperial age, while Wilson left us normalcy, the rejection of the League of Nations, and Warren Gamaliel Harding. But, whatever be the verdict here, Roosevelt ran things very close to a world disaster in 1940.

Then came the partnership with Churchill. It was not what it seemed. They were not two soul-mates, long linked in friendship, coming together across the oceans in a relationship of equality and mutual esteem to achieve common goals. There were strands of this in it, but they were not the whole, or even the main part. In the first place the basis of acquaintanceship was slight. When Roosevelt started the 'former naval person' correspondence in September 1939 they had not met for many years. Until 1941 Roosevelt knew Churchill's sovereign, King George VI, whom he had entertained for several days at Hyde Park following the state visit to Washington in the summer of 1939, far better than he knew Churchill himself. And, indeed, when the first of the nine Roosevelt/Churchill strategic meetings took place at Placentia Bay in 1941, Churchill bore with him a letter of commendation, almost of introduction, from King George to the President. Roosevelt's purpose in the correspondence with the then First Lord of the Admiralty was less to salute an old friend than to follow his well-known habit of giving the same job to several different people. The increasingly distrusted Joseph Kennedy was nominally responsible for relations with the British Government, primarily with the Prime Minister (Chamberlain) and the Foreign Secretary (Halifax). But Roosevelt wanted his own channels of communication as well.

Secondly, the partnership soon became an unequal one. In a sense it always was. Churchill's need of Roosevelt was always greater than Roosevelt's need of Churchill. But in 1940 and even early 1941 Churchill, although bounded in the nutshell of Britain, was, if not a king of infinite space, at least the unique symbol of resistance. Even then, however, by his eager although necessary acceptance of lend-lease, he underscored complete British economic dependence upon the United States. 'We threw good housekeeping to the winds', Keynes said. And once Churchill had secured his major objective of American entry into the war he rapidly became, in his own phrase, 'Roosevelt's lieutenant'.

He was not a lieutenant without influence. He could, and did, argue about grand strategy, sometimes with more eloquence than wisdom. He could delay the Second Front and give the allied effort a Mediterranean tilt. But he always knew that in the last resort he had to submit. In any real dispute Roosevelt held nearly all the cards. He was seven years Churchill's junior, but he was head of state and not merely head of government, he was commander-in-chief, and by virtue of the predominant power of the United States, he was the natural captain of the West. Nor was he in the least inclined by temperament to forego the power. He was at least as imperious as Churchill, probably more so, for Churchill was more inclined to accept the self-indulgence of a flight of eloquence as a substitute for getting his own way. Roosevelt's equivalent indulgences, telling an old story, half teasing half charming his interlocutors, were always much more subordinated to his ultimate purpose. He also believed that he had a wider and more realistic view of the con-temporary world than had Churchill, and that he could deal far more effectively with Stalin, particularly if he made it painfully clear, as he did on one or two notable occasions, that he was no closer to Churchill than he was to him.

To what extent was Roosevelt moved by genuine feelings of personal friendship towards Churchill? Not greatly so, in my view. He was amused by his exuberance and titivated by his fame and extravagance of style. But he was not captivated. He enjoyed his visits to the White House more than did Mrs Roosevelt, but he neither drank at the fount of Churchill's wisdom nor dissolved his judgement in any special bond of comradeship. Roosevelt was 'the Boss', 'the Chief', and had been so treated for at least eight years previously.

Nor did he have the same view of friendship as did Churchill. Churchill was at least as egocentric, and, tempered by shafts of humanity, saw most of mankind as part of a vast collection of toy soldiers to be manoeuvred in accordance with his noble but grandiloquent ideas. There was, however, a very limited group of persons to whom he gave friendship and loyalty. Once admitted within this category they could do little wrong. Mostly they were 'cronies', who were not on a basis of full equality with himself. Perhaps after the death of F.E. Smith (Lord Birkenhead) in 1930, they all were so to a greater or lesser extent. But this did not affect his loyalty.

Roosevelt had no such need and no such loyalty. He depended more upon women than did Churchill. With men he was much more detached. His relationships were those of occasion, with people who could be useful to him and to his often high purposes in particular circumstances. Sometimes the circumstances were manifold, as with Hopkins, but the essential basis remained. This profound difference of approach affected the balance of the Roosevelt/Churchill relationship.

Which was the better strategist? In the great controversies of 1942–3, which were not so much personal as stemming from differences of appraisal by the American and British staffs, Roosevelt was probably nearer to wisdom than Churchill. John Grigg's recent writings on this subject seem to me to have sustained this thesis. On the handling of Stalin towards the end of the war, and on the disposition of troops which affected this, there is much more room for doubt. Churchill at this stage benefited from his ability to see a single idea with greater clarity, in contrast with Roosevelt's wider but mistier approach. However, it is easy here to make over-simple judgements. Churchill's views would not have avoided the division of Europe, any more than did Roosevelt's. These views took insufficient account of the problems of a continuing war with Japan (neither he nor Roosevelt foreseeing how quickly they would be resolved). And this might have imperilled the setting up of the United Nations, which was probably an essential step towards American commitments of the late Forties, which alone made it possible for the West to live tolerably with that divided Europe. In any event, Roosevelt cannot be reasonably judged by his performance at a conference at which he was as sick as he was at Yalta.

Not merely after Yalta but after the 1944 campaign most people who had been close to him thought, with the benefit of hindsight at any rate, that Roosevelt would quickly die. They must have talked to many others. Yet when he did so there were great waves of shock throughout America and the world. It was partly that after twelve years, the longest period of continuous power for any democratic leader for a century and more, it was almost impossible to imagine a world without him in the White House. There was also a peculiar irony in the fact that he would not live to see the post-war world. He had done more to shape it than anyone else: both to experiment successfully with welfare capitalism, which gave the countries of the fortunate West 25 years of the greatest surge to prosperity in recorded history, and to lay the foundations of benevolent American dominance, which was the shield for this advance.

It was not a small legacy. Yet a major mystery remains. Did he give much thought to passing it on? Did he, like others, realise that his chances of serving out even a substantial part of his fourth term were miniscule? Did he regard the choice of his third Vice-President as being peculiarly important? All the evidence is against. Certainly he was determined not to have Henry Wallace again. But that was just getting rid of a piece of baggage that had served its use. It was quite different from giving particular attention to the choice of Truman, whom he hardly knew, and to which decision he applied his mind only fleetingly and ambiguously. It might easily have been Byrnes or Barkley, Ickes or Douglas. Perhaps he didn't care. Perhaps he subconsciously thought he himself would always be there. Perhaps he was just lucky because he was self-confident and self-confident because he was lucky in this as in so many other things, and that these qualities in combination were his greatest attributes.

Helmut Schmidt

Helmut Schmidt was born in 1918 in Hamburg. He was educated at the University of Hamburg. In 1942 he married Hannelore Glaser and has one daughter. He was a captain in an anti-aircraft regiment to the German army. Apart from a three year break in 1962–65, he was an SPD member of the Bundestag from 1953 to 1988. He was Minister of Defence, 1969–72, of Finance 1972–74. He was Chancellor of the Federal Republic from 1974 to 1982.

He has been Senior Editor of Die Zeit *since 1983.*

Helmut Schmidt has considerable claim to have been the German Chancellor who achieved the highest combination of effectiveness and respectability since Bismarck, and almost an incontrovertible claim to have been the most substantial amongst his contemporaries as Western heads of Government. He was not, however, an impeccable statesman (who is?). For that he was too moody, too prejudiced (although mostly on the right side) in his judgement of people and issues, and too impatient of everyone's monologues but his own.

His main rivals for the German accolade would I suppose be Stresemann and Adenauer, although Brandt might get some votes. But Stresemann had such a rotten hand to play and Adenauer was so concentrated on Western Europe, that as a leader of Germany as a world power Schmidt has the edge over them. And Brandt, although not geographically circumscribed, sometimes got lost in the mists swirling around the peaks of his enthusiasms.

For the contemporary international accolade Schmidt's main rival would have been his favourite partner, 'my friend Valéry' as he so frequently appeared in his conversation, President Giscard d'Estaing of France. But there is no doubt in my mind that Schmidt was the more considerable figure of the two. Giscard was arguably better at getting more for France out of the firm Franco-German partnership at the prow of Europe than Schmidt got for Germany. This apart, Schmidt had wider vision, better balance, and greater depth of personality and character.

Schmidt is a very private person who has been almost totally dedicated to public life. Notable biographical studies mostly emerge from the border country between the public and the private. This area Schmidt has done his best to reduce to waste ground. Although in many ways an arrogant man (with a good deal to be arrogant about) he has always believed in putting a semi-eclipse over both himself and the Federal Republic. This makes him a difficult biographical subject, simultaneously politically impressive and personally elusive.

He talked far more engagingly and eclectically than did any other European leader of the late Seventies. Sometimes, but not always, his talk would lead to action. When it did not it was partly because of the hobbled role that he believed German history had made necessary for his country.

His instinctive international stance was strongly pro-American, well-disposed but detached about the British, and rather against the French, hardly a word of whose language he could speak. The exigencies of his period of office made him reverse every prejudice. He was contemptuous of poor President Carter, cautious of Mr Callaghan, affronted by Mrs Thatcher, and warmed only to the rather chilly personality of President Giscard. These conflicting currents produced a certain trauma. It was added to by his conviction that although Germany (under his stewardship) was on the whole the best run economy in the world it must not for many decades ahead attempt or even accept a political rôle commensurate with its economic strength. This combination of power and self-denial made him a little like a caged lion. But as he had himself erected the bars he sniffed around them with a reasonable content.

Alfred E. Smith

Alfred Emanuel Smith was born on the Lower East Side of New York in 1873. In spite of his name he was of mixed Italian and Irish stock. His father ran a small delivery business. Al Smith left his Catholic parochial school at the age of 14 and received no further formal education. In 1900 he married Catherine A. Dunn and they had three sons and two daughters.

He was Sheriff of New York County 1915–17, President of the Board of Aldermen 1917–18, Governor of New York 1919–21, 1923–29. At the 1924 Democratic Convention he was beaten for the Presidential nomination after 103 ballots. At the 1928 Convention he was more successful but the election itself led to his heavy defeat by Herbert Hoover. He died in 1944.

Alfred E. Smith was a highly successful and progressive Governor of New York for four terms. In 1928 he was Democratic candidate for the Presidency, having only narrowly lost the nomination in 1924, when a deadlocked Convention conducted 103 ballots before relapsing into a compromise choice.

The result of his 1928 candidature was a resounding defeat. At that time he was the most celebrated politician in the United States, with a gift of easy and vote-winning relationship with his audiences. His nominator had correctly presented him to the Democratic Convention as a man with 'the habit of victory'. But he lost by 15 to 21 million votes to Herbert Hoover, who whatever his other qualities was tied to an uninspiring manuscript in every speech and had never before fought an election of any sort. Smith was the first Democrat for decades to lose States in the old South, and he failed even to carry his own State of New York.

Part of the explanation was that he was the first Catholic

to run for the Presidency. This aroused widespread antipathy in the South and in much of what would now be called 'middle America.' A 1971 biography (*Al Smith, Hero of the Cities*, by Matthew and Hannah Josephson) caught perfectly the note of menacing intolerance which assailed Smith on his first major campaign trip:

> As the train slowed down on the approach to Oklahoma City, night had fallen. Suddenly in the fields along the railroad track Smith and his party saw a line of flaming crosses: the barbarous salute of the Ku Klux Klan. The Governor was somewhat shaken by this spectacular demonstration; then he noticed on descending from the train that although a huge throng had come to the station to meet him, they were strangely quiet, suggesting a hostility he had rarely encountered in all his experience.

In those days the Klan were more concerned with Catholics than with blacks. But it was not only in the remote south-west that the old cry of 'Run, Romanism and Rebellion' was made to ride again. There was a strong rumour on the Eastern Shore of Maryland that a luxurious local estate had already been bought for the Pope in order that he might control Washington from there; and another, possibly contradictory it might be thought, that 'boot-leggers and harlots would dance on the White House lawn' as soon as Smith was installed.

In fact Governor Smith's private life was of an unusual respectability, but he had other attributes which, the passage of time apart, added to the prejudices associated with his religion and ethnic origins in a way that was not the case with John F. Kennedy 32 years later. He was the epitome of a town-bred New Yorker. His life was curiously intertwined with the moulding of the city into its present shape and appearance. Throughout his early childhood, Brooklyn Bridge, the first of the massive structures which modified Manhattan's insularity, was being built literally on top of his parents' Lower East Side home. When his White House hopes were destroyed the business job which his friends found for him was as president of the company formed to construct the Empire State Building. One of his last public rows was over the opening of the Triborough Bridge. He could never understand how anyone could want to live in the country; and in his early life he interpreted this so strictly that, admittedly then without much choice, he hardly ever went north of 14th Street until he was grown up.

Although by 1928 he had a lot of experience in campaigning far up state from Manhattan he aggressively but unsuccessfully carried this big city attitude into the South and West of the country. His campaign song was 'The Sidewalks of New York'. With prohibition a major issue, he was a defiant 'wet'. His dress and accent were unreassuring to rural America. Part Irish and part Italian by family origin (though himself third-generation American on both sides), he was the representative of the new immigrant groups, and America was not then ready to put such a clear representative in the White House. Perhaps it would not be ready now, although the groups are no longer new and so *clear* a representative could hardly exist.

When it was over Congressman Sam Rayburn of Texas, referring to Smith's constant campaign headgear, said, 'I never thought that brown derby helped'. But the defeat involved a lot of sadness and bitterness as well as some mirth. There was sadness amongst those who had greatly admired Smith's administrative skill and reforming zeal as Governor, and who were greatly disillusioned by the narrow intolerance the campaign had brought out. And there was certainly bitterness on Smith's part, made the greater by the fact that he had to sit and watch Roosevelt, whom he regarded as a political tyro, an indecisive amateur descending graciously into New York politics from his Hudson River estate, weld together and maintain the essential coalition which he had failed to fashion.

In 1924 Roosevelt had nominated Smith and, quoting Wordsworth, given him the inspired sobriquet of 'the happy warrior'. But Smith sadly lived on to become an unhappy warrior against Roosevelt himself, opposing his re-election in 1936 and sponsoring the business-financed Liberty League to oppose the New Deal.

Almost the only British politician whom Smith knew well was Churchill, his exact contemporary, and on his one visit to Europe in 1937 he spent an afternoon at Chartwell. But the British politician with whom he is strongly comparable (the late rejection of his party loyalties apart) is Herbert Morrison. They both respected political machines (Smith was a Tammany man but an honest one). They were both outstanding administrators of major but not nationwide authorities. They were both men of a great metropolis, with an instinctive relationship with its people. They both just failed to achieve a sufficient national appeal to surmount the last political hurdle. They were both a little sour towards the end of their lives.

Christopher Soames*

Christopher Soames was born in 1920 and educated at Eton and Sandhurst. In 1947 he married Mary Churchill and had three sons and two daughters. He was MP for Bedford 1950–66. He served as parliamentary private secretary to the Prime Minister (his father-in-law) from 1952–55. He was Secretary of State for War, 1958–60 and Minister of Agriculture, Fisheries and Food, 1960–64. He was appointed Ambassador to France by Harold Wilson in 1968. He served there until 1972 and played a significant part in the delicate and eventually successful process of bringing Britain into the European Community.

From 1973 to 1977 he was Britain's first Vice-President (responsible for External Affairs) of the European Commission.

In 1978 he was created Lord Soames of Fletching. He served briefly as Britain's last Governor of Southern Rhodesia, 1979–80, where he presided over the transfer of power to the independent country of Zimbabwe. From 1979 to 1981 he was Lord President of the Council and Leader of the House of Lords. He died in 1987.

Christopher Soames was a man whom it was difficult not to notice but easy to misjudge. The superficial case against him, I suppose, would be that he was a noisy hedonist who based a successful career on a wise choice of father-in-law.

This is unfair on every ground except that of noise. Nepotism may have given him a useful start but it can hardly be argued on the form that a filial relationship to Churchill was an automatic passport to political success. It was very much Soames's own verve

*This appraisal and tribute appeared in the *Spectator* the week after Lord Soames's death.

and judgement, combined with the confidence and affection which he had previously earned from Churchill, which enabled him in 1953 to exercise far more power than any other parliamentary private secretary, before or since, has ever contemplated. Furthermore, he had three times to remount his own career, and did so with considerable success, long after Churchill had disappeared from the scene.

He was a hedonist in the sense that he enjoyed the pursuit and giving of pleasure. He was a very good guest and a spectacular host, but just as much because of the buoyancy of his companionship as because of the quality and quantity of his victuals. But indulgence was only fully satisfying to him if it was part of the trappings of a major political enterprise, like a bottle of champagne which is smashed when a great ship is released into the water.

And his political purposes were never petty. There was a touch of bombast about him, but it was all above the surface. Underneath there was a large reservoir of imaginative statesmanship. His most persistent loyalty was to the European cause. I do not think that he saw the light until the late 1950s – in this he was like most of us. But once he had done so, he was unfaltering in his commitment. It informed his work as Minister of Agriculture in the early 1960s, as Ambassador to Paris from 1968 and (obviously) as a Vice-President of the European Commission in the mid-Seventies. In his last decade it was an issue which could always bring him to life, like an old general happily recalled to the colours.

His four years in Brussels were a clear success. I do not think that the Commission had ever before had a bird of such bright plumage. Much of its work is humdrum. There was an obvious danger that Soames's high-style, broad-brush approach would fail to mesh with the Commission's attachment to cautious detail, that he would become bored, and his colleagues and officials critical of his degree of application.

Nothing of the sort happened. I am told that the work of the Soames *cabinet* was conducted more by shouting through ever-open doors than by quiet reading and ratiocination, but the results were splendid. He imported a new panache into the external relations of the Community (which was his portfolio), without any loss of negotiating depth, and he quickly made himself a key figure in the hierarchy of the Commission. A little more *poire* was consumed during afternoon sessions both by Christopher himself and by those who wished to follow his style, but the effect was beneficial for Europe and for Britain.

People liked working both with and for him. In 1977 we inherited his cook, a Belgian lady of uncertain age, confirmed spinsterhood and untitillating appearance. When he came to dine and stay nearly a year later it did not surprise me that she produced a dinner even better than usual. What did impress me, however, was that she most exceptionally insisted on going out and getting her hair done in preparation for his arrival.

With all this Brussels achievement behind him he might very reasonably have expected to become President after his first four years, particularly as a British appointment was appropriate. Harold Wilson would gladly have nominated him. But there was some difficulty with Giscard, no doubt stemming from Soames's robustness, either in the Commission or when he was Ambassador in Paris. Helmut Schmidt, as often, rallied to Giscard. So I got the job, and Soames came back to England and spent 18 months unsuccessfully looking for a seat before he threw his hand in and became a peer.

The scene was therefore almost perfectly set (and was further aided by my first six months going fairly badly) for a little head-shaking bitchiness, no doubt delivered in stentorian whispers, from Christopher. How sad it was that my inexperience of Brussels and lack of Continental feel symbolised by his much superior French was messing up a great British opportunity in Europe.

Most people would have done it. He did not. Of that I am certain. The kindly bush telegraph of Europe would have relayed it back to me only too quickly. Nor do I think that he avoided it only by a rigid self-discipline. It was more a spontaneous generosity allied with a feeling that he and I were playing on the same British European side.

I had long appreciated the zest of his personality and the sense of most of his views. After 1977 I knew that they were accompanied by exceptional generosity and loyalty. The combination made him both formidable and lovable.

Professor Robert Triffin*

(Belgian Citizen, Yale Economist, Leading Architect for forty years of European Monetary Integration)

Robert Triffin was born in 1911 in Belgium. He was educated at Louvain and Harvard Universities. In 1940 he married Lois Brandt and they have three sons.

He is a prolific writer on economic and monetary matters and was Professor of Economics and Master of Berkeley College at Yale University before his semi-retirement to Brussels in 1976.

Robert Triffin is one of the most quietly remarkable men that I have known. In at least two ways he spans two worlds. He has spent most of his life in the United States, a major figure in the life and teaching of Yale, a member of the Council of Economic Advisers, and much involved in Latin American monetary problems. But he was born, and remains, a Belgian, feeling, in a fashion typical of the best traditions of that land which is more a meeting point than a country, a special responsibility for trying to make sense out of the clashing nationalisms of Europe. Equally he has been a theoretician who has always been happiest when he was trying to advance practical solutions to pressing problems.

He was the principal architect of the European Payments Union in the late Forties. He then made a unique contribution to freeing Western Europe from the shackles of a hobbling bilateralism. Thirty years later his knowledge and experience, together with his patient optimism, were essential ingredients in the setting up of the European Monetary System.

*This piece was written in 1987 as a foreword to a *Festschrift* for Professor Triffin's seventieth birthday.

167

As President of the Commission of the European Communities I tried to re-launch the idea of economic and monetary union in 1977. To begin with it fell on arid ground. But Robert Triffin was there with a watering can of intellectual refreshment. Within six months Chancellor Schmidt and President Giscard d'Estaing began to see the need for at least a limited advance. A year later the EMS was in operation. and it has worked remarkably well (although, alas, without Britain) for $2^1/_2$ years. Three adjustments have been necessary, but they have been carried through quietly and efficiently. And in a turbulent monetary sea, the Europe of the Community has been an island of relative exchange rate stability. Robert Triffin has helped to get us so far, and is constantly probing the possibility of necessary further advance.

The fertility of his ideas and the calm persuasiveness of his advocacy make it reasonable to compare him with Jean Monnet. But there is a difference. Monnet, with all his great gifts, saw things in black and white, with stark simplicity. Triffin comprehends all the complexity, but still sees the way forward.

Harry S. Truman
And the Contrast with Roosevelt

Harry S. Truman was born in 1884, the son of John Anderson Truman and Mary Ellen Young. He was educated at public schools in Independence, Missouri. In 1919 he married Bess Wallace and they had one daughter. From 1906 to 1917 he operated the family farm and then served (mostly as a captain) in the US army in Europe during the First World War.

He was elected to the US Senate in 1934 and re-elected in 1940. He was elected Vice-President of the United States in 1944 and acceded to the Presidency on President Roosevelt's death in April 1945. He was elected for a second term in 1948 and remained President until January 1953. He died in 1972.

On April 12th, 1945, Franklin Roosevelt died, suddenly if not unexpectedly, at Warm Springs, Georgia. Six hours later Truman was sworn in as the 32nd President. He was nearly 61. It was the most intimidating succession in the English–speaking world since Addington had succeeded William Pitt in 1801: 'Pitt is to Addington as London is to Paddington', Canning wrote. And Paddington did not then even have a railway station. But Addington had been an intimate of Pitt's for years and had his continuing friendship until the quarrel of 1803. Truman knew the Senate, of which he had been a member since 1934, but his experience of the executive branch, with its vastly expanded war-time complications, was minimal. He had been Vice-President for less than three months. During this period there is no evidence that he

169

had seen Roosevelt, except at Cabinet meetings, more than twice. Also, as Truman recorded, 'Roosevelt never discussed anything important at Cabinet meetings'.

Even more certainly Roosevelt never discussed anything important with his Vice-President. He looked to Truman to keep the Senate in order and to ensure that his peace treaty of the future did not meet the same fate as that which had befallen Woodrow Wilson's in 1919. He had encouraged him to do 'some campaigning' in 1944, adding rather incongruously 'I don't feel like going everywhere'. (In fact he went only to New York, Chicago, Boston and Philadelphia.) But there had been no question of treating Truman as a deputy head of government, any more than he had so treated Garner or Wallace, or indeed of recognising the essential difference between Truman and his two predecessors. They were just Vice-Presidents, threatened with the obscurity which was mostly the historic fate of those who had occupied that office. Truman, from the moment of his nomination, was a likely President. But Roosevelt was the last man who wanted to recognise that. He never thought of including him in the party of a hundred or more Americans who went to the Yalta Conference in late January. He gave him no special account of the outcome. Nor did he tell him about the Manhattan project, which was on the threshold of becoming the atomic bomb.

Roosevelt had indeed tossed the vice-presidential nomination to him rather like a bone to a dog, except that Truman was not hungry. Truman's lack of appetite came from a mixture of motives. He thought the vice-presidency itself was a grey and obscure job, and did not want it for that reason. 'I'll bet you can't name the names of half a dozen Vice-Presidents', he told his sister during a discussion of the prospect. He apprehended however that in the circumstances of 1944 it might well lead on to the presidency. And that he did not want for almost opposite reasons. He thought the responsibility was too great for him, and that in any event no man should seek the position. (Exactly how Presidents were to emerge if this rule was followed was not clear.) Furthermore he was committed to nominating James Byrnes.

Although genuine, his reluctance was not unshakeable. After he had been made to overhear Roosevelt say to the party chairman on the telephone: 'You tell him that if he wants to break up the Democratic Party in the middle of the War that's up to him', he gave in. He even made fairly strenuous efforts to find a proposer in the shape of his fellow Senator from Missouri. He was nominated on the second ballot. And so, nine months later, he found himself President of the United States. He was relatively old, more so than any new President since James Buchanan in 1857, although there have since been three older ones. Yet he was completely inexperienced in the executive side of government. He was unbriefed, and untravelled since 1919. The war against both Germany and Japan was still unwon, and he had succeeded the most charismatic figure in the world.

So, one might have thought, the Imperial Presidency came to an end, within a few years of its beginning. Truman trailed none of Roosevelt's clouds of glory. He had none of his style, none of his prestige, none of his informal patrician grandeur. A failed Missouri haberdasher had taken over from a Dutchess County country gentleman. Main Street had replaced the Hudson Valley. But the Imperial Presidency flowered with the change. Indeed in an important sense it developed only under Truman. Roosevelt had only been the leader of the free world at war, when the commitment of America was relatively easy to sustain, and the acceptance of American leadership automatic. Truman achieved the more difficult feat of being leader of the free world at peace, or something fairly near to peace. He was the first President to preside over the *Pax Americana*. It was not immediately apparent that this would be so. There was considerable early faltering. But once he had got into his stride his capacity for informed decision taking and for doing what he regarded as right, without regard to the personal consequence, became remarkable. '. . . his ego never came between him and his job', Dean Acheson wrote. Acheson believed he was clearly a better President than Roosevelt, but Acheson, for his own reasons, neither liked nor admired Roosevelt.

Truman did admire Roosevelt. He was instinctively very critical of the prominent. Of his successors in one form or another, he despised Nixon, was unforgiving of Eisenhower for his treatment of General Marshall, thought Stevenson effete, and believed that Kennedy's nomination, to which he was less entitled than Lyndon Johnson, had been bought for him by his father. But he admired Roosevelt as a great leader who was also a consummate politician. He tried to follow in his path without copying him. He would sometimes mock his grand voice and

Harvard accent, and it is doubtful how much he liked him. But he was iron in his determination never to complain about the scant notice which Roosevelt had taken of him, and he was almost completely free of the resentment against the Eastern sophistication of his predecessor's White House which devoured Lyndon Johnson. 'I see red every time (the sabotage) press starts a ghoulish attack on the President (I can never think of anyone as the President but Mr Roosevelt)' he was writing, admittedly to Eleanor Roosevelt, nearly six months after he had taken office.

Truman was in some ways the superior of Roosevelt. He did not have his style, his resonance, his confidence, his occasional sweep of innovative imagination, or his tolerance and understanding of diverse human nature. But he was less vain, less devious, and better to work for. He was more decisive, and, Roosevelt's physical disability apart, he had more sustained energy. He could always be up at 6.00 or 6.30 in the morning and be consistently fresh and on the job until however late was required. He was mostly better briefed, and not only in an immediate and superficial sense. He was almost certainly better read, particularly in history and biography, than Roosevelt. He was steeped in knowledge of the Republic and particularly of the presidency, but he was also a considerable expert upon the lives of the Roman Emperors and of almost every great military commander in the history of the world. Yet his knowledge sat less easily on his shoulders. Mr Merle Miller, who published a so-called 'oral biography' of Truman after the death of his subject, made an interesting comment:

He was a self-educated man, and he mispronounced a reasonable number of words, which in the beginning puzzled me. Then I realised that while he had often read them, he had seldom, if ever, spoken them aloud, not even in many cases heard them spoken aloud. It's like that if you are one of the few readers in town.

This gets close to the central paradox of Truman. His manner was that of a midwestern machine politician, and he was intensely loyal to his background and to those who had helped him on the way up. But a few of those he most respected and liked - Dean Acheson, already mentioned, and General Marshall

- were very different from this and from each other. He was also very family orientated, and not much at ease in female company outside his family.

It is tempting to say that he was an intellectual amongst political 'pros' and a political 'pro' amongst intellectuals. But that is much too easy an aphorism. As a boy and a young man he was more of a book-worm than an intellectual, and so he remained. He absorbed a lot of facts, and he thought about them a good deal, but his conversation involved no spinning of general theories. He neither had nor aspired to either intellectual or social sophistication. His speech and his writing - and he wrote a lot of unsent letters and undelivered speeches, even under the pressure of the presidency - were generally splendidly direct, but the choice of words was rarely distinguished and the sentiments narrow and intolerant. 'Cissy' (or 'Sissy' as he mostly spelt it) was one which he employed a good deal. He used it frequently, disparagingly, and foolishly about Adlai Stevenson. But when once asked at a school question and answer session, after he had been President, whether he had been popular as a boy, he replied:

Why no, I was never popular. The popular boys were the ones who were good at games and had big, tight fists. I was never like that. Without my glasses I was blind as a bat, and to tell the truth, I was kind of a sissy.

This interplay provided part of the formation of his personality and character. He was an 'anti-sissy' sissy, a puritan from the poker rooms, a backwoods politician who became a world statesman not just because he was President of the United States in the plenitude of its power but because he had an exceptional sense of duty and power of decision, and because he could distinguish big issues from little ones, and was generally as right on the big ones as he was frequently wrong on the small ones.

As a result, and because also of the exceptional challenges and opportunities with which he was confronted, he became the master-builder of the security and prosperity of the post-war Western world. Assisted primarily by Marshall and Acheson at home, and abroad by Ernest Bevin, the most creative British Foreign Secretary of this century, he established a framework which has preserved peace on the central front for nearly 40 years and helped to produce one of the greatest surges to prosperity the world has ever seen.

While he might not be rated with Washington, Lincoln and the second Roosevelt, I, and many other Europeans, would put him right at the head of the next rank of American Presidents.

Kurt Waldheim

Kurt Waldheim was born in 1918 and educated at the Consular Academy and the University of Vienna where he became a Doctor of Jurisprudence in 1944. In that year he married Elisabeth Ritschel and has one son and two daughters.

He entered the Austrian Foreign Service in 1945 where he served in a variety of posts before becoming Permanent Representative of Austria to the United Nations 1964–68. He was Federal Minister for Foreign Affairs 1968–70 and Austrian Permanent Representative to the UN again 1970–71. In 1971 he was an unsuccessful candidate for the Presidency of Austria. He was Secretary-General of the United Nations 1972–1981. He has been President of Austria since 1986.

From the birth of Haydn in 1732 to the death of Freud in 1939, Vienna and its hinterland of German Austria was the cradle or harbour for a remarkably high proportion of the world's men of genius. Since 1945 only one Austrian resident has become an international household name, and that is Kurt Waldheim.

Bruno Kreisky may have deserved the accolade, and had he been head of government of a bigger country might well have attained it. Karajan (doubtfully a resident) may seem to have achieved it this week*, but a week is a short time in music.

Waldheim's fame of course will not last. In two decades he will be remembered no more than any other of those figures who suddenly and briefly attain international notoriety: General Galtieri or Spiro T. Agnew or the Emperor Bokassa. But his current celebrity is as indisputable as its pre-eminence is embarrassing to his country. For Vienna to have no citizen of world renown was bad enough. For Waldheim to emerge as the exception is much worse.

*This piece was written in the week of Karajan's eightieth birthday (April, 1988).

The problem is made the greater in some people's eyes by the view that Austria as a nation is at best a convalescent from a psychiatric ward. It is certainly true that inter-war Austria was a country with remarkably exposed nerves. This was hardly surprising in view of the fact that it was not even a chicken running round with its head cut off, but had been left as just a chicken's head with its sinews twitching.

The empire of fifty million people had been reduced to a republic without much republican spirit of six million, nearly a third of whom were in the capital. The result was two decades (exactly coinciding with Waldheim's first twenty years) of a rickety economy, social divisiveness erected into a way of life, and sporadic bloodshed until the uncertain state collapsed (with a good deal of enthusiasm) into the arms of the *Anschluss*. Even before the end of the Empire and these vicissitudes, however, turn-of-the-century Vienna was a fairly febrile city. Certainly the *Sezession* movement was calm neither in name nor style.

In the thirty years after the State Treaty of 1955 had secured the withdrawal of the Russians, Austria seemed to put all this unhappy history behind her. Particularly in the Kreisky years (1970-1983) it appeared to have become the epitome of a stable bourgeois republic, prosperous with little of either inflation or unemployment, a currency able to look the D-mark in the face, social tensions vastly reduced, a very respectable just-left-of-centre government, an interesting but not rash foreign policy, and a general air of contentment except for an understandable unease at having become almost the Crewe Junction of the Common Market without having any say in how the trains were to run.

Now it is widely suggested that the existence of Dr Waldheim at once shows this to have been as big a national sham as he is himself, and also to put Austria's whole future at risk. Only, it is further suggested, by some collective act of self-immolating guilt exposure can the Austrians expiate the sin of having elected (by 53 per cent) to their not very important presidency a tawdry individual who is a sort of national portrait of Dorian Gray, exhibiting all their own hidden faults and sins.

Robert Edwin Herzstein, in his book *Waldheim: the Missing Years* (1988) puts it with sweeping certainty: 'To a remarkable extent, Kurt Waldheim *is* post-war Austria'.

I think this is dangerous nonsense. Of course Dr Waldheim does more than just exist. He has in some sense received the confidence of the Austrian people. He clings to office with a dedicated selfishness which amazes. And he is not just an internal embarrassment, for he was palmed off on the world for ten years from 1971 to 1981. Of course it is now also clear that he is a fourth- or fifth-rate individual, a congenital liar, exceptionally self-seeking and with an almost unique capacity to make himself disliked by those who have worked for him.

He is not, however, as Professor Herzstein fairly and lucidly makes clear, a war criminal. He just did not behave very well during the war, he went along, and lied about it afterwards. No doubt too there were a lot of Austrians (as there might have been in similar circumstances of many other nationalities) who behaved much as he did. This indeed becomes Herzstein's main point. He in no way presses for a full guilty verdict against Waldheim, and both in tone and in substance two-thirds of his book is objective, even almost sympathetic, towards him. But then at the end, when he begins to go for a 'fairly guilty' collective verdict, the tone changes, and he ends offering Waldheim an unctuous draft for a personal and national confession which he wants him to deliver.

Waldheim ought to go. He has already done considerable harm. No doubt too there are some very black patches on Austria's wartime history. The fiftieth anniversary of the *Anschluss* might have been a fairly embarrasing occasion even without the present President in the wings. But the idea that the way to underpin her remarkable recovery from pre-war neurosis and wartime psychosis is to keep telling Austrians they never ought to have got out of the psychiatric ward seems to me preposterous.

Beatrice and Sidney Webb

Beatrice Webb was born in 1858, the eighth daughter of Richard Potter, former chairman of the Great Western Railway and President of the Grand Trunk Railway of Canada. She was educated privately. In 1892 she married Sidney Webb (created Lord Passfield in 1929).

She was a member of numerous committees and commissions concerned with poverty in Britain and was a notable writer and diarist. She died in 1943.

Her husband Sidney was born in 1859. He was educated privately in London, Switzerland and Mecklenburg Schwerin. He served in the War Office 1878–79, as a Surveyor of Taxes 1879–81 and in the Colonial Office 1881–91. He was a university lecturer and author of many books on local government, trade unions, consumerism, poverty etc. He wrote the constitution of the Labour Party in 1918. He was MP for Seaham Harbour 1922–29 and served as President of the Board of Trade January–November 1924 and was Secretary of State for the Colonies 1929–31.

He died in October 1947. They had no children.

I never met either Beatrice or Sidney Webb, although I have it firmly in my mind that Margaret Cole (who wrote a short life of Beatrice Webb) once promised (or threatened) to take me to see her at Passfield. This however is chronologically impossible and I can only imagine that Mrs Cole was moved by some act of Fabian virtue (or vice) on my part to say that, had it been ten years earlier, a visit to Mrs Webb would have been the appropriate outcome. Had the meeting taken place I can only hope (but not with much confidence) that I would have created a better impression than did Hugh Gaitskell in 1936: 'Like Durbin, he is fat and complacent: clever, no doubt, but not attractive. Like Durbin he is contemptuous of Cripps and a follower of Morrison and Dalton, and, I think, he is anti-Communist. But as he had not read our book' - probably a fatal lack of preparation for the visit - 'it was heavy going to discuss with him the pros and cons.'

Beatrice Webb's *Diary*, unlike their joint effort *Soviet Communism*, never suffers from lack of astringency. I think she got Gaitskell wrong, but her portraits of (at the time) much better known figures are models of critical balance. She rarely misses the essential weakness. She uses a lot of faint but not foolish praise while getting into position to strike at the jugular. In the first half of the book MacDonald was naturally the compelling target. Too grand to be contemptuously dismissed like J.H. Thomas, he was nevertheless deeply disapproved of by Mrs Webb:

> He is an attractive creature, he has a certain beauty in colouring, figure and face, a delightful voice and an easy unpretentious manner, a youthful enjoyment of his prestige as a prime minister, all of which is amusing to watch. But his conversation is not entertaining or stimulating - it consists of pleasant anecdotes about political and Society personages, occasionally some episode in his own career, told with calculated discretion. . . Not once did we *discuss* anything whatsoever, and even the anecdotes led nowhere . . . Ramsay MacDonald is a magnificent substitute for a leader. He has the ideal appearance . . . But he is shoddy in character and intellect. Our great one has yet to come. Shall I live to see him? Or will it be *she* who must be obeyed? (August 2nd, 1926)

Baldwin she found 'an engaging personality with no side or solemnity', but not without variety '. . . He glories in having no expertise in political and economic equations and no cut-and-dried theories. He is a big man and an ugly-featured man, but he has a most attractive voice and the pleasantest of smiles . . . I should prefer to go round the world in his company rather than carry out a difficult job as his partner. I doubt whether he could do a good day's brainwork.' She was particularly good on Austen Chamberlain with whose father she had some sort of early romantic encounter and who remained occasionally present in her thoughts but not in her life throughout the long years of her happy, productive but quiet marriage with Sidney: '. . . Austen is undoubtedly a man experienced in affairs, with certain gifts and accomplishments, and he is personally disinterested. But he is dull and close-minded, and in his outlook on public, as distinguished from private affairs, he is morally as well as intellectually dense . . . Behind that imposing monocle there is a whitewashed but empty chamber . . .'

Of her younger visitors Keynes did about the best. 'For when I look around I see no other man who might discover how to control the wealth of nations in the public interest' (August 1926). Stafford Cripps, in spite or because of being her nephew, is seen at the beginning of his extreme period with peculiar clarity:

> In manners and morals, in tastes and preferences, Stafford would make an ideal leader for the Labour Party . . . He has sufficient personality, physical and mental, for leadership: tall, good-looking, with a good voice and pleasant gestures. But he is oddly immature of intellect and unbalanced in judgement, with a strange lack of discrimination and low standard of reasoning in picking up ideas, queer currency cranks or slapdash remedies . . .' (7 March, 1932).

The politician the Webbs respected but did not exactly admire (he was too homespun for Beatrice at least) was Arthur Henderson. Their continuing friends were the Shaws. It was an odd quartet of tolerance. Had they been anyone else Beatrice would have thought G.B.S. silly and Charlotte Shaw snobbish, and Shaw would equally have found Sidney dull, Beatrice disapproving, and the Passfield establishment inadequate for his refulgence. But they surmounted all that and a widening financial gap as the Shaws became immensely rich and the Webbs fairly poor (which meant difficulty in maintaining four servants) and continued to read the manuscripts of their plays and books to each other until feebleness took over.

Beatrice Webb was a semi-egalitarian obsessed by social differences. Her provenance was the prosperous and confident upper bourgeoisie. Her closest connection with aristocracy was Lord Parmoor, a lawyer peer who was Stafford Cripps's father. Her lost lover was Joseph Chamberlain, a 'new man' if ever there was one. Yet for some strange reason she appointed herself as the censorious social arbiter of the Labour Party's entry into government. She even ran a sort of manners-training luncheon club for the wives of Labour MPs, but mostly despaired of her pupils. They were either hopeless or progressed too rapidly up the social ladder. In both cases they were irremediably 'common'.

When her husband became a peer she refused to call herself Lady Passfield. This wholly understandable decision was only vitiated by the fact that she went on about it so much. It was the same with curtsying. She was also a considerable and slightly prurient prig. The sexual proclivities of her servants and friends caused her a good deal of concern. Anthony Crosland in *The Future of Socialism* (1956) splendidly mocked that aspect of the Webbs, quoting Beatrice's unforgettable tribute to the achievement of the Soviet Union as ensuring that there was 'singularly little spooning in the Parks of Rest and Culture'.

The accumulation of relevant facts was the *forte* of the Webbs in their joint works. But did they do much more than that? Did they have more than 'merely industry' as Mrs Webb wrote when comparing their 'dull second rateness' with the genius of Shaw? Their achievements of organisation were remarkable. They founded the London School of Economics and the *New Statesman*. Sidney launched the Labour Party on its path to government by writing its 1918 constitution, which for the first time gave it the framework of a national party. But were they just dull plodders or sparkling thinkers? I don't know. Sidney's passionless prolixity makes me think the first, Beatrice's *Diaries* the second.

Part II
Group Portraits

The Wise Men
Harriman, Acheson, McCloy, Lovett, Bohlen and Kennan

The Wise Men, as Walter Isaacson and Evan Thomas described these six in their book of that name published in 1986, were all born between 1891 and 1904 and all contributed in their different ways to the benevolent authority of the United States in the plenitude of its power.

Of the six, three were Yale men. Perhaps surprisingly only one went to Harvard College, although three others gravitated to its Law School. One went to Princeton, and the sixth to Amherst. Four went to highly privileged 'prep' schools, two of these four to Groton.

Of the three who were Yale undergraduates, two were members of a club known as Skull and Bones, which seems to combine the worst features of the Cambridge Apostles and the Oxford Bullingdon. The Harvard one got into the Porcellian, membership of which eluded FDR, although not Theodore Roosevelt, nor Richard Whitney, the President of the New York Stock Exchange, who atoned for the last 'big bang' by spending three years in Sing Sing.

Two of the six became bankers, two of them corporation lawyers, and two career foreign service officers. All of them regarded rich rewards (which only the first two occupations brought) as subordinate to influencing the direction of national policy. (At least two, and maybe a third by marriage, had such stores of wealth that this was no sacrifice.) Yet five out of the six regarded elective office with distaste, and four of them were indifferent to party affiliation.

The oldest was Averell Harriman (1891–1986), heir to a vast railroad fortune, who with Hopkins and Winant was one of a trio of laconic saviours who came to Britain out of the West in 1940–41.

He was Ambassador to Moscow, 1943-46, then briefly to London, then Secretary of Commerce, then central to the creation of NATO and the implementation of Marshall Aid, 1948-53. In the Kennedy and Johnson administrations he was back in senior State Department positions, but never at the top. Unlike the other five, he liked party politics. He was elected Governor of New York in 1954, and cherished presidential ambitions in both 1956 and 1960. To his 95th year he was never bored by the informed discussion of public events, and the authority and attraction of his personality raised the boredom threshold of others.

Next in order of birth was Dean Acheson (1893-1971), who attained the widest fame (and obloquy) of any of the six. With General Marshall as the second leg, he completed the tripod which sustained the Truman presidency. Although probably the most internationally minded of all the 59 US Secretaries of State (Kissinger is the obvious rival), Acheson never served or lived abroad. He was denounced by Senator McCarthy as a dangerous radical and protector of 'reds', possibly even one himself, but his views were never left of liberal conservative, and in later life he could be both irascibly and eccentrically right-wing. Socially he was the equivalent of a poor Etonian, the son of a bishop, a formidable man with whom to engage.

Third was John J. McCloy, born in 1895 and still alive. He was the only one of the six who had to raise himself by a combination of his own boot-straps and his mother's hair-drier, for it was as a coiffeuse that, after the premature death of his insurance clerk father, she worked with dedication to get him to a good Baptist school and then to Amherst. McCloy's central service to the Republic was to be, in the strictest sense, pro-consul in Germany, and to forge the Bonn-Washington relationship, half allied, half client, which was the crucial link in the Western world for 30 years. Paradoxically in view of his provenance (or perhaps not), Isaacson and Thomas claim that McCloy has also long been the pre-eminent arbiter of the American establishment.

Robert Lovell (1896-1986) is the first of the sextet that I have not known. As a result he appears to me to be the least interesting of the first four. President Kennedy did not agree. When he formed his administration he offered him a choice of the departments of State, Treasury or Defense. Lovett took none, although he had served Truman both as Under Secretary of State and as Secretary of Defense. He was a rich business partner of Harriman's, but in public affairs he was more of a twin with McCloy. They were both Assistant Secretaries of Henry L. Stimson, Roosevelt's Republican Secretary of War from 1941. Colonel Stimson (previously Taft's Secretary of War, 1909-13, and Hoover's Secretary of State, 1929-33) was not only their mentor but the real founder president of East Coast internationalism, a more authoritative arbiter than McCloy, an American Lord Halifax with more steel.

'Chip' Bohlen (1904-1974) and George Kennan (also born 1904 and still alive) were different from the other four. They were career diplomats and not general auxiliaries of government. They were however peculiarly influential ones, especially Kennan, who was the more awkward, the 'chippier' (in spite of their names), the more intellectually profound. He formulated the anti-Soviet doctrine at the base of American foreign policy and then spent the rest of his life complaining about the crudity with which it was implemented. There is a touch of Thomas Carlyle, the sage not of Ecclefechan but of Princeton, about him.

Bohlen was easier diplomatic currency. I can equate him with a range of British diplomats of the period, the face in the photograph beside the minister, the word in the ear, the self-confidence of an assured social position, the accumulated wisdom of many a conference, the fine posts of Moscow and Paris to crown a career.

Yet this is a snare, for the important point about Bohlen and all the others is that they were *not* like us. They were the agents of the first of the super powers, dealing across the wasteland of carnage and poverty to which Europe had reduced itself with the second of the super powers. The remarkable thing is that they did it with such a mixture of civility and authority.

The Lord Chancellors
1940–1970
Simon, Jowitt, Simonds, Kilmuir, Dilhorne and Gardiner

Collective biographical studies are in general not very satisfactory. It is not quite clear why they have been brought together. Lord Chancellors are however rather a special case. They have long been the foremost examples of the way in which the governing oligarchy fortified itself by the injection of new talent. As a result they have a good deal of sociological as well as professional and individual interest. And they have been well served by collective biographers: Campbell on the eighteenth and early nineteenth century, Atlay's Victorian Chancellors, and two widely-spaced volumes from R.F.V. Heuston taking the list on from 1885. The second of these covers Simon, Jowitt, Simonds, Kilmuir, Dilhorne and Gardiner.

Among the six, poor John Simon was in many ways the ablest, but no-one should be surprised at his being treated with a marked lack of affection. It was mostly his fate, at least from the time when as a young Attorney-General he was referred to as either 'the impeccable' or 'Sir Sympne' in his Prime Minister's private correspondence. What is more remarkable is the identity of the pair who most clearly arouse Professor Heuston's regard and admiration: William Jowitt and Gerald Gardiner. They surely have little in common beyond their political affiliation (which in Jowitt's case was carried almost embarrassingly lightly) and there is no other indication that Professor Heuston is a partisan Labour supporter.

Gardiner was a Chancellor of shy and austere integrity who sat well upon the Woolsack but found himself ill at ease in the

Cabinet, and in political life generally, and consequently was only half effective. Jowitt was nearly a bird of paradise, handsome, golden-voiced, rich-living, widely acquainted. Yet he was flawed, a minor and Anglo-Saxon Giscard d'Estaing. A geological fault ran down the middle of an otherwise fair and smiling landscape. In Giscard's case it caused dislike; in Jowitt's distrust.

This was probably unfair. Jowitt's switch of parties between Liberal and Labour in 1929 caused more recrimination than almost anybody else's. When, as Solicitor-General in 1940, he was convicted of a breach of the rationing regulations, the offence was almost technical. When, on leaving office in 1951, he facetiously complained about his lack of living accommodation and was asked whether there might not be room in the vicarage at Bray, it was crudely cruel. When the parochial church council refused permission for a memorial tablet to be placed in the Stevenage church where his ashes were deposited and of which his father had been rector, it was almost inexplicable. Yet there were too many of these incidents. There was something wrong with Jowitt.

Of more significance than the flaws in Jowitt is Professor Heuston's view of the collectivity of these mid-twentieth-century Chancellors compared with their Victorian and Georgian predecessors. His conclusion is that they came from both a more homogeneous and a more elevated social background than those whom he had previously surveyed, or indeed than those whom Atlay in 1906–08 or Campbell in 1845–47 had written about before him. The hurdle to be cleared was curiously low, as is illustrated by his lapidary sentence: '(Dilhorne) had a patrician background more splendid than that of any other Chancellor in English history, except perhaps Talbot (1733–37)'.

It was this lack of elevated provenance of the great lawyer politicians which made them such a crucial source of talented sustenance to the English governing class over many centuries. The law was a career open to the whole of the middle class, and many of its most successful practitioners (Brougham, Isaacs, Buckmaster) came from very much the petty bourgeois end of it. But there was nothing petty about their rewards. From Erskine in the late eighteenth century to Shawcross in the mid-twentieth century there were always at least one or two lawyer politicians on the scene who combined the fame of matinée idols, the emoluments of nabobs and the (eventual) rank of noblemen.

In some ways they got the best of both worlds. They were treated as professionals by the great magnates with whom they served in government, but to compensate for being so patronised they were paid more than the Prime Minister or Secretaries of State – Lord Chancellors twice as much – while Law Officers were allowed to keep their fees. And then when the match was over they were welcomed into the pavilion by the gentlemen's entrance: of the 20 Lord Chancellors in the 100 years to 1970, seven were given earldoms and 11 viscountcies.

In return they served the State well. They were by training, duties and aspiration more respectful of established values and forms than the other 'new men' who came in from a business background, such as Richard Cobden or Joseph Chamberlain. They provided shots of necessary plebeian blood in the least painful possible form.

But now Professor Heuston informs us that this ecological balance has changed. As the social background of Secretaries of State has gone down, so that of Lord Chancellors has gone up. His current six all went to public schools, to Oxford, and 'to one of the better colleges' as he quaintly and rashly puts it. Since his six Lord Hailsham of St Marylebone has been one of the only three Lord Chancellors since the eighteenth century to be an Etonian, and has consequently re-inforced Professor Heuston's perception of an up-market surge. But the present incumbant, Lord Mackay of Clashfern, has corrected by being the epitome of a Scots boy of high talent and modest origin for whom the high road of England (and the Woolsack) became the finest sight. So a clear direction is not easy to discern.

Modern Political Biography*, 1945–1970

In considering modern political biography during this period the first change to be noted is that there is much more of it. At the end of the Second World War all that was available covering the period from, say, 1870 to that time were what are sometimes a little ungenerously called 'tombstone lives' - two or three-volume commissioned works - and little else. At this stage in my life I had managed to survive the Oxford Final Honours School of Philosophy, Politics, and Economics while reading very little political biography. During the war I had managed over a period to repair some of the more obvious gaps in my readings of English fiction. Then, at the end of the war, I found myself enjoying one of those periods of paid, but almost complete, unemployment, which have always been an occasional feature of army life. In the late summer and autumn of 1945 I decided to try to repair quickly, the biographical gap as well. I read in rapid succession Morley's *Gladstone*; Garvin's *Joseph Chamberlain*; Lady Gwendoline Cecil's *Salisbury*; Churchill's *Lord Randolph Churchill;* Crewe's *Rosebery*; Mrs Dugdale's *Balfour*; Gardiner's *Harcourt*; Spender's *Campbell-Bannerman*; Spender and Asquith's *Asquith*; Trevelyan's *Grey*; Ronaldshay's *Curzon*; Newton's *Lansdowne*; and Petrie's *Austen Chamberlain*. (The most obvious gap here is Monypenny and Buckle's *Disraeli*, and that I must confess is a gap which has ever since remained unfilled. Six-volume biographies are daunting.)

A notable characteristic of this list is that of the thirteen works which make it up, five were written by family connections and

*This essay is based on a lecture given in the spring of 1972 to the Royal Society of Literature. It has deliberately not been amended to take account of books which have been published and events which have occurred subsequently.

191

the other eight by those who were enthusiastic supporters, some almost henchmen, of their subjects.

This, then, was the framework, for me at least, of late nineteenth-century and early twentieth-century political biography. Autobiography was rare. John Morley had produced two volumes, but (a warning thought, perhaps, for politicians who believe their successors will wish to read about them) the pages of this work in the House of Commons Library copy, when I came to read it in the early 1950s, were still all uncut. They had been folded together in the 16-page sets which was the practice for some publishers, at least in the first few decades of this century. No-one in the House of Commons Library had disturbed them over 35 years. Haldane and Balfour had produced fragments of autobiography. Asquith had produced two volumes of reminiscent snippets which are, I regret to say, unrewarding for the reader, and were not, I suspect, in any sense adequately rewarding for himself. I only read them when I had professional reasons for doing so.

In the practice of autobiography, there has been a sudden change of fashion. Of the eleven Prime Ministers in the sixty years between 1880 and 1940, none wrote a full-scale autobiography. One (Balfour), as I have mentioned, wrote a fragment; another (Lloyd George) wrote a major *pièce justificative* but not an autobiography. Four of the eleven (Campbell-Bannerman, Bonar Law, MacDonald, and Neville Chamberlain), it should perhaps be said, had little or no time after leaving office in which they could have written about themselves.

On the other hand, of the six Prime Ministers in the thirty years since 1940 none has remained silent. Churchill and Eden, although they wrote very full memoirs, did not in the strict sense write autobiographies. Nor has Mr Wilson.

It is often assumed that the change for the worse in the financial position of those likely to become Prime Minister, and therefore of ex-Prime Ministers, may have been largely responsible for this marked change of practice. But I do not believe that it provides a full, or even the main, explanation for the difference. This view is supported by looking, for purposes of comparison, at the position in the United States, where most of the Presidents of the former period were by no means rich, less so, on the whole, than those of the latter period. There were eleven, as with us, between 1880 and 1940; there have been nine (putting Franklin Roosevelt in the latter category) since 1940. Of the first eleven, only three (Theodore Roosevelt, Coolidge, and Hoover) wrote their memoirs. Of the last five, three (Truman, Eisenhower, and Johnson) have written; the other two (Roosevelt and Kennedy) had no opportunity of doing so. Thus, on both sides of the Atlantic, the desire to describe and justify appears to have grown enormously, independently of financial need or incentive. The result has obviously been a great new wave of political memoirs.

But biography, not autobiography, is my principal theme. Here, too, there has been an immense increase in the amount of material available. It began effectively in the early nineteen-fifties. I think I would put Harold Nicolson's *King George V,* the only commissioned royal biography with claims to be a work of art, as the starting-point of this new wave. It has been followed by works by writers like Sir Philip Magnus, Robert Blake, Lord Birkenhead, Robert Rhodes James, Sir John Wheeler-Bennett, and Lady Longford, all of whom I think have some discernible characteristics in common. As a result the whole field has, within a comparatively short period, been filled in with a dense and strongly growing crop. In the later 1940s when I first tried to write in this area myself, it was virgin territory. When I returned in 1970 after six years of compulsory absence, I found it very difficult to discover an adequate tract of open country to despoil.

What are the common characteristics of this group? First, they are none of them, with the exception of Lord Blake, academic in the strict sense of the word. They are self-taught as historians, and, I am almost tempted to add, as writers too, except that I do not think it possible to be other than self-taught as a writer. Several of them, indeed, turned to writing rather late in life, but none the less acquired remarkable skill. Sir Philip Magnus had produced a life of Burke in 1939, but his first biography of major impact was his *Gladstone* in 1954, which was published when he was forty-eight. Lady Longford is a still more striking example. She never wrote a book before she was fifty, and the first was not, in my view, a very good one. But she is now a major biographer, though writing principally about a period a little earlier than the one I am chiefly considering. This is an encouraging thought for some of us: biographers, unlike mathematicians, appear within limits to get better as they get older.

Among other characteristics they have in common is the fact

that, despite their lack of professional status as historians, the books of all those I have mentioned are written with a scrupulous accuracy, but also with a firmly selective eye for what is of interest to the general reader. Indeed, paradoxically, one of the most superficial and disappointing – almost slapdash – political biographies of the period came from a most distinguished academic historian, G.M. Young. His *Baldwin* leaves almost everything to be desired. This is perhaps explained by a strange remark which he made to me a week after the book was published, on almost the only occasion that I met him. Rather nervously searching for conversation, I said that I assumed that Baldwin, whom I had not known, was a man of singular personal charm. He looked unenthusiastic. 'I never really found him so', he said. 'As a matter of fact, I much preferred Neville Chamberlain myself.' It was an odd comment from Baldwin's chosen biographer.

All the works under consideration were also relatively detached. They were not written by relations, except Lord Birkenhead's life of his father. And this book was a revision – very substantial and much more satisfactory – of an earlier work, and is to be balanced against his very fine and non-filial *Halifax*. Nor were the writers partisan in the sense that Morley was a partisan of Gladstone, Gardiner of Harcourt, Spender of both Campbell-Bannerman and Asquith, and Garvin of Joseph Chamberlain. Indeed, even where there was a strong community of political affiliation, as with Robert Blake's *Disraeli*, this did not extend to any very strong personal admiration.

Yet they were not iconoclastic works. The authors have mostly been willing to use the scalpel and expose some aspects of the lives and characters of their subjects which it would have horrified the writers of the traditional commissioned or filial works to see exposed to the light of day. Even so, some may have skipped a little too lightly over the peccadilloes, or worse, of their subjects. I think this was true of Robert Rhodes James on Rosebery. And indeed, I have been accused of doing the same with Asquith's weaknesses, although not unnaturally I do not accept the charge. Perhaps I may deal briefly with this point, since I have not done so on any previous occasion. There are two aspects of it. There is a view that at the request, or demand, of Lady Violet Bonham Carter, I suppressed pieces of correspondence which would have thrown further light on Asquith's relations with Miss Venetia

Stanley. This is not true. The existence of the correspondence, of which she was apparently not aware until she saw the manuscript of my book, was something of a shock to Lady Violet. She asked me to make certain deletions. Questions of copyright were involved. Nor did I wish to ignore her feelings. There followed a process of bargaining, each of us, I think, behaving perfectly reasonably from the point of view of our own interest. Eventually she reluctantly withdrew her objections to about three-quarters of the deletions she had asked for. The others I agreed to make. They were not of vast significance. The principal result was that I did not fully illustrate from the correspondence the possible impact of the relationship on Asquith's handling of the transaction of the 1915 coalition. But I did not refrain from giving my own views of this. Nor did the deletions in any way change the whole picture of the relationship which I endeavoured to portray. Were I now, with Lady Violet no longer alive, to produce a new edition of this book, it would be a rather marginal question as to whether or not I would think it worth while to restore the limited excisions*. No new revelations would in any event emerge.

There is also the separate point as to whether I drew too much of a veil over Asquith's drinking habits. This must, I think, be a matter of judgement. What I did was to quote from a letter which Field-Marshal Haig wrote to his wife after a visit by Asquith to G.H.Q. in France. Haig wrote: 'You would have been amused at the Prime Minister last night. He did himself fairly well – not more than most gentleman used to drink when I was a boy, but in this abstemious age it is noticeable if an extra glass or two is taken by anyone! The P.M. seemed to like our old brandy. He had a couple of glasses (big sherry glass size) before I left the table at 9.30, and apparently he had several more before I saw him again. By that time his legs were unsteady, but his head was quite clear, and he was able to read a map and discuss the situation with me. Indeed he was most charming and quite alert in mind.' I then commented: 'Haig's picture fits in well with other accounts of Asquith's dining habits. For the last ten or fifteen years of his life, at least, he was a fairly heavy drinker. Occasionally this made him look a little unsteady (even in the House of Commons) late at night. But no one ever suggested that his mind lost its precision,

*I have since done so, in both the 1978 and the 1987 editions of *Asquith.*

or that there was any faltering in his command over what he did, or did not, want to say.' This was the picture as I saw it, from this and other written records, as well as from personal reminiscences, and I think on the whole that this gave the picture with adequate but not obsessive frankness. After that brief personal explanation, perhaps I can return to my main theme.

The group of works I have been discussing were not iconoclastic because they neither sought to break new ground in form or style – the authors had not been trying (which would probably in any event have been unrewarding attempts) to be new Lytton Stracheys – nor in the sense that the authors queried the assumptions of the political system or the society in which their subjects lived and worked. Indeed they have mostly been very much at home in this world. If they did not know their subjects personally, they knew a great number of people like them. They could understand from personal experience a good deal of the balance of their subjects' lives. This has considerable biographical advantages. It gives a sureness of touch in interpreting the nuances of letters and an understanding of what is serious and what is not. But it also gives a certain cosiness of approach, a tendency to criticise in detail and perhaps to be too sympathetic when judging with a broader brush. It is a point I shall develop further when dealing a little later with a younger school of more academic twentieth-century historians.

But first I must mention the 'Beaverbrook historians'. Lord Beaverbrook himself never wrote a biography, although each of his three main works was partly autobiographical and partly contributions towards a mammoth, unplanned, unfinished biography of Lloyd George. He was a historian of exceptional narrative power. He described events *as he saw them,* accurately as well as compellingly, always from one angle only, never in the round. His historical adjutant, Mr A.J.P. Taylor, a twentieth-century historian of great note and verve, is also so far barren of any biography of this period, although currently working upon a life of his colonel. Beaverbrook himself, and Taylor too, stand at either end of the line of Beaverbrook historians, like two substantial and impressive posts supporting a somewhat sagging clothes line. Hung from this line are some fairly soggy garments, dating from the time when Lord Beaverbrook, feeling that he had bought a large chunk of history, decided that he ought to do something with it. A few fairly bad biographies appeared as a result. The wave receded, and Lord Beaverbrook in his literary capacity is now likely to be remembered more by the good books he wrote than by the bad ones he commissioned.

I now come to what I mentioned earlier, in a rather middle-aged way, as the 'younger school'. Mr David Marquand's *Ramsay MacDonald* is well advanced. It has been long in preparation and is eagerly awaited, partly because MacDonald is the biggest almost completely unfilled gap in British political biography of this century. But Mr Marquand is in no way typical of the group I now wish to discuss. His background – son of a minister, himself an MP – is too similar to that of his subject for this to be true. The different group I have in mind has three rather curiously assorted bases: Nuffield College, Oxford; Monash University in Melbourne; and the Beaverbrook Library in Fleet Street. No full-scale biographical works have yet been forthcoming from these sources, but Professor Trevor Wilson's *Downfall of the Liberal Party*, Cameron Hazlehurst's *Politicians at War*, and the recent collection of essays on Lloyd George, written by young academics and edited by A.J.P. Taylor, as well as Robert Skidelsky's *Politicians and the Slump* and his awaited life of Mosley, all fall roughly in this category. Their distinguishing feature is that they have been, or are being, written from more outside the system than the books I discussed earlier. Their authors work on a wider variety of sets of papers, often relatively obscure ones, and their research could, perhaps, be regarded as more meticulous. But their understanding of what individuals were like and how their minds operated is, I think, less sure, or less attuned, maybe, to the conventional wisdom. Their fault is that they tend to treat all sources as equal, which they manifestly are not. Their perspectives are arguably fresher, but because they write from outside the system they are more mechanically dependent on written sources.

Thus it is paradoxically the case that this newer school of modern historical and biographical writers is more dependent on a declining industry – the accumulation of substantial sets of interesting political papers – than were the older ones. The increasing rarity of the political letter, which now almost threatens the existence of the species, is clearly a new factor, the biographical impact of which it is hardly yet possible to judge.

Letters have undoubtedly been an invaluable source. They often give a unique combination of the flavour of an event, the personality of the writer, and the quality of his relationship with the recipient. Also the fact that those used in the main line of the biographical tradition were almost entirely hand-written made them mostly reasonably terse and therefore happily quotable. Diaries have something of the same qualities. But the best have almost always been written by those who played no great part in major events, although they were close to them. A notable example of this century was provided by Sir Almeric Fitzroy, who as clerk to the Privy Council in the first decades of this century, and a man who had a good nose for the gossip of politics with no very decided political affiliations, almost exactly met the qualifications listed above. He was a more valuable source than Lord Esher who wrote at the same time and was equally well placed to observe, but who was much more opinionated and anxious himself to mould events.

For the third decade of the century Dr Tom Jones, deputy secretary to the Cabinet from 1916 to 1930, fulfilled something of the same role as Fitzroy, although his view was more concentrated upon the centre of power than upon the general political world. For a later period we have Nicolson and Channon, both more general in their interests and contacts than Jones, the latter much more frivolous but arguably giving a better picture than could filter through the literary skills and personal disappointments of Nicolson. The diarist who did play a much greater part in events feels a greater need for self-justification, and the consequent pressure upon him meant that there was usually a gap between the incident described and its committal to paper. The existence of this gap means, I fear, that we should always be a little suspicious of the full accuracy of records, even of those who write or dictate a fairly short time after the event. I know from my own experience how quickly and almost inevitably a film of retrospective wishful thinking clouds the memory. An incident, particularly one with close personal involvement, at a Cabinet in the morning is never quite the same by the evening. Already there is half-conviction that one's own arguments had a greater sharpness, and those of one's opponents a greater fuzziness or outrageousness, than was in fact the case. By the end of the week there is a substantial likelihood of full conviction that this was so.

The best published diarist amongst Cabinet members on either side of the Atlantic in the past forty years was Harold Ickes, Roosevelt's Secretary of the Interior. He wrote at great length (and produced three volumes) but gave unvarnished descriptions of his tumultuous states of mind and fluctuating relations with his colleagues which earned him the *sobriquet* of the 'old curmugeon'; and he had the great merit of not going back and attempting to iron out the fluctuations. He published the diary as he wrote it.

The best diarist in the Cabinet category on this side of the Atlantic was Hugh Dalton. He wrote as he spoke, in a somewhat declamatory style, and although he never published diaries as such, he used them to give an unusual freshness to his autobiography. And he was not over-addicted to self-justification.

Compared with letters and diaries, Cabinet minutes and papers are disappointing sources, so much so that the recent decision to reduce the restricted period from fifty years to thirty years, while in itself welcome, never aroused much excitement in me. Cabinet minutes as such have, of course, only existed since 1917. Previously there was merely the Prime Minister's hand-written Cabinet letter to the Sovereign which, although brief, usually conveyed something of the atmosphere of the meeting, although they often suffered from being angled to match particular royal interests. Since then the minutes have become highly bureaucratic documents. In recent years they have made no attempt to convey the feeling of the discussion or to pick out its sharp points. On the contrary, they smooth them off. They are essentially directed towards giving the decisions taken as precise a form as possible for the Civil Servants who have to carry them out, and supplementing them, again for the benefit of the officials, with the facts upon which the decisions were, or should have been, based. Cabinet *papers* have also become depersonalised, and most often turgid as well. Only in exceptional circumstances are they written, as distinct from being redrafted at the edges, by ministers themselves. It is a big change from the time, a little more than 100 years ago, when Palmerston conducted most of the important work of the whole Foreign Office in his own hand. Any biography based mainly upon the Cabinet papers of the subject, even fortified by the Cabinet minutes of his period in office, would be likely to be an extremely dull and unrewarding work. Most discriminating ministers can hardly bring themselves to read these documents in full at the time, let alone decades afterwards. The personal minutes of Prime Ministers to their colleagues may be more rewarding material. Churchill, who was a great exponent of the art of disseminating such minutes, made a highly successful, if somewhat one-sided, use of them in his memoirs. But this is another art which is in decline, and of which he may indeed have been the last major exponent.

Speeches are also disappointing material. By their very nature they are public from the moment they are delivered. If they contain any memorable passages these remain in the public memory and there is therefore little possibility of using speeches as a source of anything new. But it is rather worse than that. It often happens that when the actual record comes to be looked at, the memorable passage turns out to have been far less elegantly and succinctly expressed than had been hoped and believed. No doubt at the time the force of the speaker's personality more than counteracted this; but this counteraction cannot be recaptured from the written record.

The writing of letters and personal political papers being therefore in decline, first-rate diaries being a product mostly of fringe figures than of central ones about whom biographies are likely to be written, and official Cabinet minutes and papers being a somewhat barren source, to what are biographers to turn for the future? Clearly it is the telephone which has largely replaced the letter. But I would not expect this to be a very rewarding source for the biographer. One of the few uses of a recorded telephone conversation which I can remember in recent biographies or autobiographies was Macmillan's account in his third volume of a conversation with President Eisenhower in 1955. This ran as follows:

President: Hallo Harold. How are you?

H.M.: I'm fine.

President: I'm fine too. It's fine to hear your voice. How are you getting on?

H.M.: I'm getting on fine.

President: I'm going to try to see you today after my show. There will be an interval.

H.M.: That's fine.

President: How are you getting on with Foster?

H.M.: I'm getting on fine.

President: Foster's a bit sticky at first, but he has a heart of gold when you know him. You have to get to know Foster. He's all right when you get to know him. He told me that I couldn't see you because of the others.

H.M.: I only just wanted to hear your voice again. I couldn't leave America without that.

President: That's right. That's what I told Foster. I didn't want to see you as British Secretary. I wanted to see you as my political adviser.

H.M.: That's fine.

President: How's Anthony?

H.M.: He's fine.

President: That's fine. Tell Anthony I'm going to get to Geneva on Sunday morning. I figure to get there early. I want a good talk with Anthony that day.

H.M.: That's just what Anthony would like.

President: Then there's another thing. I want to have a friend of mine around, Jimmy Gault.

H.M.: Of course.

President: It will mean a lot to us if you have got Jimmy Gault over there.

H.M.: Jimmy's in the City now.

President: God, is he a stockbroker? I thought he was in shipping.

H.M.: I hope so, that's much better.

President: All right. I'll see you after the show.

This has a considerable comic quality about it, as indeed it was intended to have when recorded, but it does not suggest that there is a very rich vein here to be tapped. 'Tapped' might I suppose be regarded as the appropriate word in the context and it is indeed likely, although on reflection irrational, that a man who wrote an autobiography based mainly on recorded telephone conversations, or left them for his biographer, might be regarded with some suspicion. There is no inherent reason why they should be treated as more private than letters, and it is indeed the case when politicians are in office (although not I am happy to say when they are in opposition) that summary records of their official telephone conversations are normally kept by their private secretaries. But the versions kept are, I suspect, much more rounded than the original interchanges. They lose personality and actuality in the process. But full transcripts in nearly all cases would be hopelessly diffuse, tentative, and even inarticulate.

Personal reminiscences are the other main non-written source.

I have never found these as helpful as they should be. In the first place, they are often highly inaccurate, although usually with the best of intentions. If detailed work on the events of a period a number of decades ago is followed by the opportunity to talk to someone who was there at the time, the only too common result is that his recollections, not only of the dates, but of the sequence of events does not fit the framework of the firmly established written facts. This almost inevitably, although perhaps unfairly, arouses scepticism about the accuracy of his other recollections too. In general I have found that talking to friends and associates of a biographical subject is worth while if they themselves made sufficient impact upon his life for it to be important to know what *they* were like, but not to be worth while, except in rare cases, if the only purpose is seeking to get second-hand impressions or even first-hand accounts. Visiting the houses where your subject has lived, and the scenes which played a part in his life, is usually more vividly creative than visiting his friends.

To consider in these circumstances how the biographers of those with few personal papers are to proceed in the future it is perhaps useful to look at the examples of those who in the past have tried to make bricks without such straw. I take one discouraging and one encouraging example. Lloyd George was not a man who took very naturally to paper, and such personal records as he left have not until recently been satisfactorily available. The result has been that of the spate of biographies which have flowed from his kaleidoscopic personality, all have been in varying ways unrewarding. The conclusion may not have followed directly from the premise, but it is clearly possible that there is some causal relationship. On the other hand, Ernest Bevin was at least equally barren of epistolary output. But Mr Alan Bullock, whose third volume is yet to appear, has produced a thoroughly workmanlike, and in most ways satisfying, account of the first two-thirds of his life. He understood the subject and his background, and made remarkable use of material that sounded most unpromising - the journals of the Transport and General Workers' Union, unread by the general public, but giving intimate expression, for the eyes of its members, of the month-to-month development of Bevin's thoughts.

This suggests that determined biographers will rarely be at a loss for material which they can mould. Nor do I think there is much danger of their being driven out by the autobiographers. It is often interesting, although not invariably so, to read a man's verdict on himself. What is still more interesting is the verdict of others upon him.

Changing Patterns of Leadership
from Asquith via Baldwin and Attlee to Mrs Thatcher

Asquith became Prime Minister eighty years ago last April and held office for eight years, two hundred and forty-one days which was, until 1988, the longest continuous period since Lord Liverpool, who is the only Prime Minister to have made a reputation out of longevity. Walpole and the younger Pitt were both longer in office but their fame had other less arithmetical components. Mrs Thatcher overtook Asquith's record on 3 January, 1988 but even before that it must be allowed that she had already made at least the imprint on the pattern of government of the other three full-term Prime Ministers mentioned in my title.

I have used the word 'full-term' because I am convinced that it is essential to have a cumulative period in office of at least five years in order to rank as a Prime Minister of major impact. No-one of the last one hundred years who does not fulfil this criterion has achieved the front rank. Not Rosebery, not Balfour (although, despite the electoral ignominy of his fall, he comes nearest to being the exception), not Campbell-Bannerman, not Neville Chamberlain, not Eden, not Home, not Heath, not Callaghan. That leaves three Prime Ministers who served over five years in peacetime within my eighty-year span, and are not mentioned in my title – MacDonald, Macmillan and Wilson. I left them out because I have not written books about them, and neither do they rank as a necessary *terminus ad quem* as does the present incumbent. That at least is as good as reason as any.

So I begin my excursion with the currently ill-regarded and under-estimated Asquith. A couple of years ago I came to re-read my life of him, first published in 1964, after an interval of nearly nine years. I was struck afresh by the quality of his mind and

204

temperament, and hence his capacity to lead a government. It was not an adventurous mind that breached new frontiers, but he had knowledge, judgement, insight and tolerance. And for at least his first six years as Prime Minister he presided with an easy authority over the most talented British Government of this century.

How would I illustrate his quality in government? I give two examples. First, a memorandum, on the constitutional position of the Sovereign which he wrote on holiday in Scotland in September 1913, without any official advice, probably without any reference books to look at, and sent off direct to King George V. It was in reply to a rather pathetic *cri de coeur* from the monarch complaining that he would be vilified by half his subjects whether or not he approved the Irish Home Rule and almost suggesting that he had an equal constitutional choice between the two courses. Asquith's disabusal of this foolish idea was done with erudition and succinctness presented in a framework of muscular argument. It treated the King with a firm courtesy untinged with any hint of obsequiousness. I can think of no other Prime Minister this century who could have written out of the resources of his own mind with equal authority.

Second, as late as the eighth and penultimate year of his premiership he gave a brilliant and effective display of his talents as an effortless administrator. Kitchener (Margot Asquith's 'great poster' successfully masquerading as a great man) had become a focus of indecision at the War Office. It could be held that Asquith ought to have sacked him, but given Kitchener's hold on public opinion, that course was well beyond the limits of Asquith's effective power. What he did was to encourage Kitchener to go on a month's visit to Gallipoli, temporarily himself to take over the War Office (as he had done for four months after the Curragh mutiny in March, 1914) and quickly to lance several boils which Kitchener had allowed to fester for half a year or more. It was a last display of an exceptional administrative talent, and the fact that he enjoyed doing it contradicts the view that he was over the hill and had become indolently ineffective by 1914 at the latest. Asquith was lazy only in the sense that by his remarkable skill in the speedy, but perhaps too coolly detached, dispatch of public business he was able to keep a lot of time for pastimes outside politics.

Nevertheless, I think he was in office too long and his style was unsuited to the demands of wartime leadership. It was not so much that Lloyd George, when he replaced him, was a better war leader. His errors of strategic judgement and his ineffectiveness in dealing with a High Command backed by the King were just as great as were those of Asquith. But Lloyd George had the zest and the *brio* to behave as though he were a better war leader, and that was half the battle. Asquith did not like the frenetic drama and mock heroics of politicians' war, although he certainly did not insulate his family from the tribulations of soldiers' war, and he could not be bothered to pretend to an enthusiasm he did not feel. The lady who, as a conversational gambit in 1915, said, 'Mr Asquith, do you take an interest in the war?' was nearer the bone than she perhaps imagined.

His pattern of government should therefore be studied mainly in its peacetime manifestation, while noting that part of the complaint against him was that this pattern hardly changed when the war began. Although in general his authority in the Government was good, with no suggestion that he was frightened of strong ministers, of which he had plenty, or that they were disrespectful of him, I do not think it could be said that he operated the Cabinet tautly. There was then no written record of its proceedings, apart from his own hand-written letters to the King after each meeting. That sounds unimaginable today, but it was a practice which he had inherited from all his predecessors, including one as efficient as Peel and another as energetic as Gladstone. I think the lack of tautness had other causes. He did not talk much in Cabinet himself. He had other Cabinet occupations, notably letter-writing. But he rather believed in letting discussion run on, almost exhausting itself, before he could see developing what he liked to describe as a 'favourable curve' for bringing it to a satisfactory conclusion.

These methods made him good at holding rumbustious colleagues together and good too at avoiding foolish decisions. It made him less good at taking wise decisions ahead of time and at galvanising the less energetic members of his Government. This latter deficiency must be seen in the context of his indisputable achievement of presiding over one of the only two major reforming governments of the past 100 years. He did not greatly interfere in the work of departmental ministers and when he did it was to give them necessary but slightly reluctant support where needed, rather than to correct them. Lloyd George, ironically in some ways, was the foremost beneficiary of this support, both in getting the Budget of 1909 through a reluctant Cabinet and at the time of his Marconi peccadiloes. Asquith allowed Grey an almost complete independence at the Foreign Office, but as that priggish Whig was, in my view, one of the most over-rated statesmen in the first half of this century, even if he was also one of my predecessors as Chancellor of the University of Oxford, the results were not altogether happy.

As a butcher of ministers, Asquith was in the middle grade, about half way between Gladstone, who regarded his Cabinet colleagues, once appointed, as having the inviolate permanence of members of a College of Cardinals, and Macmillan, who in 1962, axed a third of them like junior managers in an ailing company. Asquith dropped Lord Elgin, his Colonial Secretary, when his mind became distinctly erratic, Herbert Gladstone, the son of the Grand Old Man, who was an incompetent Home Secretary but who was compensated with the Governor-Generalship of South Africa, Charles Masterman when he lost three by-elections running, and Lord Haldane, Asquith's oldest political friend, when the Tories, foolishly from several points of view, demanded Haldane's head as the price for accepting a rotten lot of portfolios for themselves when they joined the 1915 Coalition. But he left the North Sea to engulf Kitchener and the Dublin Easter rebellion to destroy Birrell, who, in spite of splendid epigrams, ought to have gone much sooner and before the rebellion also destroyed the prospect of Irish Home Rule within a United Kingdom. He reshuffled some of his ministers a good deal, although not so much as Harold Wilson, who had not a butcher's but a circus master's approach to reshuffling. Under Asquith, McKenna and Churchill, in particular, were subjected to a number of rather pointless changes.

Asquith's own attention was mostly concentrated on the high constitutional issues of which there were plenty in the peace-time life of his Government: on relations with the Lords and with the Sovereign leading to the Parliament Act, on Irish Home Rule, on Welsh church disestablishment, and, a failed measure, suffrage reform. Although he had himself introduced the first old age pension in his last Budget as Chancellor of the Exchequer before becoming Prime Minister, he left the subsequent development of national insurance as much to Lloyd George as, until late July 1914, he did foreign affairs to Grey. Nevertheless it would be quite wrong to think of him as other than the leading figure in his own Government, whom his colleagues naturally accepted as the fount of praise or rebuke, the one with the greatest command over the House of Commons, the best known to the public. In this last respect, being well known to the public, and only in this respect, Lloyd George was a near runner-up.

Stanley Baldwin came to the Prime Ministership in a totally different way. Asquith's was the calmest, the most certain and assured ascent to the premiership this century, with the possible exception of Neville Chamberlain. But Chamberlain was 12 years older than Asquith at accession and for this, amongst other reasons, will be seen in history as an appendage to the age of Baldwin, while Asquith, almost independently of merit, relegated his predecessor, Campbell-Bannerman, to being a prefix to the age of Asquith. Baldwin, in contrast to Asquith, came out of the woodwork a bare six months before he was in No. 10 Downing Street. Until then, there were at least six Conservative politicians who were much better known than he was. Asquith had become the senior Secretary of State at the age of 39, Baldwin was 50 before he became even a junior minister. Baldwin was a Conservative, Asquith was a Liberal. Baldwin was rich, Asquith was not. Asquith was fashionable, partly but not wholly through his wife. Baldwin was not. In spite of these differences, Baldwin wished to model himself more on Asquith than on any other of his twentieth-century predecessors.

Did he succeed? His main Government, that of 1924-29, was less talented than Asquith's, although with Churchill, Balfour, Birkenhead and the two Chamberlains (Neville and Austen) it could not, by any stretch of the imagination, be regarded as negligible in this respect. He was as economical with the attention he was prepared to devote to politics as was Asquith. But his intellectual equipment was much less formidable. When asked what English thinker had most influenced him, he firmly replied, 'Sir Henry Maine'. When asked which particular aspect of Maine's thought had seized his mind, he said his view that all human history should be seen in terms of the advance from status to contract. He then paused, looked apprehensively at his interlocutor, and said, 'Or is it the other way around?' That is totally un-Asquithian. Asquith might not have had many original thoughts but he could summarise the broad doctrines of any well-known philosopher or historian as well as giving you their dates at the drop of a hat.

Baldwin's authority within his principal Government in the 1920s was substantially less than Asquith's had been. Baldwin by then had escaped from the anonymity of 1923, he had won a great election victory and he had made his own Cabinet, unlike his first short spell in Downing Street in 1923 when he had merely inherited one from Bonar Law. But he made it of men who were mostly used to being his political seniors. He certainly inspired no awe. On the other hand, partly by the devotion of vast acres of time to sitting on the front bench in the House of Commons, talking in its corridors, or hanging about in the smoking room, (desultorily reading a middle-brow publication of the period called the *Strand Magazine* as he was reported on one occasion) he acquired a considerable popularity in, and, indeed, mastery over, the House of Commons. His skill at the new medium of broadcasting was also a considerable and exceptional strength.

The *Strand Magazine* incident I use to express certain differences between Baldwin and his predecessors and successors. Asquith would never have chosen the *Strand Magazine*, or the House of Commons as a place in which to read. He would have read more recondite, but equally haphazardly, in some more private precinct. Churchill in office would never have wasted time in the House of Commons smoking room without an audience. Lloyd George would never have wasted time there at all, but he might well have chosen the *Strand Magazine* had he been left waiting upon a railway station. Neville Chamberlain would never have read haphazardly. Ramsay MacDonald would never have exposed himself so apparently free from the burdens of state.

You could not exactly say that Stanley Baldwin was wasting time. More likely he was not even reading the magazine, but sniffing it, and with it the atmosphere around him, ruminating, feeling his way, nudging towards a variety of decisions he had to make. He was not indecisive. Indeed Birkenhead once unfavourably described his method of government as 'taking one leap in the dark, looking around, and taking another'. But he reached decisions much more by sniffing and then making a sudden plunge than by any orderly process of ratiocination.

He rarely applied himself to the methodical transaction of written business. Tom Jones, deputy secretary of the Cabinet who later became one of his closest confidants and best sources of information about him, at first thought him remarkably slow, with barely a fifth

209

of the speed of his predecessor, Bonar Law, in dealing with papers. It took Jones some time to realise that Baldwin did not work at all in Law's rather unimaginative accountant's sense. But his mind was nonetheless always playing around the political issues. In this sense he was the opposite, not only of Law but of Asquith, who certainly did not have an accountant's mind. Churchill wrote of Asquith, 'He was like a great judge who gave his whole mind to a case as long as his court was open and then shut it absolutely and turned his mind to the diversions of the day'. With Baldwin the court was never either wholly open or wholly shut.

It followed from this method of work that he was even less inclined to interfere in the work of departmental ministers than was Asquith. He did not bombard his ministers with declaratory minutes like Churchill, or petulant ones like Eden, or nostalgic ones like Macmillan. Nor did he exercise much control over his ministers by headmasterly promotions, demotions or sackings. He made hardly any changes during this $4^1/_2$ year period of office, except when Halifax (then Wood about to become Irwin) went to India as Viceroy, when Curzon died, or Birkenhead decided he could not live on his salary. He never seriously thought of getting rid of Steel-Maitland who was a useless Minister of Labour stationed in the most crucial and exposed segment of the Government's political front.

This at least had the effect of involving and identifying the Prime Minister very closely with his Government's handling of industrial relations. This was true before the General Strike and after it. His 'Give Peace in our Time Oh Lord' speech in February 1925 was then his most successful House of Commons foray, and the decision four months later to set up the Samuel Commission, and to pay a temporary subsidy to the coal industry, was very much his own work. During the strike itself he was deeply involved, but once the General Strike (as opposed to the coal strike) was defeated, he rather lost interest.

There were five major developments in the life of his second and central Government (1924–29), and this was the only one of the five with which he was centrally concerned. The return to the gold standard in 1925 was very much Churchill's decision at the Treasury, even though he had at first been opposed to it. The Treaty of Locarno, and the European security system created by it, was overwhelmingly Austen Chamberlain's work at the Foreign Office.

The housing and poor law reforms were even more decisively the work of his half-brother Neville at the Ministry of Health. Finally the elegant formula of the Statute of Westminster, which enabled the reality of Dominion independence to be combined with the dignity of the Crown, came from Balfour.

Baldwin was, therefore, more detached from the main policies of his Government than was Asquith and he was, in my view, a less considerable man, although not a negligible one either. He would not have had the intellectual grasp to write Asquith's constitutional memorandum. But he had the feel to deal successfully with the General Strike, although not the sustained energy to follow this up by dealing equally well with the miners' strike, which was both its cause and aftermath, continuing long after the General Strike. He dealt still more skillfully with the abdication of King Edward VIII ten years later. Like Asquith, he preferred to engage with constitutional issues more than with any other, though his lack of overseas interest (except for India which he never visited) meant that the Statute of Westminster slipped by him almost unnoticed. He continued Asquith's practice, interrupted by Lloyd George, of performing as Prime Minister without a surrounding circus. He would walk about London or travel by mainline train on his own.

Attlee arrived in No. 10 Downing Street eight years after Baldwin had left for the last time. Unlike Asquith or Baldwin, he inherited a vast government machine which the war had created, and which was used to running a great part of the nation's affairs and spending a high proportion of its income. He was also the heir to a post-Baldwin Prime Ministerial habit of trying to run a large part of British foreign policy from 10 Downing Street, and believing that Britain counted for a great deal in the world. (The latter belief was pre- as well as post-Baldwin of course). Attlee's first duty in his new office was to meet the Americans and the Russians at Potsdam. Neither Asquith nor Baldwin had ever attended an international conference as Prime Minister. Attlee, a very firmly established member of the English upper-middle class, was not rich like Baldwin, or fashionable like Asquith, but he was similar to both of them in having a natural respect for conventional values and institutions. It did not make him pompous, for his taciturnity gave him a natural talent for balloon-pricking, and it did not prevent his being the head of an effective radical Government just as it had not prevented

Asquith or, for that matter, Gladstone before him being in the same category.

Compared with Asquith and Baldwin, Attlee was the worst speaker, the least engaging personality, and by far the best Cabinet chairman. He developed this last quality even before he had the authority of the Prime Ministership behind him. Many recorded tributes testify to the way in which he presided over the War Cabinet during Churchill's frequent absences: rhetoric disappeared, and decisions were taken with speed and precision. Yet Attlee was not the dominating figure of his Government, either publicly or privately. Ernest Bevin, Stafford Cripps, Hugh Dalton, Herbert Morrison, Aneurin Bevan and latterly Hugh Gaitskell constituted a forbidable array of ministers. I do not think that they can be quite classed with Asquith's, partly because of the subsequent fame of Lloyd George and Churchill, but also because the Attlee Government had no-one to equal the non-political distinction of Morley, Birrell and Haldane. That Liberal Government apart, however, they are unmatched this century and for most of the last too. Attlee balanced them, steered them, kept them and himself afloat, but he did not exactly lead them; he was a cox and not a stroke. For his first three or four years he distributed their weight brilliantly although latterly he failed to place Aneurin Bevan properly which led to considerable trouble.

One of his strongest attributes is thought to have been his capacity for laconic ministerial butchery. This may be slightly exaggerated. He despatched parliamentary under secretaries with ease, but this was rather like shooting chickens. Of big game he was more cautious. He was probably relieved when an exhausted Dalton shot himself but he pulled no trigger on him. Arthur Greenwood he did dispose of but only when that figure had become unwilling to conduct even his morning's business from anywhere except the 'snuggery' (I think it was called) of the Charing Cross Hotel. Then towards the end he dismissed Ernest Bevin from the Foreign Office. That was an extraordinary feat. Bevin was the most important Foreign Secretary of this century, by which I mean that he was the one who left the biggest imprint on British foreign policy for a generation ahead. He was a massive but by no means a wholly amiable personality. He had been the sheet-anchor of Attlee's support throughout the life of the Government. He had given his support to 'little Clem' against Morrison, Cripps and Dalton. Yet when his health made him no longer capable of doing the job, out he went, miserable and complaining, and died six weeks later. This was an act of cold courage even more difficult than President Truman's sacking of General MacArthur.

With what aspects of government policy did Attlee most concern himself? Like both Asquith and Baldwin, even though both of them had been Chancellors of the Exchequer, I do not think that he understood or was much interested in economics. But the 'dismal science' had became far more central to government by his day. He gave his Chancellors, and especially Stafford Cripps, a very dominant position. Bevin as his Foreign Secretary had such a position *ad hominem*. Between Potsdam and Attlee's crisis visit to Washington in December 1950, when Truman had falsely given the impression that he might be about to drop an atomic bomb on the Chinese in North Korea and when Bevin had become too fragile to cross the Atlantic in less than five days, Attlee intervened in foreign policy no more than Asquith had done.

But the beginning of the end of Empire meant that there was a great range of external affairs with which a Prime Minister could concern himself without impinging on the prerogatives of even the most truculent Foreign Secretary. On relations with America, Russia and the continent of Europe, Attlee supported Bevin. On India, with a rather weak Secretary of State for India, he made his own policy. And determining the future of 450 million people, now 800 million people, was by any standards in the major league. Perhaps the two biggest impressions on history to be left by Britain in the past 300 years, have been first to govern and then to leave both America and India. So Attlee ranks as a major agent of Britain's world impact.

Internally, constitutional affairs engrossed Attlee less than they did either Asquith or Baldwin. On the other hand, he took more part in the social legislation of his Government than did Asquith in the previous wave of social advance. The Attlee Government was also memorable for six or seven major measures of nationalisation. Attlee did not much involve himself in this detail, but supported them all with commitment, even enthusiasm.

He presided over a highly interventionist Government, but he did not find it necessary to overwork. He once told me that being Prime Minister left him more spare time than any other job that he had done. It was partly, he said, because of living on the spot and avoiding the immensely long tube or Metropolitan Railway journeys to which his modest surburban lifestyle condemned him, both before and after his time as Prime Minister. The gap between Attlee's leaving 10 Downing Street and Mrs Thatcher arriving was almost exactly the same as the gap between Asquith leaving and Attlee arriving. The second gap is well within my Parliamentary recollection, the earlier gap is part of history.

The Government which Mrs Thatcher runs bears less relation to the three previous administrations I have considered, than they each do to the other two. The comparison is by no means wholly to her credit. In terms of the quality of the other ministers, I think it must be regarded as the least illustrious Government of the four. It is always necessary to be on one's guard against under-estimating one's contemporaries compared to their predecessors. It is easier to admire those on whom the gates of history have slammed shut, and there is certainly a fairly constant tendency to see things as always going down-hill: to say that the younger Pitt was not as good as his father, that Canning was not as good as Pitt, that Peel was not as good as Canning, or Gladstone as Peel or Asquith as Gladstone. Such constant digression is biologically improbable. But even with that warning, I do not think that Messrs Howe, Lawson, Parkinson, Baker and Hurd rank as outstanding political personalities comparable with the Asquith, Baldwin or Attlee lists. Nor could they match the Asquith list as men of distinction outside politics.

To some substantial extent this goes with the dominant position within the Government of the present Prime Minister. She has certainly not left ministers as secure in their offices as did Gladstone or Baldwin. Neither has she been as addicted to the annual gymkhana of a reshuffle, almost for its own sake, as was Wilson. But she has nonetheless wrought great changes of personnel in her nine years. It is remarkable that there is now no member of the Cabinet, other than herself, who has the job that he had at the beginning of her term, and there are only three of them (out of twenty) who were in the Cabinet at all in 1979. In addition, her changes have had far more of a general purpose than did those of Asquith or Attlee. They have not been primarily made on grounds of individual competence. They have been steadily directed to shifting the balance of ideology, or perhaps even more of amenability, within the Cabinet.

As a result of these various factors, she must be counted the most dominating Prime Minister within her Government of any of the four. Her control over the House of Commons I would regard as much more dependent upon the serried majorities she has had behind her than upon any special parliamentary skill. Her combative belief in her own rightness ensures that she is rarely discomfited and never overwhelmed. But she brings no special qualities of persuasiveness or debating skill which enable her to move minds where others would fail. Even an unsuccessful Prime Minister like Eden had, in my view, more capacity to do this than she has. And the serried majorities are a direct function of having a split opposition with a voting system designed only for two parties. She has never exercised any special command over a medium of communication as Baldwin did in the early days of sound broadcasting, and for much of her 13 years as Conservative leader, both before and after 1979, she has been below rather than above her party's poll rating.

Her stamp upon every aspect of her Government's policy, on the other hand, is incomparably greater than that of any of my other three Prime Ministers. There is no question of her reserving herself only for major constitutional issues. Indeed, I doubt if she has much sense of what is a constitutional issue and what is not. There is no subordinate minister who has been able to sustain an area of prerogative. It is impossible to imagine her being asked for advice, and saying to Geoffrey Howe, as Baldwin said to Austen Chamberlain, 'but *you* are Foreign Secretary'. She is equally intrusive in the military, economic, industrial, social security, Commonwealth and law and order aspects of her Government's policy. She seeks no respite from politics in the sense that Asquith, Baldwin and Attlee did. Her impact is necessarily immense by virtue of her determination and longevity in office. She will have reduced the influence of the Cabinet: if she has improved Britain's influence in the world, many would take that as more than a fair exchange. It is, however, early days to judge that.

Over the period I have been considering, the scope of government has obviously increased enormously. Public expenditure has gone up from approximately £170 million sterling (perhaps £5 billion in present day values) to about 900 times that in money terms and 30 times as much in real terms. Great new departments, like the Department of Health and Social Security, have sprung up with an entirely different pattern of ministerial duties from anything remotely prevailing before 1914. But I do not think that the essential role of the Prime Minister has changed as much as this might lead one to believe. The function of a conductor is not greatly altered by introducing new instruments into the orchestra.

The style is much more a product of a man or a woman than it is of the epoch. I would in no way exclude a reversion in the future to the calmer habits, if not of Asquith, at least of Attlee. President Reagan shows that modern government need not be too strenuous. What I think has changed permanently, however, is the necessary involvement of the head of the Government of Britain or any other comparable country in external affairs. The interdependent world, not to mention the European Community, has changed that for good. The calm insularity of Asquith and Baldwin, even to some extent that of Attlee, has gone for ever.

Presidents and Prime Ministers
Over Four Decades*

The United States

One of the most surprising features of the history of this century was the 1917 entry of America into the European War. The pressures were much less compelling than in 1941. For this there were a variety of reasons. 1914–18 was a European and not a world war. The United States had only recently and hesitantly become a world power of the first order. The notorious acts of maritime provocation in the Atlantic were relatively minor. The German influence in the United States was strong and recent. Britain and France would not necessarily have lost without America. It was a peculiarly disagreeable war in which to participate. And the menace of Kaiserism was of an altogether different and lesser order than that of Nazism.

Yet it all happened with a curious ease. It was a great contrast with the unsteady and tantalizing advance to involvement, against a background of European catastrophe, of 1939-41. Franklin Roosevelt had many qualities which Woodrow Wilson lacked, but as a resolute interventionist, Woodrow Wilson was in a different class. As a strategist he was not tested. He had no global choices to make. His wartime role was the simple and demanding one of creating the national will and machinery to mobilise an army of a force unprecedented in American history, to send it to a single theatre, and there to allow General Pershing to use it, not only to fight against the Germans, but still more to intimidate them by the sense of limitless resources behind him. At the same time

*This essay is based on two Chichele lectures given in the University of Oxford in early 1973.

217

Wilson provided uplift for the nation and for the world. Some were cynical, both at home and abroad. In 1916 he had one of the narrower victories of American history (in the electoral college it was 277 to 254, which, for once, almost exactly reflected the popular vote). Lloyd George at about the same time wrote: 'I know that American politician. He has no international conscience. He thinks of nothing but the ticket.' Whatever else Woodrow Wilston was he was not a machine politician. Tammany and most of the other big city organisations had worked very hard against him and for Champ Clark whom he had only beaten on the 46th ballot at the 1912 Baltimore Convention.

Wilson provided forthright crusading war leadership for the United States and inspiration for the world. When he came to Europe at the end of 1918 he was greeted as a saviour, almost a god. At Dover, in a somewhat un–English (and unseasonal) display, schoolgirls were organised to strew roses in his path. Keynes wrote of the visit: 'When President Wilson left Washington he enjoyed a prestige and moral influence throughout the world unequalled in history. His bold and measured words carried to the peoples of Europe above and beyond the voices of their own politicians . . . Never had a philosopher held such weapons wherewith to bind the princes of the world. How the peoples of the European capitals pressed upon the President! With what curiosity, anxiety and hope we sought a glimpse of the features and bearing of the man of destiny who, coming from the West, was to bring healing to the wounds of the ancient parent of his civilisation and lay for us the foundations of the future.'

But in Paris it was 'the princes' - if Clemenceau and Lloyd George can be so described - who did more binding of the phi-losopher rather than *vice versa*. A good deal of the gloss wore off. Still more important, his authority declined at home. No previous President had ever left the United States. Wilson was in Europe for six months, with a brief fortnight's return in the middle. No subsequent President has ever been away for more than a few weeks. When he got back he found the League of Nations sentiment crumbling, and the Senate (with a Republican majority since 1918) organising itself under Henry Cabot Lodge for resistance to rati-fication. Wilson responded with a massive crusading tour. In late September, after 34 major speeches and endless whistle-stops, he collapsed in Colorado and was forced to abandon the crusade.

On October 2nd, back in Washington, he suffered a major stroke and was incapacitated for the remaining 18 months of his presidency. From his sick-bed he resisted compromise with the Senate and announced that the election of 1920 was to be 'a great and solemn referendum'. He tied the half reluctant Democratic Party to the issue of the League.

Wilson's eruption on to the world scene had been remarkable. No other president since Lincoln, with the possible exception of Theodore Roosevelt, and that more because of the immature extravagance of his personality than because of his policy, had aroused much interest in Europe. Rutherford B. Hayes or Chester A. Arthur meant little more to Gladstone or Disraeli than did the chief of some savage tribe on the borders of the Empire. And American political practices appeared about as remote and obscure as the religious behaviour of the Mahdi, as something regarded by most otherwise well-informed people as simply not worthy of serious study, a mixture of the squalid and the comic. Wilson arose for a brief period like a saint who had been mysteriously wafted up out of the poker rooms. Then he disappeared almost in a puff of smoke. Teapot Dome and other scandals replaced the moral imperatives of the philosopher king, and Europe felt it had been right after all in its detached and superior view of American politics.

The Atlantic was very wide indeed during the Twenties. This was true in all senses. It was so in the literal sense that it still took a very long time to get across. Apart from Lindbergh and a handful of others, nobody did it in less than five days. Very few, except those who were both rich and under-occupied, did it at all frequently. The vast majority, including leading politicians on both sides of the ocean, never crossed it at all. As a result, the world of the speakeasies, of Al Capone, and indeed of Al Smith, was very remote from London or Paris. The movies in a sense accentuated rather reduced the remoteness. The world they portrayed to us was as vivid but unreal as a Verdi opera. Scott Fitzgerald was something of a bridge, but his whole approach to Americans in Europe, with its sense of breathless excitement about their being there at all, showed how wide the span had to be. And Washington seemed even more remote than New York. (It then seemed fairly remote to most Americans, it must be added. It still had much of the atmosphere of a village in a swamp, and British diplomats had only just ceased to draw an unhealthy climate allowance.)

The first President to preside over this withdrawal into 'normalcy' weak government and business dominance, was Warren Gamaliel Harding. He was a man of striking good looks and even more strikingly limited intellect. He had been Senator from Ohio for six years. He was the only Senator to be elected to the Presidency between Benjamin Harrison (in 1888) and John F. Kennedy (in 1960), but his geographical provenance was a help. He was Ohio's sixth President, a record surpassed only by Virginia (with heavy front-end loading) and New York. He emerged as a safe conservative choice after the first four ballots had been deadlocked between two more prominent candidates. He was nominated on the tenth.

Perhaps wisely in view of his limitations, he decided to imitate McKinley and fight a 'front porch' campaign. He hardly moved from Marion, Ohio. His opponent James M. Cox, the Governor of his own state, assisted as a running mate by the then athletic and loose-limbed Franklin D. Roosevelt, fought far more vigorously. Their activity was as relentless as it was ineffective. Woodrow Wilson's 'great and solemn referendum' turned into a landslide victory, the greatest since the electoral college had become vestigial, for Harding, isolation and conservative finance.

Harding made two highly respectable appointments to his Cabinet, Charles Evans Hughes, the Republican candidate of 1916 as Secretary of State, and Herbert Hoover, the world's greatest mining engineer who turned down a guaranteed life salary of half a million 1920 dollars in order to accept, as Secretary of Commerce. He also made a third which seemed even more respectable than the other two. Andrew Mellon, the Pittsburg banker and industrialist, was in many ways the most admired American of the Twenties. He was also described as 'the greatest Secretary of the Treasury since Alexander Hamilton'. Over eight years he carried through a sustained policy of tax reduction, and yet, by holding Federal expenditure at about $3 billion (barely 3% of the national income) he constantly redeemed debt. Personal taxes on an income of $50,000 were brought as low as $1000. But his own rate of progress was not enough for himself. He may or may not have been the greatest Secretary of the Treasury since Hamilton, but he was certainly the only one to be subsequently arraigned for the non-payment of personal tax (to the extent of $3 million) and escaped only by the ingenious device of getting Duveen, the great picture dealer, to testify that his interest was solely to bequeath a still greater art collection to the nation.

Harding's other Cabinet appointments were less puritanical. His Secretary of the Interior, his Postmaster General and his Attorney-General were all involved in a series of scandals of which the disposal of the Teapot Dome oil reserve was only the crowning edifice. Harding himself was not involved. But he had appointed those who were and had entertained them frequently in a White House to which (having welcomed prohibition) he gave the style of a poker-playing bar parlour. In the summer of 1923 when the scandals began to erupt, Harding, accompanied by a large entourage, set off for an extended rail and sea tour of the West and Alaska. While he was away his private intelligence made clear to him the morass of corruption over which he had been presiding and the imminence of publicity. He responded with a nervous semi-collapse accompanied by insatiable bridge-playing. Both on the train and in the ship he played from breakfast to midnight, the other players sustaining themselves by operating in shifts. When he got back to San Francisco the collapse became complete and physical. He died suddenly on August 2nd. Much of the nation was stunned with grief. As his train made its long return to Washington he was given a hero's homage.

His Vice-President was Calvin Coolidge, a Vermont farmer's son who had become Governor of Massachusetts and built much of his political reputation upon taciturnity. He was a quite different stamp of man from Harding. He was personally austere, with a passion, not for making money, but for avoiding spending it. When he left the White House he returned to a rented $40 a month half of a house in Northampton, Massachusetts. He disapproved of most of the manifestations of the great stock market boom over which he presided, but he believed it would be far exceeding his duty as President to say so. His favourite occupation was, almost literally, doing nothing. He slept several times during the course of a normal day, and always went to bed early. He told an agitated Senator that 'four-fifths of all our troubles in this life would disappear if we would only sit down and keep still'. He was known as the 'puritan in Babylon', but he continued with most of Harding's policies as well as retaining those of his Cabinet officers who were not otherwise engaged as a result of decisions of the Federal courts. He was also known as the 'prince of laissez-faire'.

'Economy is idealism in its most practical form' was one of his more notable aphorisms.

In 1924 he was comfortably re-elected – although not quite so triumphantly as Harding had been – under the slogan 'keep cool with Coolidge'. There was little danger of doing anything else. He had the advantage of being opposed by a deeply divided Democratic Party which had taken three weeks and 103 ballots at its New York Convention to choose a lacklustre, right-wing, compromise candidate in the shape of John W. Davis. (The unprecedented length of the proceedings eventually led the leader of one of the New England delegations to deliver to his followers one of the starkest of political ultimata. 'Gentleman', he said, 'we have a simple choice: either we move to a more liberal candidate or to a cheaper hotel'.) Coolidge also had to contend with La Follette as a Progressive candidate. In 1912 such an intervention has been fatal to Republican chances, but La Follette was not Theodore Roosevelt.

As the next election approached Coolidge vouchsafed his own special variant of a possible candidate's enigmatic pronouncement. 'I do not choose to run for President in 1928', he said. It was never quite certain whether or not he wanted someone else to choose for him, but as Hoover was successfully busy picking up convention votes no-one put the issue to the test, and Coolidge retired to Northampton.

Throughout the Harding-Coolidge era there had been very few stresses within the United States Government. The traditional conflict between the President and the Congress was largely in abeyance. None of the early scandals impaired the Republican control of both Houses. The bull market counted for more than Teapot Dome. And neither of the Presidents asked for very much from Congress. They were low spenders and sparse initiators of legislation. Within the Cabinet initiatives were occasionally taken. Kellogg, who succeeded Hughes as Secretary of State in 1925, achieved the pact which bore his name and that of Briand. And Hoover was constantly searching around for things to do. Coolidge mostly stopped him, referring to him sharply as 'the wonder boy' or 'the miracle worker', but he nonetheless did enough to increase the reputation he had already acquired as Food and then European Relief Administrator under Wilson. As later with Eisenhower, there had been doubts about Hoover's party affiliations. Franklin Roosevelt, who was a close friend at the end of the First World

War, canvassed Hoover's name as a possible Democratic candidate for 1920. 'There could not be a better President', he said. It soon became clear however that Hoover was neither a Democrat nor a non-partisan, but a dedicated Republican. As the end of Coolidge's term drew on he rapidly acquired presidential momentum. The party professionals were against him. He had never made any obeisance to them, he was still a little tarred with the old Wilson brush, and he had supported the League of Nations. But the popular demand for him was considerable. There was no long drawn-out Convention struggle such as was then common. He was the first non-incumbent to be nominated on the first ballot for decades. He was also, apart from Taft, the only Cabinet officer to succeed direct to the presidency since John Quincy Adams in 1825. His election was as great a triumph as his nomination. He was a dull speaker but his message was what people wanted to hear, 'A chicken in every pot and two cars in every garage' was not in 1928 the sour joke which it had become a couple of years later. Al Smith did not have a chance. He had been a highly successful Governor of New York, but he was slaughtered by Protestant middle America. He was seen as a Papist, a 'wet' (probably a drunk too), and the representative of the big-city rabble, who wanted to corrupt innocent, home-loving, individualistic America. Hoover won in a landslide. Ironically, such were the rigid traditions of American politics, only a few of the Southern states from the region in which Smith was most distrusted, held firm for the Democrats.

In his inaugural address Hoover announced: 'I have no fears for the future of our country. It is bright with hope.' Seven months later came the stock market crash, and from then on throughout the rest of his term false dawns merely heralded further plunges into still deeper depression until industrial output was down to 56% of its 1928 level, unemployment was up to nearly 20 million, and half the banks had closed their doors. Unlike his predecessor, Hoover did not believe in doing nothing. 'The Great Engineer' was an activist, too much so indeed for Andrew Mellon, who complained that his background made him want 'everything to go in a straight line and everyone to come up to the line'. His speciality had been dealing with sick companies. He would work out the solution in great detail during his long journeys about the world, and then apply it with efficiency and expedition. He never had to bother much about explaining what he was doing or why. It was the results which counted. But with the United States he could not get results, although he took a number of sensible and even bold measures. His failure – and it was one on the scale of tragedy – was his total inability to communicate, to give confidence or hope. He lived a most extraordinary life. He worked 12 or 14 hours a day, interspersed only by his appearances at the formal meals, rarely less than 24 at dinner, never fewer than seven courses, but all dry, of course, which were a constant feature of his White House régime. Mostly he sat through these meals in silence, before hurrying back to more detailed paperwork. Indeed he rarely spoke to anyone, unless it was administratively necessary. Even more rarely did he leave the White House.

But he did not lose the taste for office. He wanted to win again in 1932, and believed that he could do so. His confidence was increased by the news at the end of June that Governor Roosevelt had been nominated at the Democratic Convention in Chicago. Hoover thought him much the easiest candidate to beat. He was wrong, but he was not alone. The general view of informed opinion at the time was that Roosevelt was rather a lightweight. 'He is a pleasant man who, without any important qualifications for the office, would very much like to be President', Walter Lippmann wrote. He added, for good measure, that Roosevelt had 'neither a firm grip on public affairs, nor very strong convictions'. 'There is no bedrock in him. He is all clay and no granite', was another fairly typical contemporary comment.

The Convention itself was not overly enthusiastic. Roosevelt started with a majority, but the Democrats still required a two-thirds vote for nomination, and he stuck badly for several ballots. It even required some strong-arm work from Huey Long to keep Roosevelt's deep-South support from eroding at this stage. The balance was then tipped in his favour more by the fear of another deadlock than by any positive feeling. Even his acceptance speech, the first ever delivered at a convention itself, was only moderately received, and was indeed very much all things to all men.

But Roosevelt had one invaluable quality for the circumstances. He exuded confidence; and he knew every trick of communicating it to the public. He was the almost exact antithesis of Hoover. The picture of his drive from the airport to the convention hall in Chicago was worth much more than what he said there. 'As he rode', so it was described, 'he grinned and waved his hands

224

and tossed his great leonine head with laughter that was returned by the people on the sidewalks.' That was quite a feat in 1932. He was good under pressure. He did not turn in upon himself in a crisis. Justice Oliver Wendell Holmes made a far more perceptive remark about him than Walter Lippmann had done. 'A second-class intellect', he said, 'but a first-class temperament.'

He won just about as great a victory as Hoover had achieved four years before, and took over in the bleak spring of 1933. No one knew clearly what he was going to do. His campaign had not given much indication. Most of the time he had been against Hoover because he did nothing, but he had also attacked him for being too spendthrift. Sometimes he had vaguely mentioned a new world order, but at others he suggested that Hoover was kind to every country but his own. Nor did his Cabinet appointments give much guide. They embraced Democrats and Republicans, conservatives and liberals, inflationists and hard money men, internationalists and mild nationalists. It was not a particularly distinguished cabinet. Cordell Hull and Harold Ickes, Frances Perkins and Henry Wallace became the longest-lasting. The last three probably became the closest to the President. On matters of major policy he never took much notice of any of them. His own official family or 'brain trust' was somewhat more coherent, but even here there were a lot of differences and tensions. Roosevelt liked the tensions. Quarrels amongst his assistants were always a source of amusement rather than of agitation to him. His method of administration was, to put it at its best, creative rather than tidy. He enjoyed giving one job to two or three different people. Thus he could keep his options open, choose between the results, and, if necessary, assuage wounded feelings by the exercise of his private charm, dazzling but sometimes a little self-conscious.

So, resonantly in public, a little more hesitantly in private, the great presidency began. The next twelve years undoubtedly marked the decisive stage in the evolution of the United States to full world power. Washington changed from being a southern town to a position as near to the political capital of the world as has ever been occupied by any city since the fall of imperial Rome. The President himself became the undisputed captain of the West.

There was a great deal of happenstance about how this all occurred. The 1932 campaign was as domestic as any in American history. The first inaugural contained plenty of vision for the United States, but little for the world. And Roosevelt's first effective intervention on the international scene was to break up the World Economic Conference of 1933 rather than agree to a system of mutually agreed currency parities. This may have been good sense for the dollar and the US economy, but it certainly was not signally co-operative. The decisive embroilment of America happened rather than was planned. But this was a characteristic of the style of the Administration. A great deal was done, but not very frequently in accordance with any announced design. As a strategist Roosevelt's performance can easily be criticised. But as an internationally acceptable representative of America's power and good intentions he could not easily have been bettered.

Domestically, advance was equally subject to improvisation. Again there is room for doubt about the efficacy of the anti-depression measures and the cohesion of the programme. There were periods of energy and periods when the President seemed to be lost in a finessing lethargy. There were major political defeats, as with the plan for reforming the Supreme Court, and there were great electoral victories. But what is certainly the case is that Roosevelt changed the nature of American government. He shifted power from the states to Washington - which led after a time-lag to a major tilt from Governors' mansions to the Senate as a breeding ground for presidential candidates - and he destroyed the old habit of non-intervention in economic affairs. Whether he had any clear philosophy of what he was doing is doubtful. Although accepted in history as the great practical exponent of Keynesianism, he certainly never read the *General Theory* and at their one meeting in the Thirties, found Maynard Keynes himself 'obtruse and mathematical'.

Roosevelt's radicalism on a whole range of social and economic questions was far from clear-cut, much less indeed so than that of his formidable wife. His views, like his personality, were kaleidoscopic. Vastly different as were their physiques and backgrounds, there was a strong similarity with Lloyd George. He loved dishing his opponents and winning elections, as well as shocking his upper-class Dutchess County neighbours. But there was also a great deal of the Hudson Valley squire about him. His rôles sometimes changed but his favourite was that of the politician who could communicate with the people. This quality of communication enabled him to put together, maintain over four elections, and bequeath reasonably

226

intact to his successor, the remarkable Democratic coalition of the South, the Northern city machines with their control over ethnic votes, the liberal intellectuals, the blacks, and even a sizeable slice of the farm vote. He shed individuals on the way, including most notably James A. Farley, who had been crucial to his nomination and first election, but his electoral hold was inexorable. 1936 was even better than 1932, and this high water mark could not again be reached. But 1940 and 1944 – over 4 to 1 in the electoral college on each occasion – were by normal standards decisive victories. The third term, highly controversial in itself, and widely debated across the nation, and even for a time in Roosevelt's own mind, can easily be justified, even though it has subsequently been ensured by constitutional amendment that no president can ever repeat Roosevelt's decision. The fourth – accepted much more easily, the barrier had been broken – was almost certainly a mistake. The war was already effectively won, and even if extreme views of the evil of Yalta are rejected, Roosevelt was too ill and too tired to contribute much to the peace.

Strong partisans of President Truman may argue that the fourth term's main retrospective justification was that it made possible his presidency. It would certainly not have occurred otherwise. And there have been plenty of such partisans, many in high places. Dean Acheson, for instance, never hesitated in his view that Truman was incomparably more distinguished a president than Roosevelt and a more admirable man too. This may have had something to do with the fact that Truman allowed Acheson to have his way in policy-making far more than Roosevelt had ever done. There is indeed a certain similarity between the attitude of the internationally-minded Eastern policy establishment to Truman and that of the Foreign Office to Ernest Bevin. Both these statesmen were utterly different from their champions, but pursued with great toughness rugged policies with which these champions agreed, and defended with vigour, not only the policies, but those who helped them to be carried out.

Truman as an individual and in his way of life was far more like a late nineteenth-century president than anyone else who has been in the White House for the past half century and more. He did not come of a particularly poor background, less so than Johnson or Nixon, but went bankrupt as a haberdasher in the late

1920s, and, although he substantially improved his income, never subsequently changed his tastes and manner. Lyndon Johnson, though equally and perhaps more self-consciously a product of underprivileged America, was more Bonapartist. Truman was a machine politician, but an honest one. He came to office as the least internationally known chief executive of the past half century. But in many ways he acted more decisively in world affairs than Roosevelt had done. He laid down the lines of American foreign policy commitment for a generation. He ensured that, so far from there being a post-war recoil as from Woodrow Wilson's internationalism, there was a greater overseas United States commitment, politically, militarily, economically, than ever before.

Domestically, his performance was much more uneven. He experienced the most extraordinary fluctuations in popular support, which resulted in periods of minimal authority. His first eighteen months were a near disaster. He alienated almost every significant segment of opinion. His party begged him to keep as far away as possible from the 1946 Congressional campaign, but this abstinence did not prevent both Houses going solidly Republican. He then swung to the left and made a substantial come-back by proposing progressive measures and belabouring the Congress for turning them down. Even so, by 1948, half the liberals thought they would prefer General Eisenhower as *Democratic* candidate. Eisenhower was not available. Truman bounced back and won his wholly unexpected victory over Dewey. His second term involved further frustrations from the Congress, which again went Republican in 1950, some unpleasant whiffs of political scandal, and a general feeling that the Democrats had been in power too long. In the 1952 campaign Stevenson, deeply offending Truman in the process, thought it necessary to disassociate himself as much as possible from the Administration. Truman's main domestic achievement was to fight a defensive action for the preservation of the New Deal. By staving off retreat for nearly a decade he made it much more an accepted part of American peace-time life than was the case in 1945. Even so, and in spite of Dean Acheson, I do not think he can be compared to Roosevelt. He did some things nobly, but he did not have the stature or persuasive skill of Roosevelt which, even if sometimes devious, were necessary to transmogrify the rôle of the American Government, both at home and abroad, which process occurred between 1933 and 1945.

The 1950s were a decade of the moderate right throughout the Western world. This was true of Britain, of Germany and of the United States. General Eisenhower presided benignly over it. He was not a reactionary, but he was certainly not a radical. He was not indeed much of a politician at all, subject to the one very important qualification that he had a supreme gift of vote-getting. Aldai Stevenson's high-minded liberalism twice battled in vain against Eisenhower's confidence-giving, complacent folksiness. The general's constituency was much the same as President Nixon's in 1972 and not very different from that of Harding, Coolidge and Hoover in the Twenties. But he responded to it more moderately than President Nixon was to do, more responsibly than Harding and Coolidge had done, and more sensitively than Hoover. There were of course substantial blemishes. Eisenhower's record on McCarthyism was at best supine. He allowed the evil genius of that half-demented Senator to poison the American atmosphere for a quinquennium and to inflict permanent damage on the State Department. And when the evil was exorcised it was no thanks to Eisenhower. Paradoxically, while allowing the Department to be undermined, he placed exceptional reliance upon his Secretary of State. Foster Dulles was allowed to run United States foreign policy in a way that no previous Secretary had done since that policy became of major world importance. He was not America's most inspiring or tactful ambassador-at-large. But Eisenhower kept just enough control to make Dulles's 'brinkmanship' more of a phrase than a real danger. The world survived the 1950s and American leadership survived with it, but with little sense of enthusiasm or constructive purpose. By 1960 America was just ready for change, and the world was more than ready.

Britain

In Britain the period from 1918 to 1960 spanned nine premierships two more than the American presidencies of the period. It ran from mid-Lloyd George to mid-Macmillan. It spanned the complacency and retreat of the Twenties and Thirties, the remarkable but exhausting resurgence of the war years, and the first phase of the efforts, often faltering and uneven, to adjust the country to the circumstances of the post-imperial world. It saw politics become more democratic and more rigid, and deference replaced by the demanding expectations and sometimes cynical judgments of a mass-consumption society.

The quintessential figure of the first phase was Stanley Baldwin. His political career was highly symmetrical and slipped into the inter-war years like a hand into a well-made but loosely fitting glove. He became a member of the Cabinet two years and four months after Armistice Day, and handed over power, wholly voluntarily and with enthusiasm for retirement, two years and three months before September 1939. He first became Prime Minister at the suitably median age of 55, the same as Asquith, two years older than Peel at the start of his great ministry. He gave up within a month of his 70th birthday. He even timed his retirement, although it turned to ashes in his mouth, to last almost exactly ten years. He was nervous but not febrile. There was a sense of indolent order about his life.

What was not in accordance with an established pattern was the extraordinary speed of Baldwin's rise to eminence in 1922-3. In the summer of 1922 he was still a rather obscure President of the Board of Trade. Within three months he had played the major rôle in the destruction of the Coalition and the permanent exclusion from office of the most famous statesman in the world, the man who had won the war, who bewitched most of his colleagues, and dazzled the European conferences of the aftermath. Baldwin made himself by destroying Lloyd George, by setting, as he saw it, his honest pedestrianism against the tinsel and meretricious glitter of the Coalition. Thereafter he was to some extent a happy and voluntary prisoner of this provenance. He set himself self-consciously to be the antithesis of Lloyd George. His main rule for his style of government was to think of what Lloyd George did and to do the reverse.

Lloyd George loved performing on the European stage. He responded to the excitement and novelty of a backcloth. He liked the opportunity to refresh his matchless powers of negotiation and individual persuasiveness by exercising them upon new people, although there was often more footwork than policy in his performances. Baldwin took no such pleasure. In the whole course of his career he held only one negotiating meeting with a foreign statesman. He so disliked that 1923 encounter with M. Poincaré that he never tried again. As a result his Foreign Secretaries could not complain of interference. In his main Government Austen Chamberlain, although as an ex-Coalitionist far from being a solid Baldwin man, was left almost entirely free to pursue his generally pro-French policy. The same independence was given to Churchill, another ex-Coalitionist, at the Treasury.

It was not so much a question of Baldwin's being lazy, although he was moderately so. It was more that he believed in concentrating upon day-to-day issues of government, keeping the administration upon as even a keel as possible, and either leaving the longer-term issues alone, or allowing them to be settled by the more important departmental ministers, if they had the will. Thus the apparent successes with which his name is most closely associated – the handling of the General Strike and the Abdication – were issues, particularly in the latter case, which arose casually and had to be handled by instinct and improvisation. To cultivate his sensitivity for 'nudging' solutions he believed in keeping in the closest touch with parliamentary opinion. He spent more time in the House of Commons than any other Prime Minister of this century. He was always available for little chats, both with his own supporters and with Opposition members. He spent endless hours sitting on the Treasury Bench, half listening to debates, or rather watching the men, and half reading bare details about them in the familiar pages of Dod's Parliamentary Companion. This gave him a considerable House of Commons mastery. Most Prime Ministers, at least until they begin to outstay their welcome, achieve a parliamentary dominance. But most use it only for the negative purpose of repelling attacks upon their actions and policies. Baldwin, unusually, used it to do more. He did not so much win debates as seduce and mould parliamentary opinion – often with dangerous results.

As a communicator he was highly professional. He was the first Prime Minister to whom the wireless was available. He mastered it with skill and application. He devoted much of his attention to a rather passive form of political management. Yet he was n without courage, even rashness. As an untried Prime Mini he lurched into Protection and the unnecessary and unsuy a election of 1923. Rarely if ever has a party leader thrownd the majority so casually. Yet in a longer-term sense it workeuously ghost of a Coalition revival which had haunted him; st Labour turned the awkward corner (for a Conservative) o

Government; and it led on to the solid Tory majority of 1924. Then in 1929-31 he was stubbornly moderate over India, sustained the combined onslaughts of Churchill, Beaverbrook and Rothermere, found his leadership more endangered than anyone since Balfour, waited until he had got to the line he had to defend, and then hit back with a skill which was almost vicious.

His governing thoughts were to maintain effective power, to assuage the industrial conflict while making sure that his own side won, and comfortably to channel the Labour Party into the mainstream of British politics. In the first objective he was more than adequately successful. He held office for eleven out of the fourteen years of his leadership. His fault towards the end was to set too high a store by power, although not by place, for he served uncomplainingly under MacDonald for four years. I doubt if the result of the 1935 election was ever in serious doubt. And his somewhat melodramatic confession that he had to conceal the truth about Britain's defence weakness in order to win it has always seemed to me unconvincing; but if true it deserved to be as damaging as it proved to be.

His record on industrial conflict is more difficult to appraise. He postponed the General Strike. He defeated it. He ground the miners into the dust. He encouraged the Mond–Turner climate which gradually emerged thereafter. Arguably he got the result he wanted: a transition from the semi-revolutionary strikes of the Twenties to the TUC of Bevin and Citrine in the Thirties. His handling of the political Labour Party, by which he always set great store, was less successful. No one could fault his personal relations with individual Labour members. But his strategy was less sure. He never much feared or disliked Ramsay MacDonald. He saw him as infinitely preferable to Lloyd George. He was as satisfactory a Labour leader as Baldwin could have hoped for; misty, moderate, elevating, not very strong on administration. That being so, he should have wanted to keep him exactly where he was, leader of the Labour Party, and of a reasonably to u Labour Party. He allowed his reaction to the 1931 crisis the ba his. To solve a temporary difficulty Baldwin allowed himself of British politics to be seriously upset. He gave majority ibility without the first place, with the top-heavy driven tempo ational Government, and with a Labour Party extremism by the magnitude of its defeat.

232

The result was a sterile decade of dismal politics. It was Baldwin's biggest error.

When Baldwin went Neville Chamberlain was the automatic successor. At 67 he hardly brought a breath of youth, but he appeared to many to bring an infusion of efficiency. Cabinet business was much more expeditiously despatched, and the old immunity of the major departments from Downing Street interference was rudely shattered. Chamberlain came to the top job after a Treasury tenure so long that he had been able to work through a substantial number of Dickens titles (*Bleak House, Great Expectations* etc) as the themes of his successive Budgets. Perhaps because of the natural attraction of the unfamiliar it was however to the Foreign Office that he turned his primary attention. The first result, eight months later, was the resignation of Anthony Eden. Eden was replaced by the more accommodating Halifax, and major British foreign policy came to be made much more in Downing Street than in the Foreign Office. Eventually Halifax made a mild revolt, but for the first year at least the power relationship was well summed up by Halifax seeing Chamberlain off to Berchtesgarten with a dignified and uncomplaining wave. The results were hardly inspiring.

Nevertheless Chamberlain's powers of stubborn, uncompromising leadership should not be underestimated. His enemies hated him, far more than they had done Baldwin. But he also, curiously, inspired a greater degree of personal devotion, and even admiration, amongst his followers. He never attempted to cosset his opponents. His self-righteousness made him contemptuous of them, and his narrow-sighted honesty made him unwilling to conceal it. He had no gift of persuasive speech. Nevertheless, he got his way on all major policy issues and he could almost certainly have won a decisive election victory in the autumn of 1938. His nemesis arose from the fact that he was wrong, and, as his policies were clear-cut, demonstrably so. He was a harsh epilogue to the Baldwin era, just as Bonar Law had been a bleak prologue.

Churchill both acceded to the Premiership and lived through most of his first period of supreme office in such exceptional circumstances that it is difficult to apply normal criteria to his leadership. It was by any standards a remarkable surge to power. He had been out of office, with his own party in for most of the period, for just over ten years, from the age of 54 to 64. Only $3^1/_2$

years before he became Prime Minister, at the time of the Abdication, he had appeared one of the most isolated and discredited figures in the House of Commons. Even at the moment of crisis his accession had been by no means a foregone conclusion.

Once in, Churchill's power was great yet curiously vulnerable. He had no organised opposition in the House of Commons to worry about. An election he occasionally used as a threat, but as a worry to him it was far off over several ranges of hills. He had a major task with public opinion: but it was to inspire it to resistance to the enemy rather than to mould it for political purposes. His real problem after the first year or so was in Parliament, even without any formal opposition. His majority on an issue of confidence was never in doubt. But, just because his nominal position was one of overwhelming all-party support, so any sizeable revolt was disproportionately damaging. In terms of reality he took over at the bottom, in a desperate position. But in parliamentary terms he was like a share floated at the top of a bull market. Starting with almost unanimous support there was only one way which he could go, and that was down. Hostile votes therefore counted for more than they would have done with a regular and therefore innocuous pattern of party voting. There was always the memory that what had destroyed Chamberlain and made Churchill Prime Minister was not a defeat in the House of Commons but a 'victory' by 280 to 200, with less than a third of the membership voting against the Government. Churchill was careful never to get near to such a 'victory'. One of his motives in insisting on becoming Leader of the Conservative Party after Chamberlain's death, even though it marginally and temporarily weakened his national position, was to guard against this by giving himself control over the whips and the party machinery. (Another was to avoid a Lloyd George-like position after the end of the war; but there is clearly room for argument as to which of the two was left more stranded by victory.)

Churchill never had any real trouble (until 1945) with the party partnership of the coalition. There were strains, almost entirely over domestic affairs - the Beveridge report, coal rationing - but little affecting the central direction of the war. He was at least as well-served by Attlee as Lloyd George had been by Bonar Law. The only two ministers who on occasion challenged the central direction were Beaverbrook and Cripps, neither of whom at the time – Beaverbrook hardly at any time – had party anchors. Beaverbrook was not a serious danger, partly because he was not really a serious man and partly because he was much subject to late-night influence by Churchill. Cripps was more serious, and at the beginning of 1942 achieved briefly and rather fortuitously a strong national popularity, amounting almost to a competitive pole of power. Churchill corralled him with skill. And Cripps played his hand, which was in any event shaky, in too gentlemanly a way. He offered a challenge to the organisation of the War Cabinet which was not in substance very different from that which Lloyd George offered to Asquith. But he did it privately and allowed the issue to be postponed until after the Battle of Alamein, victory in which (although not wholly foreseeable) destroyed his challenge. Cripps wanted a small War Cabinet, independent of the Chiefs of Staff, to make strategic decisions. Churchill wished to keep the existing organisation, by which he made the decisions, nominally endorsed by others – Attlee, Anderson, Eden – who were engrossed in strategically non-central work.

Despite these occasional checks and challenges Churchill's power was far greater than Lloyd George's between 1916 and 1918. Lloyd George had no effective control over the generals, and was not therefore in full command of strategy. Churchill had no such problem. There was no comparable power of a military establishment, no general who could not be moved if he lost the Prime Minister's confidence. Balancing this was the fact that Churchill had to subordinate himself more to his principal ally than did Lloyd George. In World War I Britain and France needed each other equally. In World War II Britain needed America more than America needed Britain. One of the most notable acts of self-discipline which Churchill had to impose upon himself – in a not notably self-disciplined life – was never to quarrel with Roosevelt. In Britain, however, the concentration of power in a single pair of welcoming hands was greater than it had ever been before.

The transition to Attlee was correspondingly abrupt. Massive changes in the whole framework of politics took place within a fortnight. The shift of parliamentary power was greater than on any occasion, other than in 1906, in the past 140 years. But this was by no means all. Britain's hour of perilous but spectacular glory was over. The inheritance was bleak. Our nominal membership of the triumvirate of world power was guaranteed by our recent record. But it was as unsustainable as it was temporarily incontestible. The temporary reconciliation of these two facts was one of the most awkward processes in our history. In addition, on a lower level, there was the reversion to party politics, and to a normal system of Cabinet Government under a Prime Minister who, in the sharpest possible contrast with his predecesor, was a less famous figure than several of his ministers.

It is always tempting to make a comparison between Attlee and Campbell-Bannerman. Yet this can easily be pushed too far. They shared certain speaking characteristics. Neither could make an inspirational appeal, either in the House of Commons or in the country. But they both developed an effective balloon-pricking technique for dealing with their principal opponents. Attlee had much tougher intellectual fibre than Bannerman. He ran his Government with much greater internal efficiency. Campbell-Bannerman gave the Government of 1905 a more acceptable start than Asquith could have done, but it was a political benefit that he died when he did. This would have been far from the case had Attlee died in 1947. Despite the rumblings and plots of that year he established a balance which no-one else could have done. He left a lot to his principal ministers. With such powerful satraps he had no alternative, although it was also in accordance with his own inclinations. Bevin and Cripps had great independent power in their own fields. In this respect he was like Baldwin, but with the important difference that there was much more co-ordination of overall Government policy.

Attlee was a man in whom rather conservative habits of mind sat a little uneasily with firm radical purpose. He believed in exercising strong discipline over almost all the members of his Government. There were at the time many fairly derogatory anecdotes about Attlee's anonymity and colourlessness. But the main aspects of his character and command are, I believe, much better illustrated by the reply which he gave to John Strachey, when as a middle-rank minister he put in a routine request to be allowed to publish some verses, 'Certainly not', Attlee told him, 'they don't scan'.

The second Churchill premiership was a vastly different affair from the first. He was very old and failing. A great part of his effort had to be devoted to being allowed to stay on, to assuaging the natural and growing impatience of Sir Anthony Eden. As a result he allowed Eden an unchallenged suzerainty over all aspects of foreign policy which did not concern his own attempts at summitry. The consequence was that Britain failed to be represented at the Messina Conference which led to the Treaty of Rome and entered Europe fifteen years late and with unnecessary difficulties. At home he was anxious to avoid confrontation, and gave Monckton, as Minister of Labour, a very accommodating brief for industrial relations.

Eden, the clear heir for over a decade, Foreign Secretary on and off for 20 years, at last succeeded in the spring of 1955. His premiership was a tragic epilogue to this long period of distinguished waiting. It provided almost the only example of a Prime Minister being broken by a single event. Chamberlain was destroyed by a single policy and its aftermath, but that involved a whole chain of events leading up to a five-year world war. Lord Avon's Suez disaster was a much more limited event, a few days of ineffective hostilities on an isolated issue. He had previously been a politician unusually insulated from the clash of party warfare. He had not avoided difficult issues. He had been through an exceptionally testing period in the Thirties, and had come out with high credit. But what he was then involved with was an intra-party dispute, with a lot of support from the opposition and from non-party opinion. During his second and third terms as Foreign Secretary, he had usually been able to carry three quarters of the House of Commons with him. In these circumstances he was a persuasive and conciliatory speaker. But he was unused to being in the centre of a direct encounter of fairly evenly matched party armies. In 1956 not merely was this the case, but the House of Commons became more bitter and violent than at any time since the pre-1914 Home Rule disputes.

More important, however, was the effect which these events had upon the development of Britain's world position and policy. Suez was our last imperial military adventure. As such it might have been expected to mark an important even if unpleasant stage in our evolution from an imperial to a European orientation. In fact it operated only unevenly in this direction. Suez was an Anglo-French failure, but both the Governments and the peoples of the two countries reacted very differently. The British, chastened and a little guilty, drew the conclusion that, tiresomely admonitory though some thought Foster Dulles and even President Eisenhower to have been, the main lesson was that no more enterprises would be attempted without the support of Britain's principal ally. Hilaire Belloc's 'keep a hold of nurse, for fear of finding something worse', became for the next decade Britain's motto for dealing with Washington. In France the reaction to Suez was quite different. There was less guilt and more anger. The lesson there learnt was never to trust the Americans and probably not the British either. The 'Anglo-Saxons' became the main object of obloquy. Suez therefore both turned the British away from the remnants of our imperial tradition and deeply divided, for a decade or more, the two principal powers - as they then were - of Western Europe.

Conclusion

If we look for the difference between the evolving patterns of British and American leadership over these four decades, there are five points which stand out.

First, the method of selection in America was much more haphazard. Ramsay MacDonald apart, and the circumstances were then quite exceptional because of the emergence to government of a new party, no British Prime Minister came to office without having served a s a major minister for at least two years, and in most cases nearer to ten. No American President other than Hoover had held Cabinet office. Three had served brief terms as Governors. The others had virtually no combination of administrative and political experience. Yet I do not think it could be argued that this produced any clear difference of quality. No British Prime Minister was as bad as Harding, but this apart, the spread of performance was about equal between the two countries.

Second, United States Presidents once elected were in a more secure position than British Prime Ministers. Only one, again in very special circumstances, failed to be re-elected when he wanted to be. The Cabinet was no limitation on the power of the President. Throughout the period only three Cabinet officers, Mellon filling a vacuum until Hoover came to office and then exiled to London as Ambassador, Marshall as Secretary of State under Truman, and Dulles, wielded a share of power which a British senior minister would consider normal.

To balance this, Congress was far more of a limitation upon

Presidents than Parliament was upon Prime Ministers. Parliament occasionally unseated a Prime Minister. That of course has never yet happened to a President. But all Presidents who wanted to do anything were sometimes frustrated. It was much worse when there was a majority of the opposing party, but it could happen without that, as with Roosevelt's Supreme Court plan in 1937, and with much of Truman's legislation in 1948–50.

Third, in neither country was there a steady evolution over the period towards or away from a more popular, even demagogic appeal. Roosevelt and Lloyd George were the best at playing upon audiences. Wilson and Churchill were the best at set-piece oratory, Baldwin and Eisenhower at quietly cosseting their hearers. Hoover and Chamberlain were the most arid, Bonar Law, Coolidge, Attlee and Truman were the least high-flown.

Fourth, in America, clearly as a result of the changing world position of the country, there was a decisive shift in the balance of attention which Presidents devoted to domestic as opposed to world affairs. The last term of Wilson was dominated by special factors but from then until Roosevelt's second term domestic affairs took overwhelming priority. From 1938 onwards, the new pattern of external orientation has persisted. There has been no reverse change in Britain to correspond with our declining power. Baldwin was rigorously detached from the outside world, but Lloyd George and Ramsey MacDonald gave about the same amount of attention to international affairs as did Churchill (in his second Government) or Harold Macmillan.

Fifth and last: Probably all generalisations are at least partly false. No rules are fixed. No patterns are wholly regular. Individual performance, as I have endeavoured to show, has made, and continues to make, a lot of difference to politics and to government.

Oxford Installation Speech

On 24 June 1987 I was installed as Chancellor of the University of Oxford and delivered the following speech in reply to the speech of commemoration of the previous Chancellor and felicitation of the new one by the Public Orator. The first paragraph only was delivered in Latin and the text of this follows the English version.

I thank the Public Orator for the warmth and erudition with which he has welcomed me to this ancient office, the apogee of unearned university honours, the list of whose incumbents is more redolent with great names, at least since the seventeenth century, than almost any other in our national life. Between Oliver Cromwell and Harold Macmillan that list was undefiled by the name of any commoner, but Mr Macmillan survived for a quarter of a century in this office unadorned by rank although fortified by fame. So I do not feel unduly naked solely on this account.*

[Oratori publico, viro eloquentissimo, gratias ago maximas, qui me in hunc vetustissimum magistratum ineuntem blande et docte salutarit; quo munere nihil sublimius nihil a doctorum certaminum molestiis remotius inter academicos exstat. Si qis enim viros quaerit de re publica optime meritos, Cancellariorum nostrorum fasti hos trecentos fere annos nescio an ceteris omnibus excellant. Quid si hoc addam, inter Oliverum Cromwell et Haroldum Macmillan nomen plebeium ne unum quidem occurrere? Cum hic autem sua magis quam maiorum laude nobilitatus istum magistratum viginti quinque annos gesserit, in hac saltem parte egestas mea mihi non nimis displicet.]

Mr Macmillan's Chancellorship was memorable, more so I

I did not become a peer until six months later. Harold Macmillan did so only in 1984.

think than any other since that of Lord Curzon. He did not emulate that noble marquess in trying to run the University, and by such restraint set an example which it is no doubt wise for his successor to follow. What he did was to preside over the great ceremonial occasions with an inimitable panache, which became greater not less as infirmity of limb and sight added the suspense of waiting to see whether he could mount slowly to this seat and remember or improvise his lines when he got here. I shall not forget his last performance on the occasion of the King of Spain's degree by diploma, fourteen months ago today.

In addition, beyond what his predecessor Edward Halifax had done, he devoted himself to intimate college commemorative occasions and illuminated them with his unique combination of mordant wit and romantic nostalgia. For a Chancellor now there are new tasks involving both the harnessing of mammon and the defence of learning. But the old ones must not be neglected, and in the discharge of these Mr Macmillan set a model which is at once inspiring and unrepeatable.

During the past three months I have been involved in two electoral contests. I must say that I preferred the first to the second. Not only was the outcome more satisfactory, but my opponents were rather more distinguished and the weather for the poll was incomparably better. It is not only in my memory, I think, that 12 and 14 March will remain engraved as days of magical light when an unclouded sky presided over a notable reunion of the University with a surprisingly large number of its alumni.

My pleasure was the greater because in January and February it had appeared to me only too likely that I might repeat the record of one of my biographical subjects who, sixty-two years ago, lost both a Thames-side chancellorship and a Clydeside constituency within the span of a few months. From the first I was rescued by the votes of Convocation, more eclectically cast than in Asquith's day. Oxford did not, alas, save Glasgow by its example, but it has certainly fortified me to take that defection in my stride.

One result is that I shall have somewhat more time available for the University. But, let me hasten to assure Mr Vice-Chancellor and his successor, not too much time. The Chancellor, as I understand it, is required to be occasionally heard as well as seen, but with neither the sound nor the sight being available for everyday consumption. Legally he is necessary because degrees can only be conferred under his authority, and students, even before the device of contracts to regulate the output of degree factories was thought of, went to universities at least partly in order to obtain degrees.

In the earliest days he was the Chancellor and agent of a bishop rather than the choice of the University itself. This was repaired as quickly as the thirteenth century, although in the fifteenth century there was half a move back when the election of bishops or archbishops themselves began. After the Reformation those who were thought to have the ear of the King became favoured, although this did not preclude Oxford having at least two notable archiepiscopal Chancellors as late as the seventeenth century.

Paradoxically, in view of later developments, it was Cambridge which chose the more controversial Reformation figures. Five of its nine sixteenth-century Chancellors were beheaded. Oxford has its martyrs, but it never subjected my predecessors to that degree of hazard. Cambridge, however, learned its lesson even if slowly. Its most controversial recent Chancellor has been Stanley Baldwin. Subsequently it has found unchallenged unanimity in a military commander, a former Vice-Chancellor, and a royal prince. But Oxford has self-confidently continued to elect – now an unvarying habit over 250 years – only those who have been embroiled in political controversy. It is one of the few remaining compensations for a parliamentary life.

The advantage of such a controversial tradition is that it should produce Chancellors who are willing to engage in controversy. And the University today needs a voice which will speak out, if necessary against the ruling opinions. In its long history Oxford has not often had to fight to *maintain* achieved academic standards. Sometimes it – or parts of it – has fought to resist the imposition of better ones, and happily has mostly lost.

There is a clear and present danger to the University's ability to perform its twin and inseparable rôles of educating the young and advancing the frontiers of knowledge. The fame of Oxford as both a training ground and a repository of humanistic learning has long been worldwide. In recent decades there has been added to this a major research capacity in the natural and applied sciences. That capacity is not only a vital part of this University. It is also an immensely valuable national asset at a time when this country needs to cling with an iron determination to those few rôles which it can pre-eminently perform.

Yet the shadow is there. In Oxford we inherit the resonance of our name and the framework of man-made beauty which surrounds us. They will both continue, unless we wantonly damage the framework. But if the depredations of the wave of anti-intellectual philistinism which sometimes seems to be sweeping this country and its government, or any dereliction on our part, were to mean that we did not continue with all the attributes of a world-class university, they could be almost an embarrasment and not an embellishment.

Nothing in my life has given me greater pleasure than my election as Chancellor. That pleasure will only continue if I can increasingly feel that the University over which my successor will preside is as secure in the intellectual firmament as it has ever been. So my interest and my duty are clear. I believe that they coincide with yours.

Oxford Inaugural Degree Ceremony

Speeches and Allocutions

On 20 October, 1987, to mark the beginning of my Oxford term of office, I bestowed honorary degrees on a special list of 12 honorands, many of whom represented particular phases or aspects of my life: His Majesty, King Baudouin of the Belgians; the President of the Italian Republic, Signor Francesco Cossiga; Sir Patrick Neill, Q.C., Warden of All Souls College and Vice-Chancellor of the University; Dr Garret Fitzgerald, former Taoiscach (Prime Minister) of Ireland; Sir Nicholas Henderson, former Ambassador to Warsaw, Bonn, Paris and Washington; Dr Anthony Kenny, Master of Balliol College; Mr Robert S. McNamara, former President of the World Bank; Sir Alwyn Williams, Principal and Vice-Chancellor of Glasgow University; Sir Isaiah Berlin, O.M.; Dame Iris Murdoch; Professor Arthur Schlesinger, Jnr; and Professor Dorothy Hodgkin, O.M.

To the two heads of state, who by Oxford custom received degrees by diplomas, I made brief speeches in English as well as allocutions in Latin, which were also delivered to the other ten. These were as follows with the English of the allocutions, in which language they were first written, preceding the Latin:

The King of the Belgians
Wise and dedicated sovereign of the European Community, who has counselled both his own people and the leaders of Europe towards fusion not fission, I, acting on my own authority and that of the whole University, and by the power and force of this Diploma, admit you to the Degree of Doctor of Civil Law.

Belgarum Rex prudentissime, de civibus tuis optime merite Communitati Europaeae hospitium praebentibus liberalissimum, qui cum inter tuos tum inter ceteros Europae duces unitatem ita fovisti ut in atomos non dissipetur, ego auctoritate mea et totius Universitatis nec non vi ac virtute huius Diplomatis admitto te ad gradum Doctoris in Iure Civili.

One of the pleasantest though not one of the easiest tasks of the new Chancellor of this University is the compiling of a list of those whom he wishes to propose to Congregation for honouring with doctorates. My aim was to produce a list somewhat shorter than, though at least equal in total distinction with the inaugural lists of my recent predecessors. In the first aim I have demonstrably succeeded. Arithmetic cannot be argued with.

I *believe* I have also succeeded in my second objective. My further aim in selecting those to be honoured was to propose only those to whom I thought the University as a whole would enthusiastically wish to pay respect. I also considered that as this special list is unrepeatable and specifically linked to my installation, it was appropriate that it should to some extent, compatibly with the other criteria, represent different phases and interests in my life.

My four Brussels years as President of the European Commission were clearly for me an important phase. I wished to mark them, and express my appreciation of that combination of hospitality and inspiration which the Belgian state and people have always given to the European Community. That national approach was singularly epitomized in you, Sir. The consideration and friendship which you and Her Majesty the Queen extended to us were a great encouragement. Happily I do not recollect your frequently warning me, but you certainly fulfilled Bagehot's other two prescripts for a constitutional monarch. You constantly encouraged, and you were always open to consultation, and in such interchanges were full of wisdom and hope.

You do us great honour by coming here today, at the beginning of my Chancellorship, as did your brother sovereign, the King of Spain, on the occasion of the last appearance of my predecessor, Mr Macmillan, in this theatre. We respectfully salute you and your country, and look forward to your words.

President of the Italian Republic

Familiar of this University and most cultivated head of the country which has long embellished our civilisation, more recently refreshed our vacations, and now threatens to outpace our economy, I, acting on my own authority and that of the whole University, and by the power and force of this Diploma, admit you to the Degree of Doctor of Civil Law.

Academiae nostrae amice familiarissime, Italiae omnium nationum humanissimae Praeses humanissime, quae nobis diu mores expolit, nuper otia delectat, mox nisi contendemus vectigalia superabit, ego auctoritate mea et totius Universitatis nec non vi ac virtute huius Diplomatis admitto te ad gradum Doctoris in Iure Civili.

The President of the Italian Republic and I first met when we were fellow home or interior ministers, both much racked at that time by terrorism. I escaped to Brussels. He was crucified upon the cross of the kidnapping and subsequent murder of Aldo Moro. He was in no way to blame, but he resigned and with a dignity and abnegation rare in the politics of any country withdrew to Sardinia. Even more rarely, his abnegation did not lead him to be forgotten. Eighteen months later he came back as Prime Minister, and his subsequent year of office was crucial to a resolution of the first phase of Britain's budgetary argument with the Community.

In 1985 he was elected President of the Italian Republic and is clearly the most intellectually distinguished incumbent since Progressor Einaudi left that high office thirty years before. I welcome him today both as an individual who has maintained scholarly standards in politics and as the head of state of the large country which in my experience, before all others, has given the most consistent support to the idea of European unity.

It is a country which for me, as for many others in this University, has been a magnet as well as a pillar. This occasion today has provoked my over-arithmetical mind to discover that in the past forty years I have spent in Italy a total of 432 days, almost exactly fourteen months, spread over seventy-three separate visits. I ought in these circumstances to be able to address you , Mr President, in a near perfect version of your native tongue, rather than in a mixture of English and our hard and un-Italianate Oxford Latin, which always reminds me more of pebbles plopping into a cold

clear Northumbrian stream than of any sounds which were ever
likely to have been heard on the banks of the Tiber.

Your English words will, I know, combine the warmth of Italian
with the precision of Latin.

Sir Patrick Neill, Q.C.
Persuasive advocate and wise arbitrator who returned to Oxford
to preside over All Souls and quickly became the courageous
spokesman of all Colleges, I, acting on my own authority and that
of the whole University, admit you to the Honorary Degree of
Doctor of Civil Law.

Advocatorum eloquentissime, arbitrorum peritissime, qui idcirco
inter Oxonienses regressus ut praesideas Collegio Omnium
Animarum mox causam omnium Collegiorum animosus pro-
pugnator suscepisti, ego auctoritate mea et totius Universitatis
admitto te ad gradum Doctoris in Iure Civili honoris causa.

Dr Garret Fitzgerald
Irish statesman who has striven for reconciliation in his own
island and who from the westernmost limits of the Community
has achieved high esteem in the heart of Europe, I, acting on my
own authority and that of the whole University, admit you to the
Honorary Degree of Doctor of Civil Law.

Hibernensium praeclarissime, qui in eo elaboravisti ut omnes
Hibernenses offensas deponant concordiam diligant, quo in ultimis
occidentis oris orto nemo est ipsis Europae praecordiis acceptior,
ego auctoritate mea et totius Universitatis admitto te ad gradum
Doctoris in Iure Civili honoris causa.

Sir Nicholas Henderson
Most experienced of modern diplomats, closest adviser to five
Foreign Secretaries and four times the Queen's ambassador to
some of the greatest republics of the world, I, acting on my
own authority and that of the whole University, admit you to
the Honorary Degree of Doctor of Civil Law.

Vir omnium virum hodiernorum in legationibus versatissime,
qui praetoribus peregrinis quinque continuis a secretis fuisti,

quem Regina augustissima ad quattuor liberas res publicas easque valentissimas legavit, ego auctoritate mea et totius Universitatis admitto te ad gradum Doctoris in Iure Civili honoris causa.

Dr Anthony Kenny

Preceptor and philosopher, master of my humble house, whose writings have memorably illuminated the path from Rome and much surrounding landscape, I, acting on my own authority and that of the whole University, admit you to the Honorary Degree of Doctor of Civil Law.

Praeceptorum doctissime, philosophorum sapientissime, domunculae meae magister amplissime, cuius scripta non solum tramitem istum quem sequitur si quis Romam deserit sed ceteras quoque regiones amplectuntur, ego auctoritate mea et totius Universitatis admitto te ad gradum Doctoris in Iure Civili honoris causa.

Robert S. McNamara

Former lord of military might, who has subsequently striven not only to beat swords into ploughshares but to spread the ploughshares throughout the world, I, acting on my own authority and that of the whole University, admit you to the Honorary Degree of Doctor of Civil Law.

Exercituum moderator olim potentissime, qui in eo nuper laboras ut gladii in vomeres conflentur, vomeres autem per totum orbem terrarum dispertiantur, ego auctoritate mea et totius Universitatis admitto te ad gradum Doctoris in Iure Civili honoris causa.

Sir Alwyn Williams

Son of Wales, who after academic services in Northern Ireland is now honoured in the heart of England as the *doyen* of Scottish education, I, acting on my own authority and that of the whole University, admit you to the Honorary Degree of Doctor of Civil Law.

Cambriae alumne, de Hiberniae septemtrionalis academicis optime merite, quem in ipsius Angliae penetralibus tamquam omnium praeclarissimum Scotorum praeceptorem honoramus, ego auctoritate mea et totius Universitatis admitto te ad gradum Doctoris in Iure Civili honoris causa.

Sir Isaiah Berlin
Penetrating thinker and critic, delicate ironist, iridescent talker, who over six decades has epitomised and strengthened the spirit of Oxford, I, acting on my own authority and that of the whole University, admit you to the Honorary Degree of Doctor of Letters.

Intelligendi auctor acutissime, criticorum subtilissime, facete in cavillando, in colloquendo corusce, qui per duodecim lustra nobis ipsius loci genium sub oculos ponis in mente confirmas, ego auctoritate mea et totius Universitatis admitto te ad gradum Doctoris in Litteris honoris causa.

Dame Iris Murdoch
Daughter of this University and philosopher–novelist who has led us enchanted from net to brotherhood, safely past sandcastles, unicorns, black princes, fire, sun and sea, I, acting on my own authority and that of the whole University, admit you to the Honorary Degree of Doctor of Letters.

Huiusce academiae filia dilectissima, cum inter philosophos tum inter fabulatores eminentissima, quae nos reti primum inlaqueatos praeter castella harenosa, monocerotes, principes nigros, ignem solem mare denique ipsum ad amorem fraternum usque deducis, ego auctoritate mea et totius Universitatis admitto te ad gradum Doctoris in Litteris honoris causa.

Progressor Arthur Schlesinger, Jnr
Eminent historian of the American Republic who has informed us of the ages of Jackson, Roosevelt, and Kennedy and strenuously reconciled personal commitment with academic accuracy, I, acting on my own authority and that of the whole University, admit you to the Honorary Degree of Doctor of Letters.

Rei publicae Americanae annalium conditor doctissime, qui in aetatibus Jacksoniana Rooseveltiana Kennediana exponedis ita sententias tuas signifacavisti ut ab exactissima accuratione numquam declinares, ego auctoritate mea et totius Universitatis admitto te ad gradum Doctoris in Litteris honoris causa.

Professor Dorothy Hodgkin
Nobel scientist of world renown whose eyes have penetrated matter, including living things, and created new understanding

of their nature, I, acting on my own authority and that of the whole University, admit you to the Honorary Degree of Doctor of Science.

Rerum naturae indagatrix praestentissima, praemio Nobeliano nobilitata, cuius oculorum mentisque acie ipsius materiae compages, ipsorum animalium structura perspecta et intellecta est, ego auctoritate mea et totius Universitatis admitto te ad gradum Doctoris in Scientia honoris causa.

Royal Society of Literature Awards*

Iris Murdoch, V. S. Pritchett, Steven Runciman and Rosamund Lehmann

The last third of this October of monsoon and tempest has been for me a remarkable ten days – not alas of receiving but of presenting honours. On Tuesday last week I conferred 12 Oxford doctorates on my own inaugural list. This evening I bestow four Companionships of Literature, to add to the small number of six, which already exist.

There are considerable differences between the ceremonies, although some similarities too. First it should be said that the Royal Society of Literature list is a much more exclusive one. There are far more Oxford D.Litts, let alone DCLs than there are Companions of Literature. Second, to-night's quartet, although they arouse my enthusiasm and admiration, are unlike last week's dozen, not my own unilateral choice. Tonight I am delighted to be the agent: I cannot claim to be the principal. Third, I do not propose to conduct the evening's ceremony in Latin.

Dame Iris Murdoch

Those are some of the dissimilarities. By far the most notable of similarities is the presence on both occasions of *Iris Murdoch*, at the Oxford ceremony of good average age, but this evening appearing almost presumptuously young. If I may paraphrase Housman and take only a little arithmetical liberty with an exact contemporary of mine as an undergraduate, I am tempted to say:

On 29 Ocotber 1987, not then President of the Royal Society of Literature, I was asked to confer these awards.

251

'What C of Litt at sixty-two
A fine upstanding lass like you'

Whether or not she wins the Booker prize for the second time later this evening, she is this year undoubtedly the most concentratedly honoured writer since Saul Bellow almost took the gilt off my gingerbread, when we paraded together for a Harvard degree in 1972, by informing me that he had only just managed to get there from Yale, which had also given him an honorary degree the day before.

Iris Murdoch has become a Dame, received an Oxford D. Litt. and a Companionship of Literature in one year. With what envy would have popped the eyes of Evelyn Waugh, so barrenly desiring and yet so deserving of public honour, as a writer if not as a man, Noël Annan's brilliant lecture on whom provided my last occasion for visiting this room and this society–and that is a sentence almost worthy of an Ali Forbes *Spectator* review.

At Oxford, I had to try to encapsulate Dame Iris in 25 words and did so as 'Daughter of this University and philosopher-novelist who has led us enchanted from net to brotherhood, safely past sandcastles, unicorns, black princes, fire, sun and sea.'

After only nine days I cannot either subtract from or add to that, but it gives me renewed pleasure to bestow the first of these accolades upon Dame Iris Murdoch.

Sir Victor Pritchett

Next, having disposed of presumptuous youth, we come to Sir Victor Pritchett, whom I had long admired from afar but came to know only when after 1975 we coincided as members of the Literary Society, a dining club only too familiar to those who have read the Hart-Davis/Lyttelton correspondence. That august club in its elections policy sometimes seems to place greater weight upon the word society in its title than upon the word literary, although to have written a book is not an automatic disqualification, but by no means a necessary recommendation either. Sir Steven Runciman is however also a member, although not, needless to say, Rosamund Lehmann or Iris Murdoch. The view is firmly taken that literature and women do not mix. (I think a compromise of having two of them in at a time as guests was tried a few years ago, but that was given up as being too expensive.)

Victor Pritchett I there regard as the captain of the literary team (Steven Runciman comes less often) so that the competition to sit next to him is strong. To my disappointment I only occasionally win.

I salute him this evening as the last and in many ways the best of the great general reviewers who wrote before the literary pages of the Sunday newspapers came to look like patchwork quilts of snippets from semi-specialists; whose *Books in General* review-fronts gave to the second half of the *New Statesman* in its heyday an unique combination of literary authority and wide appeal; and for whom 'the cab at the door' may in childhood have symbolised yet another domestic misfortune but for whose readers over the past 60 years, it has come more to promise another acutely chronicled and deeply rewarding literary excursion.

Sir Steven Runciman

Sir Steven Runciman, recent Companion of Honor, a knight for 29 years, a fellow of the British Academy for still longer, a fellow of the R.S.L. since 1952, would also have received the offer of an Oxford degree, had he not already possessed one, as from a dozen other universities. There are now few awards that can be conferred upon him, but a Companionship of Literature is one, and it is entirely appropriate that its highest accolade should be forthcoming from this Society.

It was here, under the chairmanship of Dame Veronica Wedgwood, that, almost exactly 25 years ago, he delivered one of the most notable lectures to find its way into *Essays by Divers Hands*. It was entitled 'Medieval History and the Romantic Imagination' and contained for me one particularly striking passage on his purposes in writing history . . .

'I am no seer who can interpret and foretell the rhythm of the universe', he wrote '. . . Nor can I believe that the statesmen of to-day will trouble to profit from whatever I may be able to tell them of bygone ages. I merely find a fascination in the study of human beings in times and conditions very different from our own, and in the attempt to bring a sympathetic vision to bear on that study sufficient to make some sense of it and to arrive at some understanding, and then to reproduce what I have learnt and understood in a form that will rank – as one continues to hope – as literature.'

I salute Steven Runciman as one whose history, infused by

imagination but disciplined by fact, indisputably ranks as literature; native of Northumberland, which Proust, Harold Nicolson *via* a Runciman essay has informed us, thought provided the most sonorous base in all Europe for an echoing title; now resolute resident of the almost adjacent Scottish county of Dumfries-shire: whose writings for a wide but discriminating readership have long constituted the most exciting but best constructed 'bridge to the East'.

Rosamund Lehmann

I come to the fourth, and, alas, only absent member of the quartet. Our desire to do her honour is in no way diminished, as I hope her son and grand-daughter, both here present, will convey to her, by her incapacity. Her books have given me exceptional pleasure. Yet they have never been designed for self-indulgence. Her evocative writing has had the very special taste of romance without lushness, astringency without sourness.

Her titles have been superb. They are almost all so, but it is perhaps *The Weather in the Streets* which most remains in the mind. When first heard it raises a quizzical eyebrow. Once assimilated, it is unforgettable. That is perhaps a good recipe for a title. But of course great titles are no use without sustaining contents. Otherwise there is a danger of bathos, a peanut rattling round in a coconut, a Hofburg without Hapsburgs. There has never been a danger of that with Miss Lehmann. Her titles have enhanced her books; they have never oppressed them.

I therefore salute her as a quintessential English writer who nonetheless earns high esteem amongst critical French audiences; a novelist of sensibility who gives sentiment its proper place and no more; and a literary figure whose renown now grows with each year of her life.

Should Politicians Know History?

The first question to which I address myself is whether or not a lively awareness of history is going the way of a classical education and becoming a discarded attribute for the leaders of the Western world? And secondly if it is, does it matter? And thirdly, are there any great differences in this respect between the main states of, say, the Atlantic Alliance?

First, has there in fact been a significant and secular decline in historical knowledge and interest? Cromwell said when laying down a prescription for the education of his third son Richard: 'I would have him learn a little history'; and it has been written (by Professor Dumas Malone) of Jefferson and his contemporaries that compared with modern statesmen 'they thought more about the future and know more about the past'. But I am by no means sure how consistent was the historical erudition of nineteenth-century Presidents or Prime Ministers. I would not put Andrew Jackson – or indeed Andrew Johnson – very high in this respect, less so indeed than Lyndon Johnson 100 years later. British mid-nineteenth century Prime Ministers were probably more informed, although I do not think that the knowledge of Wellington or of Grey or even of Melbourne was very meticulous.

What is however certainly the case is that for nearly 25 years from 1940 British Governments were led by a series of men whose minds were to an exceptional extent moulded, refreshed and stimulated by their historical knowledge. Churchill was of course the outstanding example. Although he had no formal training, he wrote history with a verve unequalled by any other British statesman and with a professionalism which could be rivalled in this category only by John Morley and James Bryce. Beyond that, his imagination was constantly seized by the tides of historical events and an epic view of how great men could divert them. He was undoubtedly much motivated by an awareness of his own historical destiny.

Attlee saw himself and events less grandiloquently. He had no gift of narrative prose. But his training was historical, as were his continuing intellectual interests. He had an acute instinct for balance between change and continuity, and his laconic sense of proportion, which cut men and events down to size, owed much to his knowledge of the past.

Eden knew a lot about Persian and Arab history and came to acquire an encyclopaedic knowledge of the minutiae of diplomatic exchanges of the first half of this century. But his interests were more aesthetic than intellectual, and his mind was probably the least conditioned by history of this quartet.

Its fourth member was Harold Macmillan. He, like Attlee, had little of Churchill's command over written English, and he could not therefore compete as a chronicler. But his knowledge was at least as great as Churchill's, and covered a wider span. He knew Greek and Roman history in a way that Churchill, whose interests were always concentrated on the past 300 years, never did. Harold Macmillan may not have been a great writer of history, but his most characteristic speeches moved easily from the Peloponnesian War to the Battle of the Somme.

Since Harold Macmillan's resignation in 1963 it has in Britain been gradually downhill nearly all the way so far as historical knowledge and interest are concerned. Alec Douglas Home has a history degree, but has maintained the amateur status of a gentleman commoner of Christ Church, Oxford; Harold Wilson's knowledge, while by no means negligible, is somewhat over-concentrated upon the American Civil War. Bruce Catton has long been his favourite author and I have little doubt that he is now deep into James Macpherson's *Battle Cry of Freedom*. Edward Heath, although he thinks in broad and generous terms, has never much illuminated his speeches or writings with historical parallels going back beyond his own, now long experience.

James Callaghan does not break the pattern, even though he, too, now likes to think broad. Margaret Thatcher, while her own impact upon history may be great, is curiously bounded by her own period of office, and that of the previous Labour Government. She is fond of argument by historical comparison, but it is almost invariably done in a scale of two, and her history does not often go back before 1974. Nor does any likely alternative British Prime Minister show much sign of ability to reverse the trend.

The case could therefore be regarded as superficially proved: 23 years from 1940 to 1963 producing four Prime Ministers, of whom at least three were impregnated with historical sense; and 23 years from 1963 to 1986 with five Prime Ministers on an incline of descent towards indifferrence or ignorance. History appears to be in retreat.

Yet might it not have been the first rather than the second period which was exceptional? If we consider the eight preceding Prime Ministers who took office since 1900, this looks quite plausible. Arthur James Balfour brooded on the likelihood of cosmic doom when 'the energies of our system will decay, the glory of the sun will be dimmed, and the earth, tideless and inert, will no longer tolerate the race which has for a moment disturbed its solitude', but this grand pessimism did not encourage much detailed historical application, even though he was determined not to be like Peel and 'betray his party'. Sir Henry Campbell-Bannerman was an indolent Cambridge classicist who preferred French novels to English political biography, and managed more on a mixture of shrewdness and niceness than on historical thought or erudition.

H. H. Asquith had absorbed a lot of history, as his smoothly purring brain absorbed almost everything, and could have easily held a historical conversational candle to Attlee or Macmillan, as he frequently did to Churchill. But he was no writer - except of personal letters to ladies, frequently penned with great fluency during Cabinet meetings over which he was presiding. Lloyd George made a lot of history, but he was always too much a man of the moment to be greatly influenced by historical lessons. In his oratory he preferred topographical imagery - 'the great peaks . . . of honour, duty, patriotism and . . . sacrifice' contrasted with 'the enervating valley' of selfishness - to historical analogy.

Bonar Law knew the works of Thomas Carlyle inside out, and his historical reading beyond the works of 'sage of Chelsea', eclectic though these were, was remarkably thorough and wide for a commercially educated accountant of rather rigid views.

Stanley Baldwin loved the rhythms of the English countryside and had a strong sense of continuity, but although he claimed (not wholly plausibly) to have been most influenced by the writings of Henry Maine, his favourite historical author was probably Arthur Bryant.

Ramsay MacDonald attached considerable importance to political theory, but found more parallels in biological evolution than in historical precedent for the form of socialism which he wished to introduce. Neville Chamberlain's practical and somewhat intolerant mind did not much require the support or the recreation of history.

Nevertheless, I think that on balance this group of early twentieth century Prime Ministers knew more history than do their successors of the last decade or so, and they were certainly buttressed by other ministers - Lloyd George by Curzon and Milner and H.A.L. Fisher, MacDonald by Haldane and Sydney Webb, the early Baldwin by Churchill and L.S. Amery, the later Baldwin and Neville Chamberlain by Halifax and Duff Cooper, to take some random examples - who knew incomparably more than do those who are ministers or likely ministers today.

The case for secular decline can therefore be regarded as substantially if not overwhelmingly proved for Britain. And the early part of the twentieth century was already a significant decline from the habits which had prevailed in the nineteenth century.

What about other countries? I begin here for obvious reasons with America. It appears to me that here the US pattern of decline is much less clear. The early Virginian and Massachusetts Presidents are naturally thought of as gentlemen of easy eighteenth century squirearchical culture, as at home in their libraries as in the open air, and of Jefferson, the two Adams, Madison and probably Washington, this must be allowed, although with the exception of John Quincy Adams' diary their literary output was exiguous, even if, in the cases of Jefferson and Madison at least, its constitutional imprint was vast. Their minds were set in a constitutional and historical mould by the objective circumstances of creative flux in which they lived. Monroe does not seem to me to be in the same category of library culture.

Nor were the mid-century Presidents between Jackson and Lincoln. Lincoln acquired his considerable historical knowledge rather in the way that Truman did 70 years later: through solitary, sometimes unselective reading more than through structured teaching or the interplay of ideas with members of a peer group. But as a composer of memorable prose and an importer of a sense of the sweep of history into oratory he was clearly in a different category from Truman. 'The buck stops here' and 'If you can't stand the heat get out of the kitchen' are good adages but not exactly of the quality of 'four score and seven years ago . . . .'. Post Lincoln we have to wait until the turn of the century before we get back into significant historical hills let alone into the commanding peaks of knowledge. I suppose the twentieth century might be very crudely categorised by saying that Wilson knew a vast amount, that Theordore Roosevelt, Franklin Roosevelt (in a not very applied way), Truman (in a plodding way) and Kennedy (perhaps more through associates than by detailed study) knew quite a lot. That Taft, Hoover, Lyndon Johnson and perhaps Carter know some, Coolidge, Nixon and Ford a little, and that Harding, Eisenhower and President Reagan have practised a very rigid economy of historical reading.

In Europe I have mostly found the French to be more interested and better informed than the Germans and most others, with the Belgians and possibly the Italians inclining to the French category. Both Presidents Giscard and Mitterrand combine knowledge and interest, although the former has more detail and the latter, like De Gaulle in this respect, more sweep. Chancellor Kohl clearly has little historical interest. But nor did Helmut Schmidt, who was the most constructive statesman of my time as President of the European Commission. I think that for someone of Schmidt's generation the immediate past constituted a noxious barrier which discouraged him from retrospective peering.

Does this catalogue tell us much about how desirable a qualification for statesmanship is historical knowledge? On the whole, and surprisingly cautiously, I think it can be said that those with knowledge and interest performed better than those without, with, on the European side of the Atlantic, Lloyd George and Schmidt providing notable exceptions one way, and Eden a less certain one the other. On America I am more hesitant to pronounce.

Why should this be so? The most obvious explanation is that history helps to lengthen perspective and by so doing discourages extreme partisanship. This must however be qualified by saying that it applies to a reasonably detached study of history and not to living in its shadow with an obsessive concentration. No communities are more difficult to bring together – Northern Ireland, Cyprus – than those where the contemplation of ancient wrongs is a way of life. And even beyond this it could be cited in contrary evidence that few politicians have been more short-sighted than the elegant biographer Harold Nicolson, with his five switches of party, or more partisan than were the great constitutional historians, Dicey and Anson, at the time of the Parliament Bill of 1911. I suspect it is more that historical knowledge stems from a mixture of curiosity and a generally well-stocked mind, and that those with these attributes are better equipped than those without.

There has been another recent development which seems to me of possible beneficial importance: this is the enormous growth of memoir writing. This applies on both sides of the Atlantic. of the eleven British Prime Ministers between 1880 and 1940 none of them wrote full-scale memoirs. Balfour wrote a fragment of autobiography and Lloyd George a major *pièce justificative*, but not an autobiography. Of the nine Prime Ministers since only the present incumbent and Edward Heath, said to be busily writing, have been silent. In the United States there were twelve Presidents between 1880 and 1945. Three of them (Theodore Roosevelt, Coolidge and Hoover) did write memoirs. But since 1945, of the seven who have gone from the highest office, no one has remained silent except for President Kennedy who obviously had no choice. The inevitability of the political memoir had become a fact of political life. This may not produce much good literature, or even in some cases satisfactory narrative reading, but it does I believe make the prospective authors a little more aware of how their actions may look in longer perspective and of their comparative performance *vis-a-vis* others who will be working at the memoir face alongside them. And the effects of this are more likely to be good than bad.

I therefore give my vote in favour of history rather than Henry Ford's dictum upon it, but I do so with suitable caution and reservation. What I really believe is that those with curiosity, whatever their educational and occupational backgrounds, are bound to have interest in and acquire some knowledge about the past; and that those without it are likely to be dull fellows and uncomprehending rulers.

INDEX

261

INDEX

INDEX

INDEX

INDEX